How to Do Everything™

Microsoft® SharePoint® 2013

Stephen Cawood

Mc
Graw
Hill
Education

New York   Chicago   San Francisco   Lisbon
London   Madrid   Mexico City   Milan   New Delhi
San Juan   Seoul   Singapore   Sydney   Toronto

Cataloging-in-Publication Data is on file with the Library of Congress

McGraw-Hill books are available at special quantity discounts to use as premiums and sales promotions, or for use in corporate training programs. To contact a representative, please e-mail us at bulksales@mcgraw-hill.com.

How to Do Everything™: Microsoft® SharePoint® 2013

1234567890   QFR QFR   109876543

ISBN   978-0-07-180983-2
MHID   0-07-180983-X

Sponsoring Editor Roger Stewart	**Technical Editors** Sean Wallbridge Colin Phillips Keith Tuomi	**Production Supervisor** Jean Bodeaux
Editorial Supervisor Patty Mon		**Composition** Cenveo Publisher Services
Project Manager Harleen Chopra, Cenveo® Publisher Services	**Copy Editor** Marilyn Smith	**Illustration** Cenveo Publisher Services
Acquisitions Coordinator Amanda Russell	**Proofreader** Debbie Liehs	**Art Director, Cover** Jeff Weeks
	Indexer Jack Lewis	**Cover Designer** Jeff Weeks

To Mom and Joan. Thank you both for all you've done for Christa, Robin, and me.

About the Author

Stephen Cawood has written nine books, including *Microsoft Content Management Server 2002: A Complete Guide*, *Augmented Reality: A Practical Guide*, and *Microsoft XNA Game Studio Creator's Guide*. Stephen is a former Microsoft Program Manager on the MCMS and SharePoint product teams, but more recently, he has joined the management team at Aquatic Informatics. Stephen lives in Vancouver, Canada, with his wife and daughter.

About the Technical Editors

Sean Wallbridge, president and principal consultant of itgroove Professional Services Ltd., is a SharePoint MVP and Evangelist. Sean likes to characterize himself as a "SharePoint Jedi" (there are no experts, just those who continue to explore the enormous ways of the SharePoint force), and there is no better way to describe Sean's enthusiasm for SharePoint. In addition to being a SharePoint Server MVP, Sean has a rich background in the Windows world and carries many certifications, including CISSP, MCSE, MCT, and MCSA. His blog can be found at http://blog.brainlitter.com, and he utters the odd tweet @itgroove.

Colin Phillips is a SharePoint consultant and developer with itgroove Professional Services Ltd. He brings more than 12 years' experience in information technology and software development, including stints at small and large software firms such as Cognos (now IBM). Colin provides capable and competent expertise on a variety of SharePoint topics, such as custom development solutions, business intelligence, workflows, Nintex, branding, page layouts and design, search, infrastructure, and many more. His blog can be found at http://mmman.itgroove.net.

Keith Tuomi, is a SharePoint-focused consultant and developer at itgroove Professional Services Ltd. With extensive experience designing, coding, testing, and supporting Microsoft technologies, he works consistently to improve his proficiencies in creative technical development and administration. A programmer's approach to detail combined with the inspiration of an architect means there is plenty for him to explore in the world of SharePoint. He blogs regularly at http://yalla.itgroove.net.

Contents at a Glance

v

Contents

Foreword

The latest version of SharePoint makes collaboration very easy. With a focus on user design, the new user experience enables many new end-user scenarios. Whether it's sharing a document, assigning permissions, or searching for information, SharePoint empowers users to get work done. Project collaboration features, such as rich task management and new timeline view, make SharePoint a great place to start new projects.

A big investment in this latest version is social. SharePoint has never been this social before! There are a many terrific features, such as microblogging, community, improved tagging and following, and improved personal sites—just to name a few. End users can connect and interact with others very easily with SharePoint, on-premises or in Office 365.

While the new user experience makes it easy for end users to collaborate, training and education continues to be important if you want to take advantage of SharePoint's rich capabilities to transform your business processes. Whether you're new to SharePoint or someone more experienced looking for tips and tricks, this is a great resource to have. I've known Steve for almost a decade, and what I admire most is his ability to communicate technology topics in a very simple way. Whether it's his Halo books or *How to Do Everything™: Microsoft® SharePoint® 2010*, he's done it over and over, and this time is no different.

I hope you enjoy this book and get the most out of the latest version of SharePoint!

Arpan Shah
Senior Director, Office 365
Microsoft Corporation

Acknowledgments

I would like to thank my agent, Neil Salkind (www.studiob.com), for nine book projects in nine years. To Roger Stewart and McGraw-Hill, thanks for another great book project. I've said it before, but all authors should be so lucky to have such a professional publisher backing them. Thanks again to Sean Wallbridge, Colin Phillips, and Keith Tuomi; the itgroove (www.itgroove.net) technical editors on this project. You did a fantastic job, and not only assured technical accuracy, but also helped shape the final result.

Thank you once again to my old friend Arpan Shah for writing the foreword and the section on SharePoint history.

Finally, thanks once again to my wife, Christa. I'll try to keep that promise of not taking another book project for a while.

Introduction

I'm pleased to have an opportunity to write another SharePoint end-user book. *How to Do Everything™: Microsoft® SharePoint® 2010* was my first end-user book, and my goal was to keep it highly approachable. I believe I accomplished that goal, but this time around, I'm aiming for a bit more balance for the readers who want to go one step further. I've added more "real-world examples" and a couple of chapters that introduce the topics of SharePoint administration and SharePoint development.

As with the previous book, I have included some reference material as well. Each chapter begins with a bulleted "How to..." list that provides a summary of the topics covered in that chapter.

- **Chapter 1, "Introduction and SharePoint History"**   This chapter provides the back story of SharePoint and introduces the reader to the new SharePoint 2013 user interface.
- **Chapter 2, "SharePoint Concepts"**   The fundamental components of SharePoint are discussed in this chapter. For example, the differences between sites, lists, and items are described.
- **Chapter 3, "Working with Documents"**   The focus of this chapter is document management—still one of the primary use cases for SharePoint users. Topics such as working with documents and the content approval workflow are discussed.
- **Chapter 4, "Collaboration"**   Various SharePoint collaboration and social features are discussed in this chapter. These include new features that have become available only with the release of SharePoint 2013.
- **Chapter 5, "Tagging and Taxonomy"**   This chapter provides an introduction to Enterprise Managed Metadata (SharePoint taxonomy) functionality in SharePoint 2013, as well as how to use tagging to create a "folksonomy" within your SharePoint user community.
- **Chapter 6, "Publishing Sites"**   Publishing sites are becoming more and more popular with SharePoint users. They are being used not only for intranet sites, but also for public-facing websites. This chapter introduces publishing pages and discusses how they can be used to empower SharePoint users to create their own web pages.

- **Chapter 7, "Personal Sites and Personalization"** This chapter is about personalization. My Sites (now commonly called "personal sites") are discussed, as well as features that allow users to tailor SharePoint to their needs.
- **Chapter 8, "Web Parts and App Parts"** Web parts and SharePoint apps are nuggets of functionality that can be used on many SharePoint pages, and this chapter will help you make the most of the out-of-box options.
- **Chapter 9, "Customization"** Customizing SharePoint sites, lists, views, and pages is a huge topic within the SharePoint community. This chapter covers many of the ways that SharePoint can be customized without anyone needing to write a single line of code.
- **Chapter 10, "Using SharePoint with Client Applications"** The SharePoint web interface has many advantages, but it isn't the only way to interact with a SharePoint server. This chapter introduces some of the rich client applications that you may want to use with SharePoint. Examples include Microsoft Outlook and Microsoft SharePoint Designer. A couple of examples of third-party client applications are also discussed in this chapter.
- **Chapter 11, "Introduction to SharePoint Administration"** This chapter introduces the topic of SharePoint administration for those who want to go beyond end-user features. Subjects covered in this chapter include PowerShell and SharePoint Central Administration.
- **Chapter 12, "Introduction to SharePoint Development"** For anyone curious about SharePoint development, this chapter provides an introduction. Topics covered include setting up a SharePoint development environment, developing SharePoint visual web parts, and developing SharePoint apps.
- **Chapter 13, "Template Reference for Apps, Pages, and Sites"** This is a reference chapter that provides you with a list of all the site templates, list templates, and page types that ship with SharePoint Foundation 2013 and SharePoint Server 2013.
- **Appendix, "SharePoint Resources"** A collection of links for SharePoint training, community forums, and blogs.

I feel fortunate to have had a front-row view as content management systems evolved from obscure applications (that few people had heard of) to mainstream business requirements that millions of people use every day.

I'm pleased to have had a chance to work on another SharePoint book, and I hope you find it useful. Have fun, and feel free to contact me through my blog (www.geeklit .com) or Twitter account (@cawood) if you have any questions.

1

Introduction and SharePoint History

HOW TO...

- Understand SharePoint's history
- Work with the SharePoint 2013 user interface
- Identify the differences between SharePoint Server 2013 and SharePoint Foundation

A book titled *How to Do Everything: Microsoft SharePoint 2013* has an obvious practical issue. SharePoint is an enterprise server product with an incredibly diverse feature set. Each SharePoint release has added a great deal of functionality, and has established SharePoint as both an application for quickly deploying websites and a platform for building almost any web-based functionality imaginable. SharePoint Server 2013 users will take advantage of features such as document management, team collaboration, wikis, taxonomy, blogs, and social features. The list of what you can do with SharePoint is long and diverse, and it gets longer with every release.

SharePoint has gotten so big that it's actually becoming difficult to explain SharePoint in a succinct fashion. Microsoft CEO Steve Ballmer took a stab at defining SharePoint when SharePoint 2010 was released. He described SharePoint as "a general-purpose platform for connecting people with information."

Rather than trying to imagine what all readers might want to do with their general-purpose platform, this book will focus on what's available in SharePoint Server 2013. Once you've been introduced to the features, how you choose to use them is up to you.

Because this book is meant for end users, we won't cover subjects such as using SharePoint to manage a large, distributed SharePoint server farm. However, we will look at many real-world examples that will help you get going on common tasks more quickly. The book also has a couple of short chapters that introduce SharePoint development and administration, which will be useful to readers who want to go beyond the SharePoint end-user functionality.

That gives us a great deal of material to discuss, but before you get your feet planted in the present, we'll start with a look into the past. Arpan Shah, a Director on the Office 365 team at Microsoft, has written the following retrospective section about the genesis and evolution of SharePoint.

SharePoint History, by Arpan Shah

It's interesting to look at how SharePoint has evolved over the years. Most people had their first experience with SharePoint with the 2007 release.

SharePoint has its roots as early as the mid- to late 1990s during the dot-com hype. Businesses were very interested in getting websites up as fast as possible, and Site Server, first released in 1996, played a significant role in providing packaged software to the industry. Site Server 3.0, released in 1998, was especially popular and came in a special Commerce Edition. It delivered content and product management capabilities, along with search, personalization, and order processing.

The first official branded SharePoint technologies were released in 2001: SharePoint Portal Server 2001 (codenamed Tahoe) and SharePoint Team Services (STS). SharePoint Portal Server was positioned as a portal product that helped businesses aggregate corporate information through navigation and search. SharePoint team sites enabled teams to get sites up and running very quickly to organize documents, events, and other digital information. And while both these technologies were great for the scenarios they targeted, they had little integration between them. Customers wanted to use the two technologies in conjunction, and provided strong feedback to Redmond that portal and collaboration were very similar, and should be delivered on a common platform to give businesses more flexibility.

Over the next few years, the two teams worked closely together to deliver a common platform. As part of redesigning the architecture, a few fundamental big bets were made: SQL Server as the back-end data store and ASP.NET as the development platform. This made sense given Microsoft's focus on its database storage and development platforms. Web parts were ASP.NET server controls that were based on the Microsoft Digital Dashboard design present in SharePoint Portal Server 2001.

In 2003, SharePoint Portal Server (SPS) 2003 and Windows SharePoint Services (WSS) 2.0 were born. While SPS 2003 was licensed separately, WSS 2.0 was licensed as a part of Windows Server. These two products were built on a common base platform, with SPS 2003 offering deep portal and search functionality at its core and WSS 2.0 delivering core collaboration capabilities (see Figure 1-1). Because of the ease with which WSS 2.0 could be deployed, businesses began deploying WSS 2.0 in spades, leading to mass viral adoption.

During the time that Microsoft was designing and building the SharePoint products and technologies in the 2003 wave, Microsoft acquired a Vancouver-based web content management (WCM) company, NCompass Labs, whose flagship product was a content management platform called Resolution. Shortly after acquiring NCompass in 2001, Microsoft released Microsoft Content Management Server (MCMS) 2001, which used ASP technology for creating web pages. The following year, Microsoft released MCMS

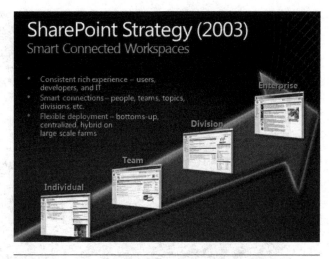

FIGURE 1-1   SharePoint strategy in 2003

2002, which added ASP.NET functionality. MCMS 2002 was a very popular product that was quickly adopted by many enterprise companies for their public websites.

When SPS 2003 was released, MCMS was a popular WCM solution, and SPS 2003 quickly gained momentum and was widely adopted in the enterprise as an intranet solution. With collaboration and portal technologies integrated in SPS 2003, customers were excited about the ability to create team sites and departmental solutions on the same platform.

With the successful delivery of collaboration and portal technologies in one product, the primary customer and partner feedback to Microsoft was to deliver a platform that combined collaboration, portal, and WCM technologies.

In 2004, to address customer and partner feedback, Microsoft released the Microsoft Content Management Server Connector for SharePoint Technologies (codenamed Spark). Spark consisted of code and prescriptive architecture guidance that helped customers with some integrated portal and WCM scenarios; for example, customers could use SPS 2003 as their WCM site search engine, and surface WCM page summaries and links within SPS 2003.

Spark was a stopgap that helped address some customer requirements. But what customers and partners really asked for was one integrated platform for WCM, portal, and collaboration. In October 2006, Microsoft released Microsoft Office SharePoint Server (MOSS) 2007 and Windows SharePoint Services 3.0 (see Figure 1-2).

SharePoint 2007 was built on top of Windows Server, SQL Server, and the .NET Framework, much like SPS 2003. However, SharePoint 2007 heavily leveraged the .NET Framework (ASP.NET 2.0), which was more mature and had rich functionality, such as master pages and web parts.

SharePoint 2007 had tremendous business success, with more than 17,000 customers, 100 million licenses, 4,000 system integrators, and $1.3 billion a year in revenue. It changed the way customers and partners think about business collaboration. It delivered

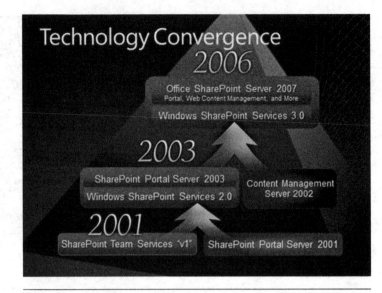

FIGURE 1-2 The convergence of Microsoft technology

an integrated platform that featured collaboration, portal, search, content management, business forms, and business intelligence technologies.

Figure 1-3 represents the integrated capabilities that SharePoint 2007 delivered. Building these different features on a common platform provided a common and consistent experience for IT professionals and end users. For example, a SharePoint list

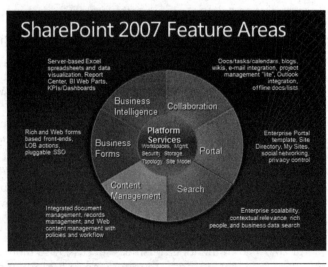

FIGURE 1-3 SharePoint 2007 feature areas

now stored documents, blog posts, wiki pages, WCM pages, and much more. This meant that all the different SharePoint list features—from single-item security to workflow to RSS—accrued to all sorts of scenarios. SharePoint 2007 not only delivered an integrated set of features, but also delivered top-notch capabilities in each functionality area and was rated at the top of many analyst reports.

After the 2007 release, Microsoft continued innovating and making strategic acquisitions to deliver the best value to customers and partners. From acquiring FAST search technology to delivering a cloud-based SharePoint service (SharePoint Online), Microsoft has continuously delivered value while building the next-generation platform for business collaboration.

On May 12, 2010, Microsoft launched SharePoint 2010—at the time, the most anticipated release of SharePoint. It was designed to deliver the most comprehensive and best productivity experience available (see Figure 1-4). SharePoint 2010 came in three main flavors: SharePoint Server 2010, SharePoint Foundation 2010 (which replaced the WSS branding), and SharePoint Online, available in the Microsoft Business Productivity Online Suite (rebranded as Office 365 for this version). SharePoint 2010 was a hugely successful release and helped galvanize SharePoint as a mainstream solution that is now used by more than 80 percent of enterprises with more than 1,000 employees.

SharePoint 2013 adds a number of improvements such as better social features, the new SharePoint app development model, and a more sophisticated version of Office 365. This book focuses on the end-user experience in SharePoint 2013, and the vast set of features that will once again change the way business collaboration is done in the enterprise and on the Internet.

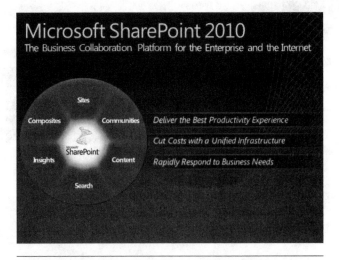

FIGURE 1-4   The SharePoint 2010 wheel

The SharePoint User Interface

SharePoint has always been a web-focused system, and the improvements that come with SharePoint 2013 are largely aimed at enabling SharePoint Online, which is provided in Office 365, to be an attractive alternative to SharePoint on-premises.

Since SharePoint is primarily concerned with web technology, the main interface to SharePoint is through web browsers such as Internet Explorer, Apple Safari, Google Chrome, and Mozilla Firefox, although Internet Explorer may be the most feature-rich option. The main value of a web-based user interface (UI) is clearly the "access anywhere" aspect. You don't need to worry about being on a certain computer or installing any software; you can just open a web browser and access SharePoint lists, libraries, and sites. This section explains the main elements that compose the SharePoint 2013 UI.

Note Although many people use SharePoint only through this web interface, there are many rich client applications that can add value to the SharePoint experience. Accessing SharePoint from a rich client is discussed in more detail in Chapter 10.

Most SharePoint pages use common elements, such as the global navigation at the top of the window and the quick launch navigation down the left side (see Figure 1-5).

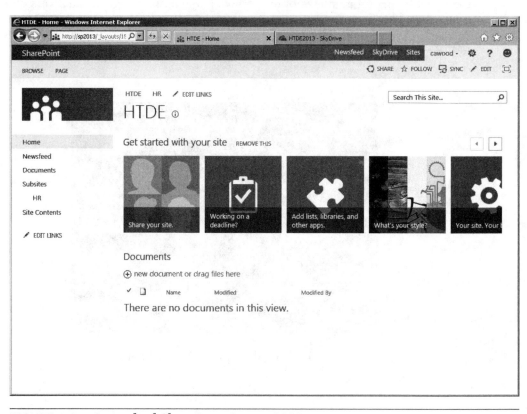

FIGURE 1-5 A standard SharePoint Server 2013 page

Below the quick launch area are links to the Site Contents page and the Edit Links option. In the top-right corner of the page, you'll see the Search This Site... box and the Follow option. SharePoint users will use many of these features daily. Sites, lists, and other key SharePoint concepts such as the Recycle Bin are discussed in Chapter 2. SharePoint social tagging and following are discussed in Chapter 5.

 To get started with SharePoint 2013 training, browse to this URL: http://technet .microsoft.com/en-us/sharepoint/fp142366.

Navigation and Breadcrumb Links

There are two layers at the top of the screen: the navigation links on the right and the breadcrumb links. The breadcrumb is a simple means for navigating to containers above the current page in the SharePoint hierarchy, such as a library page or the home page of a site. Above the breadcrumb links is a menu that includes the Fluent UI options and a few handy links on the ribbon menu band on the right, including the following:

- **Share**   Provides a quick means to grant another user permission to the current page.
- **Follow**   Gives you the option to get updates about the current site or document in your newsfeed.
- **Sync**   Uses the new SkyDrive Pro features to create a local copy of SharePoint content on your computer.
- **Edit**   Puts the current page in edit mode.
- **Focus on Content**   Provides a handy way to remove some of the navigation elements on the page and simplify the presentation of the current content.

Top Menus

Above the ribbon bar, there are some options that are new to SharePoint 2013 and some that have been moved (see Figure 1-6).

FIGURE 1-6   The menus at the top of SharePoint

The following options appear in the top-right area of the page:

- **Newsfeed** Newsfeed is new to SharePoint 2013, and it is a welcome improvement to SharePoint's social features. Newsfeed will help you keep up with changes to sites and documents that interest you.
- **SkyDrive** For users familiar with SharePoint 2010, the new SkyDrive Pro feature will largely replace the SharePoint Workspace client that you may have used with SharePoint 2010.
- **Sites** This link provides a shortcut to the list of sites that you're following—in other words, sites that you have decided will interest you. This is an easy way to add convenient links to sites.
- **Username** This is a drop-down menu with your username (some call this a "callout menu"). This menu provides a logout link, as well as links to your profile and the personalize page option.
- **Settings** This link (a little gear icon) provides options to add an app, view the site contents, and open the Site Settings page.
- **Help** If you're brand-new to SharePoint, you should take a look at the Help articles.

The Fluent UI

If you click the Page link on the home page, you'll see that SharePoint Server 2013 pages in edit mode make use of the Fluent UI (see Figure 1-7) that was introduced in SharePoint 2010. The Fluent UI, or "ribbon" as it's commonly known, was first introduced in Microsoft Office products and is meant to give you quick access to the most frequently used options.

In SharePoint, the ribbon provides contextual options. When you are on a site that contains pages, such as a publishing site, you'll see a tab called Page. If you are editing a page, you will be offered choices for formatting text, such as bold, italics, and underline. Editing pages is discussed in Chapter 6.

When you are viewing a list or library, you will see a Files tab and a Library tab. If you're viewing a library, you can switch to the Library tab to see the options available for customizing the library (see Figure 1-8). These include options for e-mailing a link to the library, switching the view, creating a new column, modifying the current view, and even creating your own custom view (if you have sufficient rights).

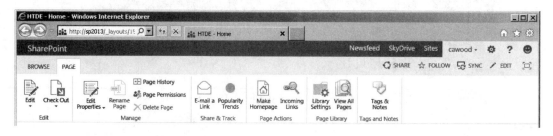

FIGURE 1-7 The Page tab of the ribbon

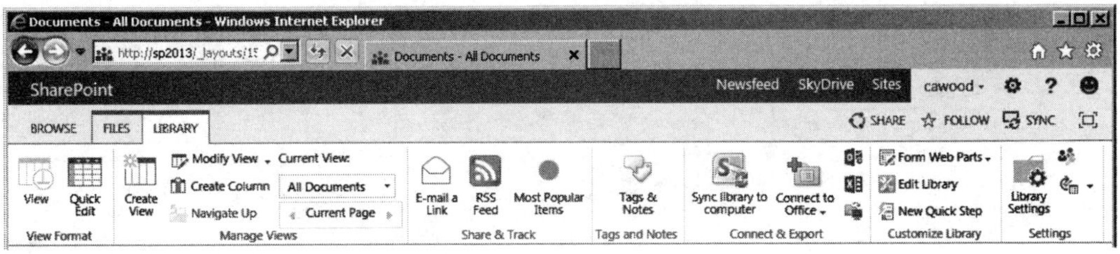

FIGURE 1-8   The Library tab of the ribbon

If you click the Library Settings link, you'll be taken to a page chockablock full of links to various settings options (see Figure 1-9). The specific options available will vary based on the list or site template and also on your particular permissions. However, options such as list name, description, and navigation are standard.

If you click the ellipsis (...) link for a particular item in a library (such as a document in a document library), you will see the options currently available to you for managing that item (see Figure 1-10). These options will change based on the context, type of list (or library), and your rights. For example, you might have rights to edit the item or delete it, and if content approval is enabled, you might be able to check it out or approve a change. If versioning and workflows are enabled, you might also be able to manage the versions or pass the item through a workflow process.

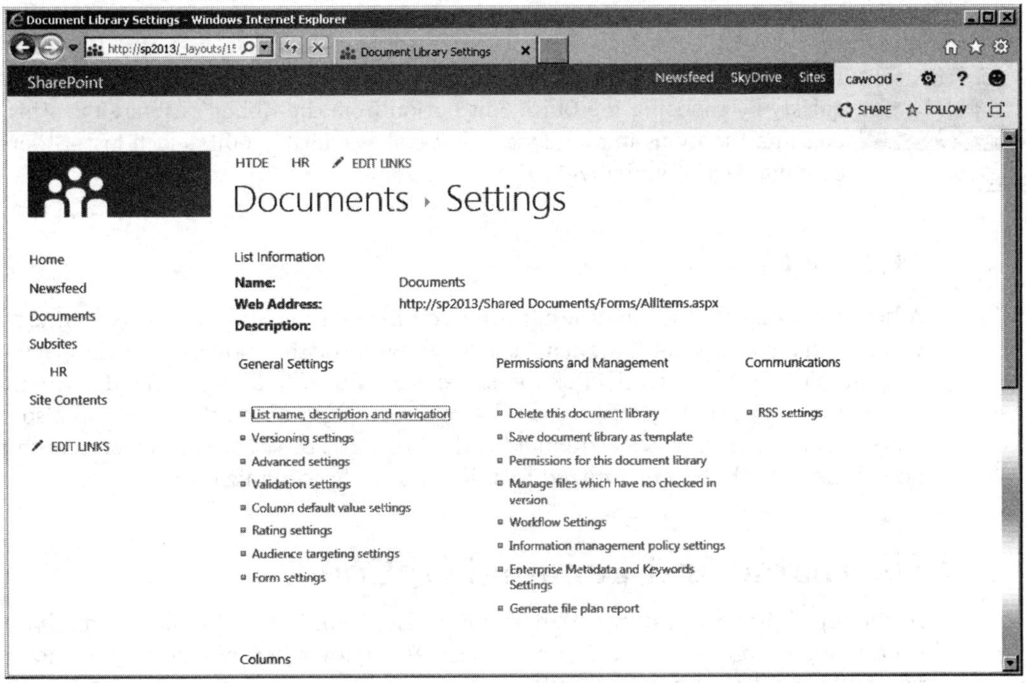

FIGURE 1-9   The Library Settings page for a document library

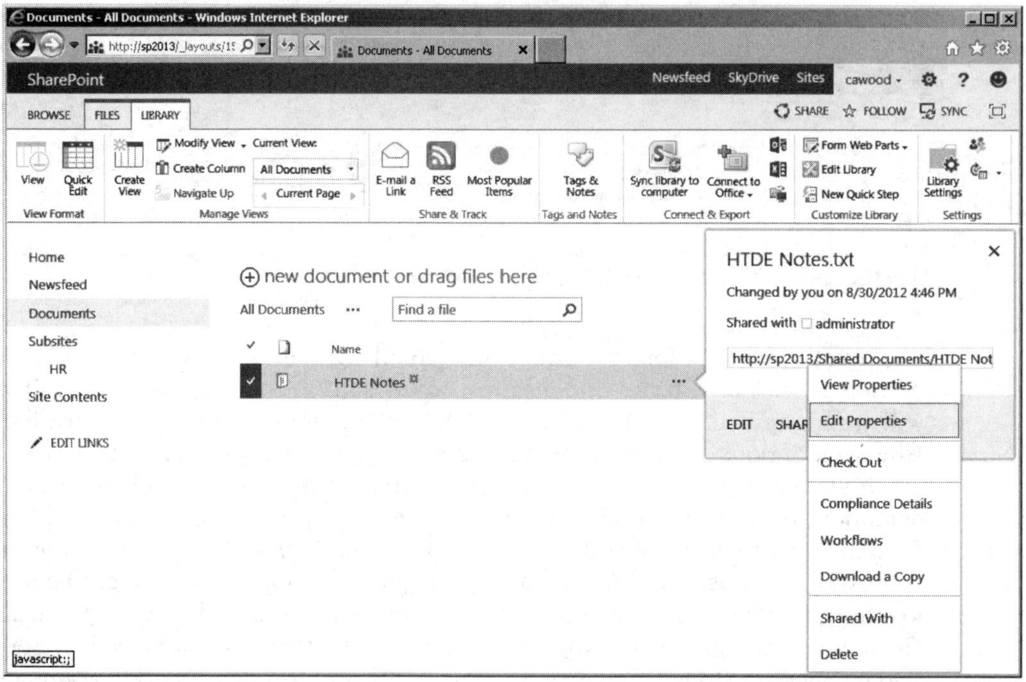

FIGURE 1-10 The item options for a document in a document library

> **Note** If you'd like to edit the properties of multiple list items, you can do this more quickly by choosing the Quick Edit option from the ribbon's Library tab. This presents the items in a grid view that makes multiple edits much faster than opening each item individually.

Hover Cards

A hover card is a helpful element employed in the new SharePoint user interface. As you may have guessed—it appears as a small window that hovers over the page. To see an example of a hover card, click the ellipses icon next to an item in a document library or other type of list. The hover card shows information about the item and also provides links to actions if they are available for the item. In some cases, such as search results, hover cards might be customized to suit a particular organization's needs.

Username and Personal Options

In the top-right corner of most SharePoint pages, you'll see the username that you've used to log in to the server. If you click the drop-down arrow next to your username, you will see various personal options. You can access your personal site (via the About me link) or sign out. Personal sites are discussed in Chapter 7.

Site Navigation Aids

Generally, you'll be able to find the sites and lists you're allowed to view using the global navigation, the Sites link, or quick launch options. However, including unique links in these navigation controls is also possible.

You might be looking for a list, library, or subsite and find that you need some help. Of course, you can use the search box to try to find what you're looking for, but sometimes that isn't sufficient. If you find yourself searching without success, one of the best ways to look is to use the Site Contents page (see Figure 1-11). A link to this page is available at the bottom of the quick launch navigation on the left side, and also under the gear icon callout menu. Customizing SharePoint Server 2013 navigation is discussed in Chapter 9.

Navigating between lists and sites can be time-consuming. If you're looking for a more task-centric view of your SharePoint hierarchy, you're in luck. It's called Site Content and Structure. This option will be available only if you have sufficient privileges on the site and the site has the publishing features enabled.

To access the Site Content and Structure interface, choose Site Settings from the gear icon callout menu and then select Content and Structure from the Site Administration category. This opens the Site Content and Structure page for the current site (see Figure 1-12).

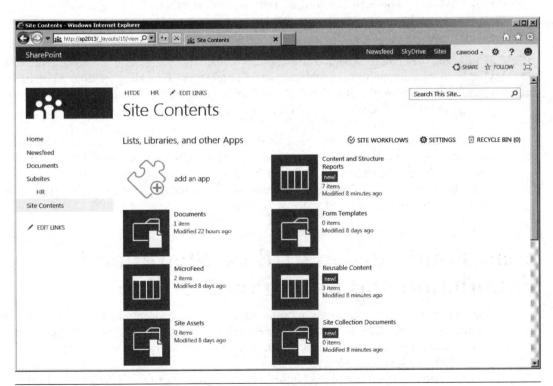

FIGURE 1-11   The Site Contents page in a SharePoint site

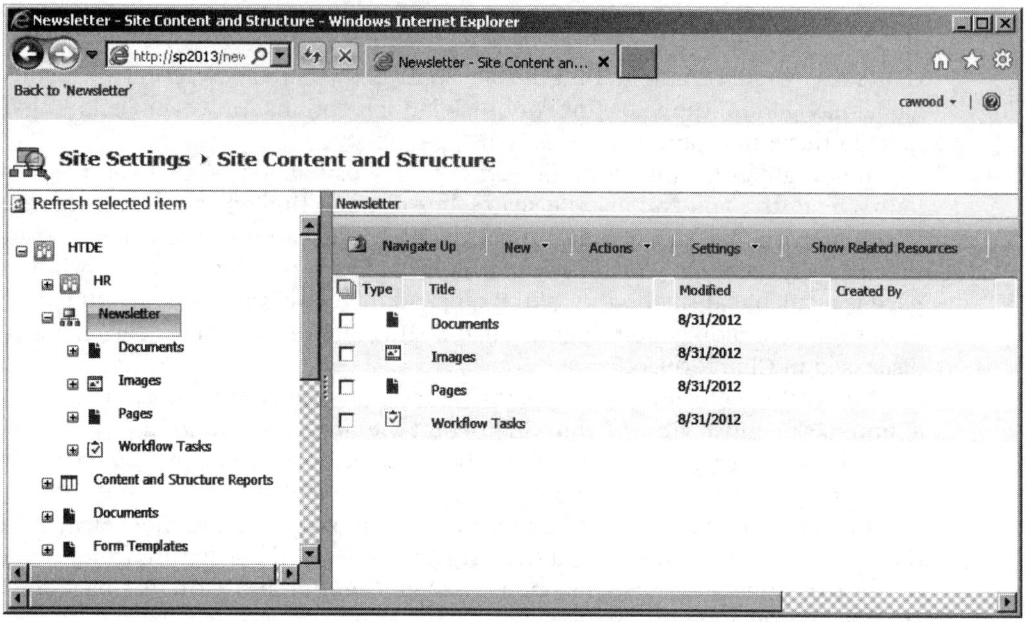

FIGURE 1-12 The Site Content and Structure interface

Note You may not see any publishing options, such as Content and Structure, available to you. The publishing features within SharePoint—including creating a publishing site—require the SharePoint Server Publishing Infrastructure feature to be activated on the site collection. Activating features is discussed in Chapter 11.

The Site Content and Structure page allows you to perform tasks such as creating and deleting sites or lists. In some cases, you'll even be able to move them. Using the check boxes next to items, you can make multiple selections to perform some operations on multiple items at the same time—something that might otherwise be quite cumbersome.

SharePoint Server 2013 vs. SharePoint Foundation and SharePoint Online

SharePoint 2013 comes in three main flavors: SharePoint Online in Microsoft Office 365, SharePoint Server 2013, and SharePoint Foundation. SharePoint Server 2013 is the more feature-rich, on-premises version, and the version primarily targeted by this book.

Office 365 includes a hosted version of SharePoint that differs slightly from the other versions. If you are using SharePoint Foundation or Office 365, you'll find that the majority of this book is still applicable. SharePoint Foundation—as you may have guessed from the name—is the platform that serves as the solid base for the server version. You can think of SharePoint Server as a superset of the functionality you'll find within SharePoint Foundation, but under the hood, they share a great deal.

Note Office 365 is a cloud-based service offering from Microsoft. Office 365 includes Exchange Online, Lync Online, the Microsoft Office Web Apps, and SharePoint Online. For more information, refer to www.microsoft.com/office365.

One clear difference between the two on-premises options is that SharePoint Foundation offers fewer out-of-the-box web parts, list templates, and site templates. However, many people would say that the most notable difference is that SharePoint Foundation is a free add-on for Windows Server (covered under the Windows Server license), whereas SharePoint Server 2013 is licensed from Microsoft based on the number of servers and client access licenses.

Summary

This chapter introduced you to SharePoint with topics such as the history of SharePoint, an overview of the SharePoint user interface, and a discussion of the differences between the on-premises version of SharePoint and SharePoint Online. Hopefully, this chapter has given you enough background and information that you feel you know SharePoint a little better.

2

SharePoint Concepts

HOW TO...

- Work with sites
- Work with lists, libraries, and apps
- Work with items and documents
- Use SharePoint permissions
- Work with pages
- Work with web parts and app parts
- Use the Recycle Bin

The goal of this chapter is to get you familiar with SharePoint terminology and the types of containers, pages, and items you'll find inside SharePoint Server 2013. Unlike with so-called traditional websites, you can't look through the directories on a SharePoint server and find the site hierarchy and other assets that comprise the SharePoint content. This is because SharePoint is a dynamic, database-driven application. The site hierarchy is just one example of something that is stored within the SharePoint SQL Server databases and then dynamically retrieved by SharePoint`s web server, Internet Information Services (IIS), when a user browses to a SharePoint site.

Inside a SharePoint server farm, the largest organizational container is called a *site collection*. Site collections contain sites and allow administrators to define permission boundaries and separate resources such as space quotas and features. Since this book is not focused on the administrator's perspective, we're going to skip site collections and cover what you'll be working with on a day-to-day basis, such as SharePoint sites, apps, lists, libraries, and items.

Note Technically, there are two other ways to organize SharePoint that are higher level than site collections: web applications and farms. Web applications can be used to add administrative security boundaries. SharePoint farms can contain multiple SharePoint servers, each of which can have specific functions within the farm—for example, indexing content for search or serving pages to end users.

Sites

It's not hard to argue that sites are the most important containers in SharePoint. Security is often defined at the site level, and the various site templates determine what type of functionality is enabled by default within each site. It's true that list templates also define functionality, but sites do it at a macro level.

Although there has always been a platform component to SharePoint, it`s fair to say that SharePoint was originally designed as an application for easily building collaborative intranet websites. Over the years, it has grown into an enterprise class, general-purpose platform, but it has also maintained its value as a means to quickly deploy a website.

> **Note** Historically, SharePoint farms have been freely customized. However, when Microsoft Vice President Jeff Teper introduced the SharePoint 2013 Preview, he encouraged organizations to use the out-of-the-box functionality. In the Microsoft SharePoint Team Blog (http://sharepoint.microsoft.com/blog/Pages/BlogPost.aspx?pID=1012), he wrote, "Use SharePoint as an out-of-box application whenever possible ... we designed the new SharePoint UI to be clean, simple and fast and work great out-of-box. We encourage you not to modify it which could add complexity, performance and upgradeability and to focus your energy on working with users and groups to understand how to use SharePoint to improve productivity and collaboration and identifying and promoting best practices in your organization."

Site Templates

To help users create sites easily, SharePoint provides multiple site templates out of the box. Site templates determine the functionality that comes with a particular type of site. These templates allow users with sufficient rights to effortlessly roll out a new team collaboration site, publishing site, or maybe even a record center. For those with sufficient permissions, it is possible to augment a site or remove functionality from it at any time. For example, you can add or remove apps or lists. However, the site template defines the starting point, so it makes sense to choose the template that comes with the functionality that most closely matches what you require for your site.

SharePoint Foundation 2013 includes site templates organized by category, as listed in the following sections, with the descriptions provided by Microsoft.

> **Note** Although the site template descriptions are available in the UI, going through all the categories—as I have for the book—and looking up the descriptions for each one is not exactly a quick exercise (especially when some of the descriptions are only visible as tooltips). I've included the descriptions here to make them readily accessible. In some cases, the description from SharePoint 2010 was more detailed, and I've included both the old and the new descriptions.

Collaboration Templates

The following templates are in the Collaboration category:

- **Team Site** *A place to work together with a group of people.*
- **SharePoint 2010 Description** *A site for teams to quickly organize, author, and share information. It provides a document library, and lists for managing announcements, calendar items, tasks, and discussions.*

Tip The Team Site template is one of the most popular site templates—if not the most popular—because it provides a good base of functionality for collaborating on a project.

- **Blank Site** *A blank site for you to customize based on your requirements.*
- **Document Workspace** *A site for colleagues to work together on a document. It provides a document library for storing the primary document and supporting files, a tasks list for assigning to-do items, and a links list for resources related to the document.*
- **Blog** *A site for a person or team to post ideas, observations, and expertise that site visitors can comment on.*
- **Group Work Site** *This template provides a groupware solution that enables teams to create, organize, and share information quickly and easily. It includes Group Calendar, Circulation, Phone-Call Memo, the Document Library, and the other basic lists.*
- **Project Site** *A site for managing and collaborating on a project. This site template brings all status, communication, and artifacts relevant to the project into one place.*
- **Community Site** *A place where community members discuss topics of common interest. Members can browse and discover relevant content by exploring categories, sorting discussions by popularity or by viewing only posts that have a best reply. Members gain reputation points by participating in the community, such as starting discussions and replying to them, liking posts and specifying best replies.*

Publishing

In a SharePoint Server 2013 server, with the publishing feature activated, the following site templates are added in the Publishing category:

- **Publishing Site** *A blank site for expanding your Web site and quickly publishing Web pages. Contributors can work on draft versions of pages and publish them to make them visible to readers. The site includes document and image libraries for storing Web publishing assets.*
- **Publishing Site with Workflow** *A site for publishing Web pages on a schedule by using approval workflows. It includes document and image libraries for storing Web publishing assets. By default, only sites with this template can be created under this site.*
- **Enterprise Wiki** *A site for publishing knowledge that you capture and want to share across the enterprise. It provides an easy content editing experience in a single location for co-authoring content, discussions, and project management.*

Enterprise

The SharePoint Server Enterprise Edition also includes the following templates:

- **Document Center** *A site to centrally manage documents in your enterprise.*
- **Records Center** *This template creates a site designed for records management. Records managers can configure the routing table to direct incoming files to specific locations. The site also lets you manage whether records can be deleted or modified after they are added to the repository.*
- **Business Intelligence Center** *A site for presenting Business Intelligence content in SharePoint.*
- **Enterprise Search Center** *A site for delivering the search experience. The welcome page includes a search box with two tabs: one for general searches, and another for searches for information about people. You can add and customize tabs to focus on other search scopes or result types.*
- **Basic Search Center** *A site for delivering the search experience. The site includes pages for search results and advanced searches.*
- **Visio Process Repository** *A site for viewing, sharing and storing Visio process diagrams. It includes a versioned document library and templates for the Basic Flowcharts, Cross-functional Flowcharts, and BPMN diagrams.*

Opening a Site

Getting to a SharePoint site is as simple as entering the site's URL into your favorite browser (see Figure 2-1). If you have read permission, you'll be able to open the URL.

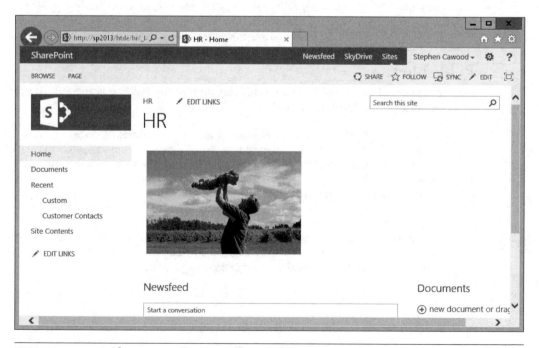

FIGURE 2-1 A SharePoint Server 2013 site home page

It's important to note that content with any URL under the site (for example, a library URL) is being managed by the settings at the site level. For example, lists, libraries, apps, and items commonly inherit their user permissions from their parent site. It is possible to set more granular permissions, but in many cases, this complicates the security model, so list-level permissions—and especially item-level permissions—are often avoided.

Configuring Site Settings

Site templates are one way that SharePoint provides flexibility at the site level, but another key aspect to flexibility is the options in each template's site settings.

To change the configuration of a site, you need to open the Site Settings page. From most locations within SharePoint, you'll be able to access the settings for the current site from the Settings menu (see Figure 2-2).

 SharePoint administration options are security trimmed, so if you do not have sufficient rights, you will not see some configuration options.

The options on the Site Settings page are extensive (see Figure 2-3). The following sections list these options by category, along with the descriptions provided

FIGURE 2-2   The Settings menu

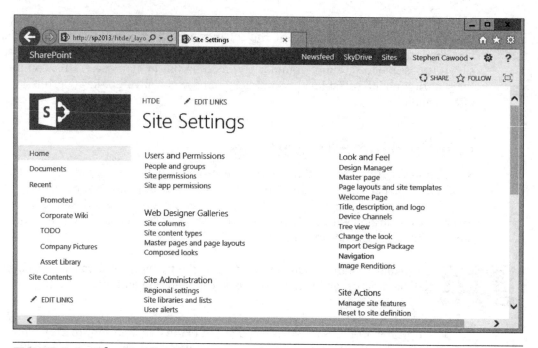

FIGURE 2-3 The Site Settings page

by Microsoft, for your convenience. Many of the options are not the sort that you'll use in your day-to-day SharePoint activities; however, some of them will be covered in more detail in later chapters.

In addition to the site settings, you'll see some general information about the site on the right side of the Site Settings page. For example, you can see the site URL and the mobile site URL listed under the heading Site Information.

Users and Permissions

The following Users and Permissions options are available:

- **People and groups** *Specify users and user groups who have access to this site and any subsite which inherits permissions.*
- **Site permissions** *Define what capabilities each user or user group can perform on this site and all subsites inheriting permissions.*
- **Site collection administrators** *Add or remove users from the site collection administrators group, which allows members full control over all sites in this site collection.* (Available only if you're a site collection administrator.)
- **Site app permissions** *Manage app access to content in this site.*

Web Designer Galleries

The following Web Designer Galleries options are available:

- **Site columns** *Manage the collection of columns available when defining lists.*
- **Site content types** *Manage the collection of content types, which enables consistent handling of content across sites.*
- **Web parts** *Select which web parts are available to page owners.* (Available at the root site level.)

> **Note** You can also manage web parts here. For example, you can upload web parts you may have created or acquired elsewhere.

- **List templates** *Upload templates that are available when creating lists.* (Available at the root site level.)
- **Master pages (and page layouts)** *Manage the collection of look and feel templates available to sites.* (If the site is using publishing features or the collaboration portal template, you will also see "and page layouts" here.)
- **Solutions** *Upload and manage solutions, which can contain additional functionality and templates for sites.* (Available at the root site level.)
- **Themes** (Available at the root site level.)
- **Composed Looks** *Select a style which defines the fonts and colors for this site.*

Site Administration

The following Site Administration options are available:

- **Regional settings** *Configure regional settings such as locale, time zone, calendar format, and work week for this site.*
- **Site libraries and lists** *View and customize the lists and libraries in this site.*
- **User alerts** *Manage alert settings for site users.*
- **RSS** *Enable or Disable syndication feeds for this site.*
- **Sites and workspaces** *Review and create subsites and workspaces.*
- **Workflow settings** *Manage the workflows that are associated with this site.*
- **Site Closure and Deletion** *View or change the information management policy used on this site and configure dates that drive site lifecycle actions.*
- **Term store management** *Manage taxonomy metadata and keyword used by this site.*
- **Popularity Trends** *Review popularity trends reports, which provide insight into how and what content is being accessed.*
- **Content and structure** *Use the content and structure application to rearrange the physical layout of all your sites, lists and libraries.*
- **Content and structure logs** *Review the long running operation logs, which provide a history of operations and recovery information for operations in error.*
- **Translation status** *Review variation logs, which provide tracking and history for the variations publishing process.*

Search

The following Search options are available:

- **Result Sources**   *Manage search result sources.*
- **Result Types**   *Manage Result Types.*
- **Query Rules**   *Search Query Rules.*
- **Schema**   *Manage crawled and managed properties.*
- **Search Settings**   *Change the behavior of Search for this site.*
- **Searchable Columns**   *Select which site columns should not be crawled by the search engine.*
- **Search and offline availability**   *Define whether this site should appear in search results and how search should handle pages with advanced security restrictions.*
- **Configuration Import**   *Import a search configuration file.*
- **Configuration Export**   *Export a search configuration file.*

Look and Feel

The following Look and Feel options are available:

- **Design Manager**   *Create and modify page templates and more.*
- **Master Page**   *Select the look and feel template to use on this site.* (Available for publishing sites.)
- **Page layouts and site templates**   *Define set of page layouts and site templates available to other sites.* (Available for publishing sites.)
- **Welcome page**   *Specify the default page for this site.* (Available for publishing sites.)
- **Title, description, and logo**   *Configure the title, description, and logo displayed on this site.*
- **Device channels**   *Create and organize device channels to optimize the way your site is rendered to mobile and alternate devices.*
- **Tree view**   *Show or hide the quick launch and hierarchical tree view of sites, lists, and folders.*
- **Change the look**   *Select a style which defines the fonts and colors for this site.*
- **Import Design Package**   *Import a Design Package or Design Files.*
- **Navigation**   *Manage the links on the quick launch* (within a site) *and global navigation* (across sites). (Available for publishing sites.)
- **Image Renditions**   *Use this page to configure the image renditions that are available for every image uploaded to this site.*

Site Actions

The following Site Actions options are available:

- **Manage site features**   *Activate or deactivate features that provide additional web parts, pages, and other functionality to your site.*
- **Save site as template**   *Save this site as a template, which can be reused when creating other sites.* (If site publishing is not enabled.)
- **Enable search configuration export**   *Activate features to enable export of search settings.*
- **Reset to site definition**   *Remove all customizations from a single page or all pages in this site.*
- **Delete this site**   *Permanently remove this site and all contained content. Click to see more information about this operation.*

Site Collection Administration

The following Site Collection Administration options are available:

- **Recycle Bin**   *Restore or permanently remove items that users have deleted on this site.* (Available at the root site.)
- **Search Result Sources**   *Manage search result sources.*
- **Search Result Types**   *Manage Result Types.*
- **Search Query Rules**   *Search Query Rules.*
- **Search Schema**   *Manage crawled and managed properties.*
- **Search Settings**   *Change the behavior of Search for this site.*
- **Search Configuration Import**   *Import a search configuration file.*
- **Search Configuration Export**   *Export a search configuration file.*
- **Site collection features**   *Activate or deactivate features that provide additional Web Parts, pages, and other functionality to sites in this site collection. Some features may require activation at the Site Administration level.*
- **Site hierarchy**   *Review the complete list of sites in this site collection.*
- **Site collection navigation**   *Configure navigation settings to improve the usability of navigation across the site.* (Available at the root site.)
- **Site collection audit settings**   *Configure auditing, which tracks user actions on all sites in this site collection.* (Available at the root site.)
- **Audit log reports**   *Review available audit log reports, which provide comprehensive event tracking for content activity, security, policy, or other filters.* (Available at the root site.)
- **Portal site connection**   *Define a parent site which will appear in the breadcrumb of this site collection.* (Available at the root site.)
- **Site collection policies**   *Manage information management policies, which provide policy statements, labels, auditing, expiration, and barcodes to all sites in this site collection.* (Available at the root site.)
- **Storage Metrics**   *View site storage metrics.*
- **Site collection app permissions**   *Manage app access to content in this site collection.*
- **Site Policies**   *Site policies define how a site and its content are managed and disposed. They can be shared across Site Collections via the Content Type Publishing mechanism.*
- **Popularity and Search Reports**   *Review popularity trends reports, which provide insight into how and what content is being accessed.*
- **Content type publishing**   *View content types consumed by the site and the corresponding shared applications.*
- **Variations Settings**   *Configure variations settings, which allow you to configure variations source locations and propagation behavior.*
- **Variation labels**   *Create variations labels for managing different language or branded versions of the source site structure and content.*
- **Variation logs**   *Review variation logs, which provide tracking and history for the variations publishing process.*
- **Translatable columns**   *Define which site columns in the site collection should be translated when variations content is exported for translation.*
- **Suggested content browser locations**   *Add or remove locations that will be suggested to users when they use the Content Browser to select images, rich media or other assets.*
- **HTML Field Security**   *Control the security settings for HTML fields under this site collection.*
- **Help settings**

- **SharePoint designer settings**
- **Site collection health checks** *Run pre-upgrade health checks for the site collection.*
- **Site collection upgrade** *Perform upgrade or review upgrade status for the collection.*

Creating New Sites

Creating SharePoint sites is probably not something that you'll be doing every day. However, when you first set up your SharePoint server, you'll obviously need to create some sites. You'll need to plan in advance exactly which sites you need and where to put them. Many SharePoint users do not do this, and they end up creating sites in an ad hoc fashion as the sites are needed. This can lead to the dreaded problem of *SharePoint sprawl*—out-of-control SharePoint servers that grow without a unifying architecture or plan.

To keep the lid on SharePoint sprawl, there are many cases where the average SharePoint user does not have sufficient permissions to create or delete sites. However, if you are able to do so, this section shows you how to perform these operations.

To create a new site under the current site, click the gear icon to open the Settings menu and choose View Site contents, or simply click the Site Contents link if it's available in the left-hand navigation. Once you're on the Site Contents page, scroll down until you find the Subsites section and click new subsite (see Figure 2-4).

The Create dialog opens and asks you to choose from a list of the available site templates (see Figure 2-5). The site template determines the features that will be

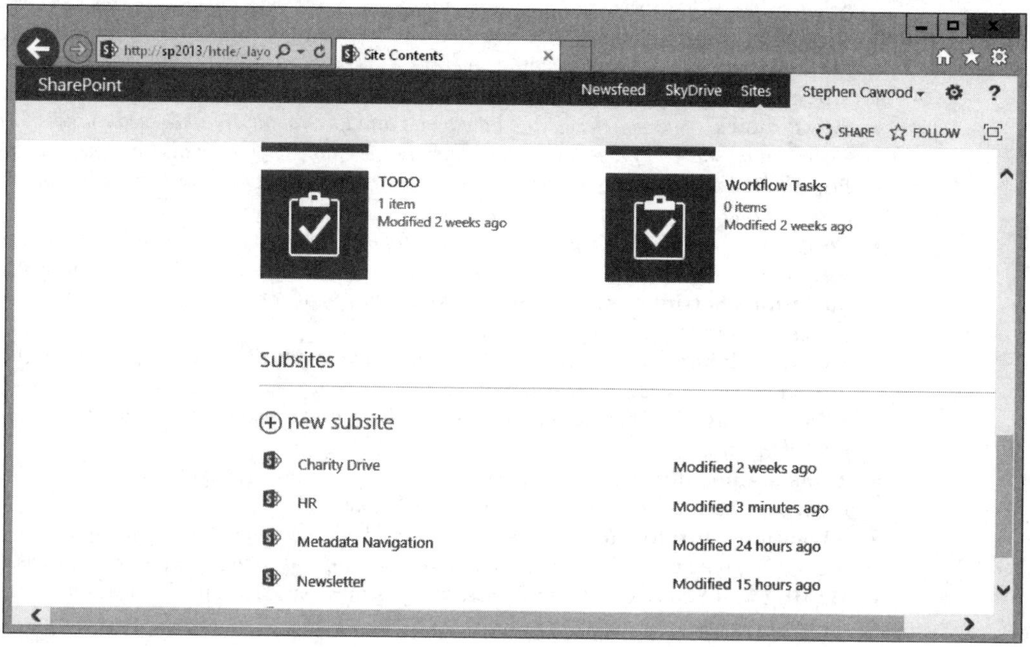

FIGURE 2-4 The new subsite option on the Site Contents page

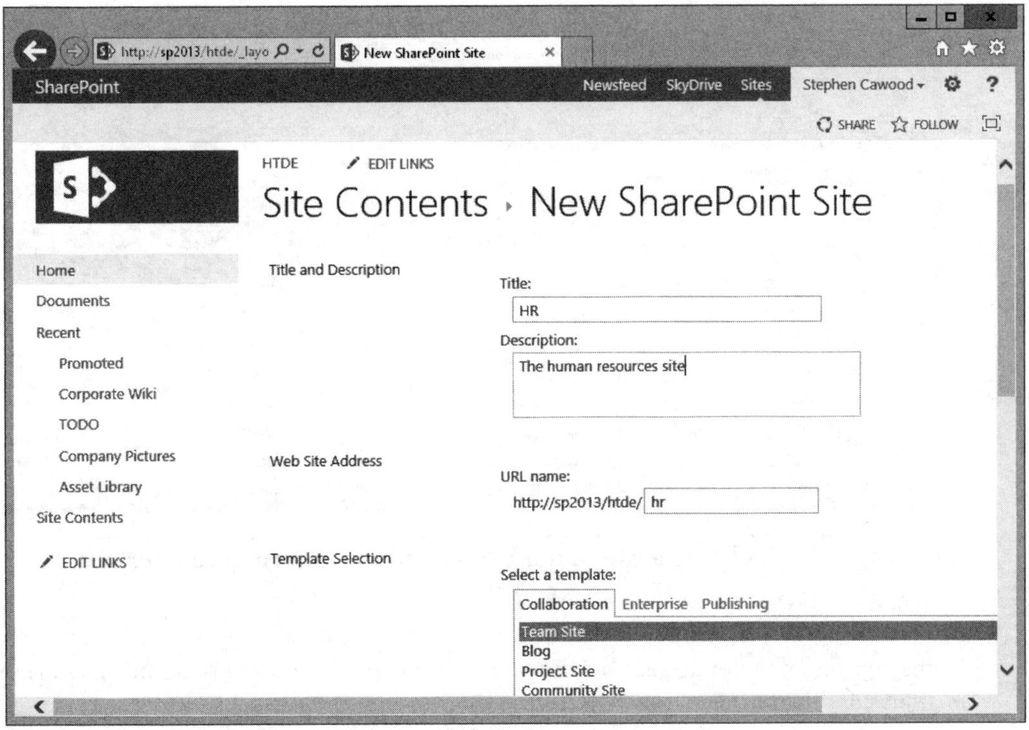

FIGURE 2-5   Creating a new site

available within the new site, so it's important to understand what each offers and to choose wisely.

> **Tip**   There are third-party SharePoint management tools that will let you convert lists or sites to a new template. This can be useful when you upgrade to a new version of SharePoint and want to migrate your content to a template that offers new or more appropriate functionality.

If you need to delete a SharePoint 2013 publishing site, the easiest way to delete a site is to use the Delete this site link from the Site Settings page. You can also delete a site through the Site Content and Structure interface, as described in the next section.

Managing Content and Structure

When you're working with publishing sites, there is a handy interface for performing a number of operations. Whether you want to delete a site, move a list, or just see a tree view of your site structure, the Site Content and Structure interface is the place to go. To open the page, choose Content and Structure from the Site Settings page. If

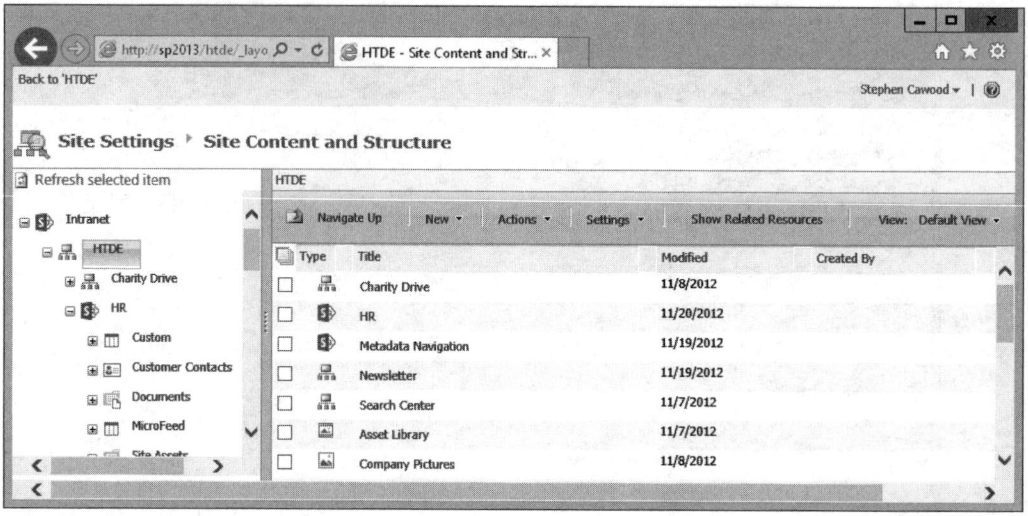

FIGURE 2-6 Deleting a site in the Site Content and Structure interface

the option does not appear on the Site Settings page, you likely do not have rights to manage the SharePoint hierarchy.

To delete a subsite, click the down arrow that appears when you hover over the name of the site and select the Delete option (see Figure 2-6).

Note You cannot delete a top-level site from the Site Content and Structure interface.

You might want to take some time to explore the options available on this page. Understanding your management options will help you decide which decisions about your site structure need to be made in advance and which you can play by ear.

Apps, Lists, and Libraries

Sites may be the primary building blocks within SharePoint, but there's no doubt that the workhorses are lists. In SharePoint 2013, there are three terms associated with lists. This is a change from SharePoint 2010, which used the terms *list* and *library*. In SharePoint 2013, the concept of a SharePoint *app* has been introduced.

There are now apps available for download from the SharePoint app store. These apps can be developed in-house and added to a private corporate catalog, or they can be installed from the public SharePoint app store. However, that's not the only reason for using the term *app* when referring to functionality that would have previously been called *lists*. Due to the success of various app stores (for example, those that sell apps for mobile phones), most people are now familiar with the concept of an app. To make SharePoint more accessible, Microsoft has decided that *app* would be a good term to use both for the new SharePoint app store and as a general label when referring to functionality that can be added to a SharePoint site.

Lists, apps, and libraries contain pretty much all of the content within SharePoint, and the list templates determine the sort of information and functionality available to users accessing that content. SharePoint libraries are special types of lists that have been augmented for particular functionality. You can think of them as lists with attachments. For example, picture libraries have an option to display a slide show of the images in the list. As you'll see in the next chapter, document libraries have a great deal of functionality added for managing documents.

SharePoint Foundation includes these list and app templates:

Lists	Libraries
Add Access App	Asset Library
Announcements	Data Connection Library
Calendar	Document Library
Contacts	Form Library
Custom List	Picture Library
Custom List in Datasheet View	Promoted Links
Discussion Board	Report Library (new in SharePoint 2013)
External List	Slide Library (new in SharePoint 2013)
Import Spreadsheet	Wiki Page Library
Issue Tracking	
Links	
Promoted Links	
Survey	
Tasks	

Viewing App, List, and Library Content

As with sites, any app can be opened by navigating directly to the app URL. If the app has been added to the site navigation, it might be easy to find by navigating to its parent site. However, you can always choose the View Site Contents option from the

Settings menu and find all the apps, lists, and libraries that have not been added to the navigation.

Apps, lists, and libraries are displayed using SharePoint views. Some standard views are provided out of the box (see Figure 2-7), but if you need something slightly different, you're free to create your own custom view by clicking the List or Library tab in the ribbon and choosing to create a new view. Some customizations, such as which columns to display, can be made quickly using the SharePoint web interface. However, it is also possible to make more substantial changes using Microsoft SharePoint Designer and Microsoft Visual Studio.

If you are looking for something specific in a large list, you might need to sort the data to find what you want. Many of the list columns are enabled for sorting. To use one of them to specify a sort order, simply click the column heading. If you click the column heading a second time, the sort order will be reversed, just as with sorting in Windows Explorer. When you choose to sort by a column, a little up or down arrow appears, indicating that a sort order has been applied to the view (see Figure 2-8).

If a column supports filtering, you will also see filtering options when you open the callout menu for a column. Filtering allows you to clear out items that don't meet the criteria that interest you (see Figure 2-9).

FIGURE 2-7 The default list view for a document library

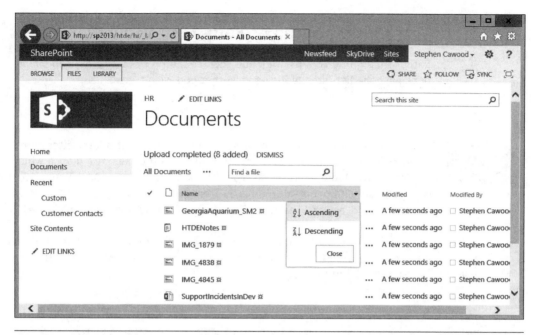

FIGURE 2-8   Column sorting options

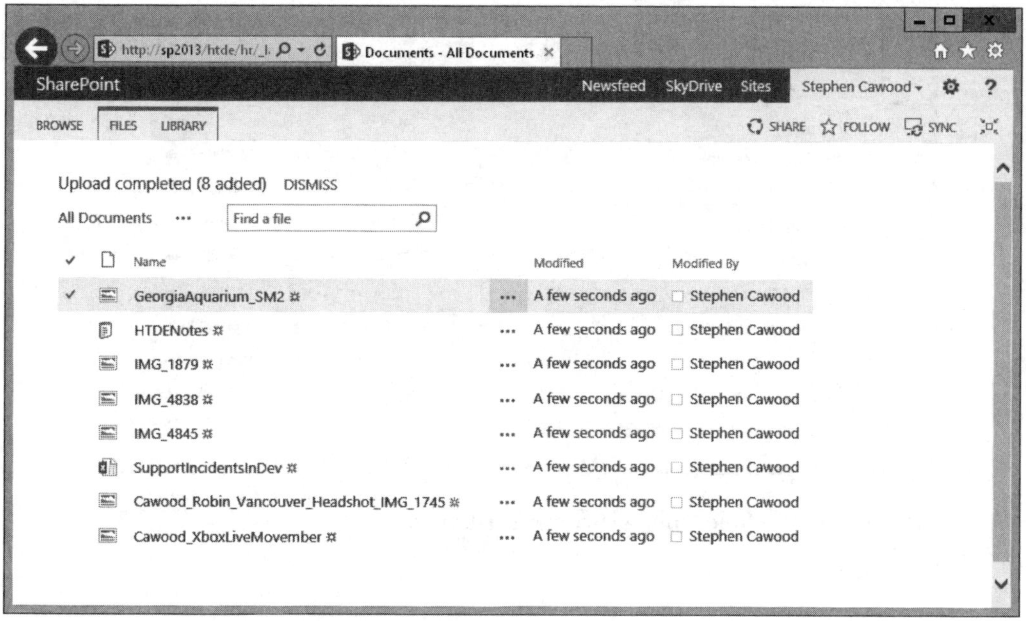

FIGURE 2-9   A list sorted by the Name column

You Can Bookmark Your List Views

Rather than going to a list URL and then changing the view, you can simply bookmark the list already in the view that you wish to use.

Tip You can add visible drop-down menus to each column that allows filtering by adding ?Filter=1 to the URL of a list. This allows you to see at a glance which columns are available for filtering. For example, http://sp2013/_layouts/15/start .aspx#/Shared%20Documents/Forms/AllItems.aspx would become http://sp2013/_ layouts/15/start.aspx#/Shared%20Documents/Forms/AllItems.aspx?Filter=1.

Sometimes, just sorting the data isn't enough. If the default view does not show you the data that you need to see, or in the format that you prefer, you can alter the list view, as shown in Figure 2-10.

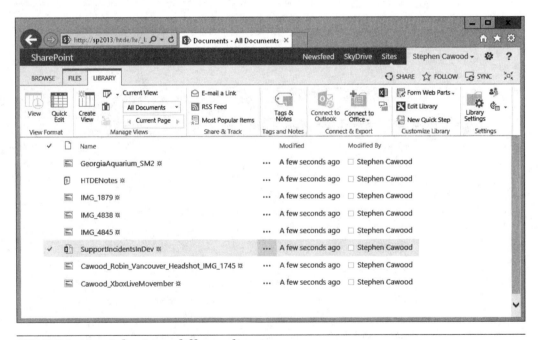

FIGURE 2-10 Selecting a different list view

Configuring a List or Library

In the same way that you can customize site settings, apps; lists; and libraries also have many configuration options. For example, when you click the Library tab on the ribbon, you'll see the list options that are available to you in the Library section (see Figure 2-11). Note that not every type of list will have this option.

When you open the Settings page, you will have the option to adjust settings such as workflow, versioning, and permissions.

Customizing apps, lists, and libraries is discussed in more detail in Chapter 9.

Creating and Deleting Lists

If you would like to add an app to your site, the quickest way to do that is to click the Site Contents link in the quick launch navigation, and then click the add an app link at the top of the Site Contents page (see Figure 2-12).

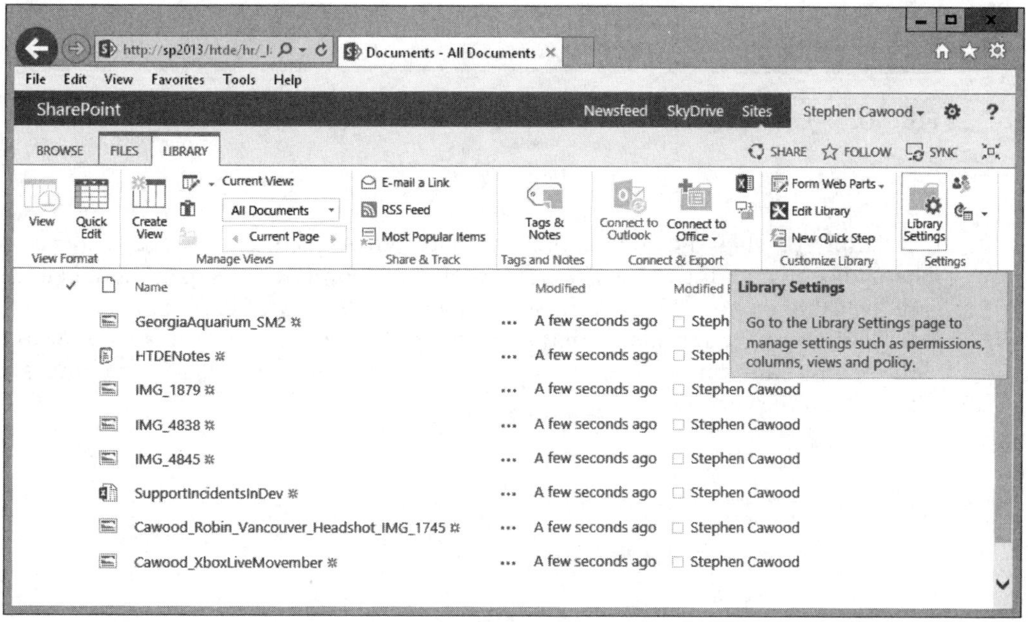

FIGURE 2-11   The Library Settings option in the ribbon

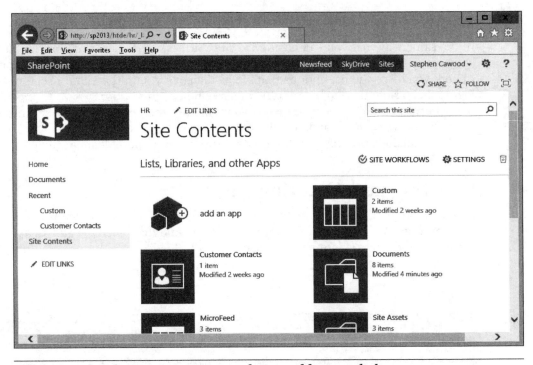

FIGURE 2-12   The Site Contents page has an add an app link.

After you click the add an app link, the Your Apps page opens, and gives you the choice of creating the various types of apps, libraries, lists, pages, and sites that are available on your SharePoint server (see Figure 2-13). These choices are defined by the list and site templates that have been installed on your server. For example, SharePoint Foundation users will find that they don't have as many choices as SharePoint Server users.

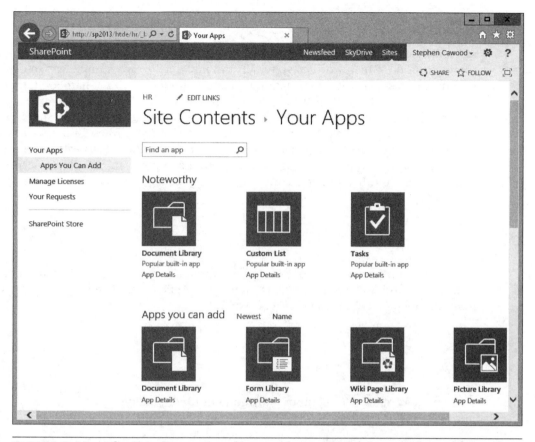

FIGURE 2-13   The Your Apps page showing the available choices of app, list, and library templates

Items and Documents

Items make up the content that fills apps, lists, and libraries. For example, the items inside a tasks list are tasks, and the items within a picture library are images. Another way to think about items is that they are rows in the SharePoint content database, and each piece of information about an item is stored in a column for that row.

Documents are a type of item. Many specific options are available in document libraries, and documents are so popular that they receive special treatment in this book; see Chapter 3.

Metadata

Metadata is the invaluable information associated with content in SharePoint. The term comes from the Greek word *meta*, which can mean *with*. So a simple way to explain metadata is to say that it's information that goes with data, and in SharePoint, that data is your content—documents, lists, folders, sites, and more. However, if you're more technically inclined, you might prefer to think of content as rows in the SharePoint database and metadata as the columns associated with those rows. Either way, when you look at the properties associated with items, documents, lists, sites, or any other SharePoint assets, you are looking at metadata. Examples can include something as simple as the title of a document to taxonomy data or workflow status—it's all metadata.

Pages

An important aspect of an enterprise content management (ECM) solution such as SharePoint is the web content management (WCM) facilities. The following types of pages are included with SharePoint Server 2013:

- Content page
- Publishing page
- Web part page

These pages are used for content management functionality.

App Parts and Web Parts

App parts and web parts are certainly one of the most fundamental benefits of SharePoint. You can think of them as pieces of functionality that can be added to pages within your SharePoint sites.

Did You Know?

SharePoint WCM Is Based on MCMS

The WCM features within SharePoint Server are fundamentally based on functionality from a former Microsoft product called Microsoft Content Management Server (MCMS). When both SharePoint and MCMS were being developed, there was confusion as to why Microsoft was producing two different products that could be used as platforms for building websites. Having heard the feedback, Microsoft decided to add the MCMS development team to the SharePoint team and consolidate on one platform. They were introduced together for the first time in Microsoft Office SharePoint Server 2007 (MOSS 2007).

App parts and web parts can be used to show all sorts of information and add a wide range of functionality. For example, you might choose to add a web part to show your Outlook calendar or track a list of tasks you need to complete.

A number of app parts and web parts come with SharePoint. Roughly 70 come with SharePoint Server 2013, but using the SharePoint framework, developers can write custom code and deploy it to SharePoint as a web part.

Web parts and app parts are covered in depth in Chapter 8, but to get you going, this section presents a run-through of how to add an app part or a web part to a SharePoint page.

Note App parts are much the same as web parts, but unlike web parts, they are used by developers to create the user interface for SharePoint apps. In other words, an app part allows a SharePoint user to interact with a SharePoint app.

Adding an App Part or a Web Part to a Page

To add an app part or a web part to a web part page, first navigate to a page that you have rights to edit. Once there, choose the Edit Page option from the Settings callout menu, or click the Edit link in the top-right area, and the page will be refreshed in edit mode (see Figure 2-14).

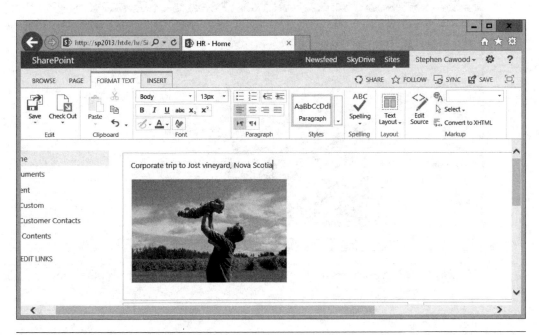

FIGURE 2-14   A page in edit mode

With the page in edit mode, you'll be able to see various editing options available to you. On some pages, this will include the ability to add app parts or web parts. Click the Insert option on the ribbon to add app parts or web parts to a page (see Figure 2-15).

Another way to add a web part or an app part to your page is to simply click the Add a Web Part link within one of the web part zones. Once you click the link, you'll be asked to choose from the available app parts and web parts. The options available to you at this point are determined by which app parts and web parts have been installed on your server. SharePoint Foundation users will see a subset of the app parts and web parts available on a SharePoint Server 2013 server. Also, if any custom or third-party app parts or web parts have been installed on your SharePoint installation, these may also appear among your choices. To make it easier to find what you're looking for, the available web parts are divided into categories (see Figure 2-16).

As noted earlier, the functionality of the out-of-the-box app parts and web parts is covered in Chapter 8.

FIGURE 2-15 Web parts and app parts can be added into web part zones.

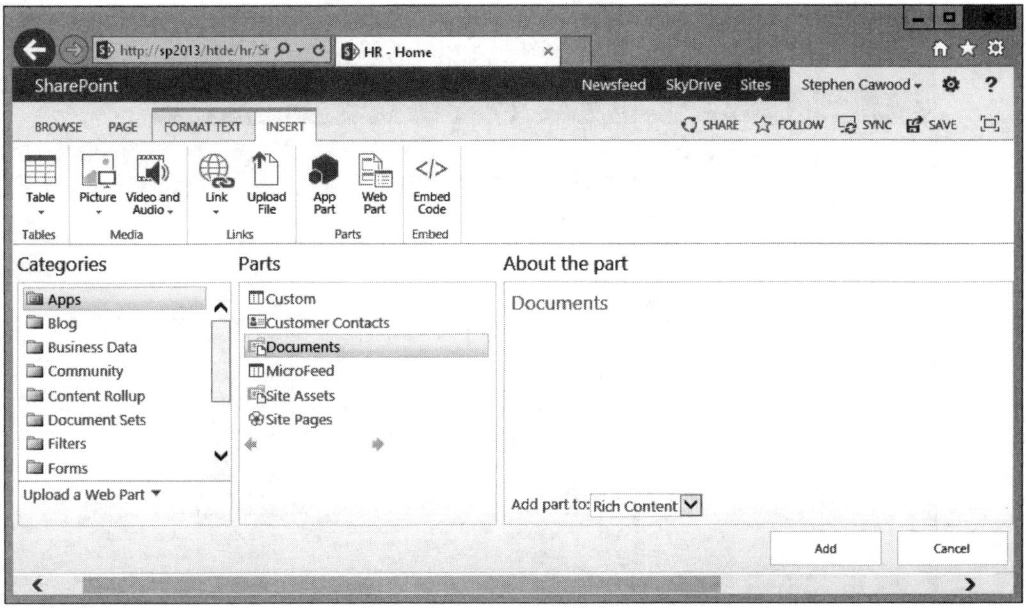

FIGURE 2-16 You can choose from various types of app parts and web parts.

The Recycle Bin

I'm sure everyone has experienced that "oh no!" second that comes immediately after accidentally deleting a file that should not have been deleted. In a feature that is similar to the Microsoft Windows Recycle Bin, SharePoint users also have access to a Recycle Bin. With SharePoint, however, you have access to the Recycle Bin from anywhere because you access it through the SharePoint web-based UI.

The Recycle Bin stores documents, list items, lists, folders, files, and even sites. If you delete an app, you will not find it in the Recycle Bin. To navigate to the site Recycle Bin, click the Site Contents link, and then click the Recycle Bin link on the right side of the page.

There are other ways to access the Recycle Bin. For example, if you navigate to the Site Settings page, the Recycle Bin link is also available (see Figure 2-17). When the Site Settings page is open, you'll see a Recycle Bin link on the left side. Click this link, and the Recycle Bin page will open (see Figure 2-18).

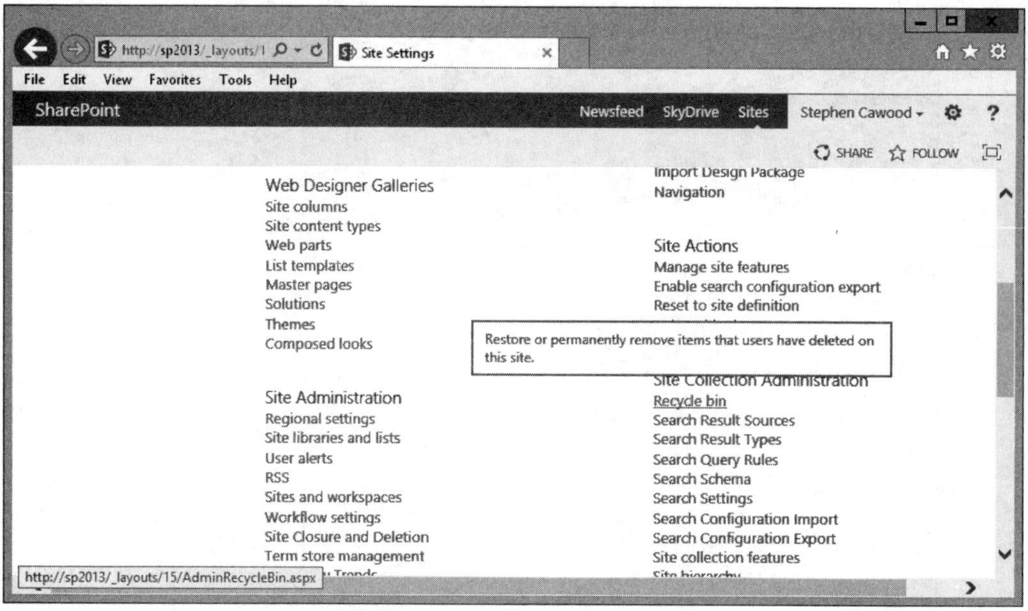

FIGURE 2-17 The Recycle Bin is also accessible from the Site Settings page.

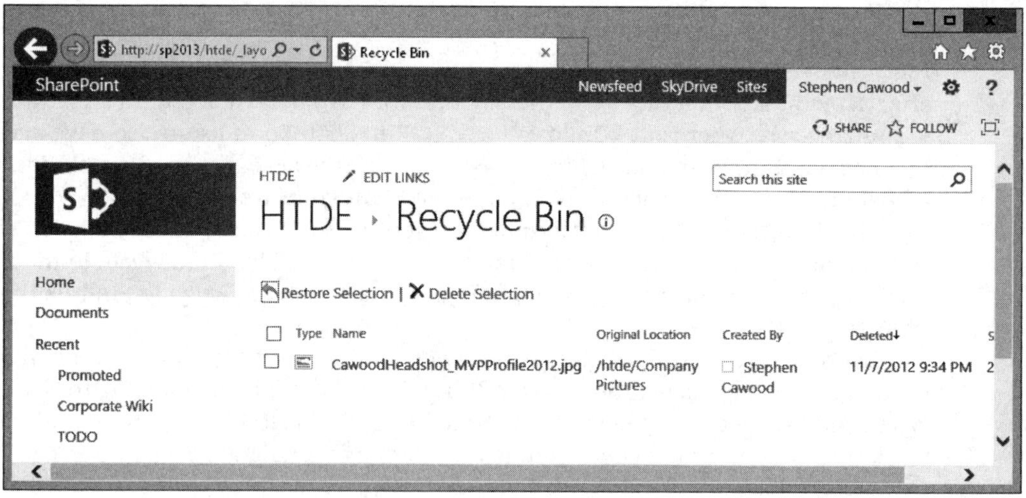

FIGURE 2-18 Viewing the Recycle Bin

It is paramount to think of the SharePoint site Recycle Bin as a last resort. Items within SharePoint's site Recycle Bin are emptied after 30 days, so there is no guarantee that your deleted content will be there when you realize that you need it back. There is another Recycle Bin that administrators can access, but that Recycle Bin has rules about how much data to store, so you can ask, but you might not be able to get your content back from that bin either.

Permissions

SharePoint permissions fundamentally define two things: who can see things and who can do things. Permissions can be applied at many different levels, but for ease of management, they are usually defined at the site level. Generally, groups are then used to control which users have rights to each site. This makes permissions for the most common collaboration scenarios relatively easy to manage.

Furthermore, many SharePoint sites, lists, and items are configured to use permissions inheritance. This means that many assets in SharePoint don't have their own permissions applied—they inherit permissions from their parent. This is not only convenient, but it is also a SharePoint best practice.

To modify the permissions on a site, go to the Site Settings page and find the Site Permissions link. Click it to open the Permissions page (see Figure 2-19).

![Screenshot of a site's Permissions page in SharePoint showing the ribbon with Manage Parent, Stop Inheriting Permissions, Grant Permissions, Create Group, and Check Permissions options, and a list of SharePoint groups including Approvers, Designers, Excel Services Viewers, and Hierarchy Managers.]

FIGURE 2-19   A site's Permissions page, accessed via the Site Settings page

Caution Although it is possible to assign permissions to SharePoint items, it is generally not considered to be a good idea. Once you start using permissions other than at the site level, it becomes vastly more difficult to manage and track the permissions of each user.

In SharePoint 2010, a feature called Check Permissions was added. This allows you to go to the settings of a list and quickly see which rights a particular user or group has to the list. To use the feature, go to the Permissions page for a list and click Check Permissions (see Figure 2-20).

After you enter the name of a user or group, the results will show the relevant rights and whether those rights have been granted directly or as a result of group membership (see Figure 2-21).

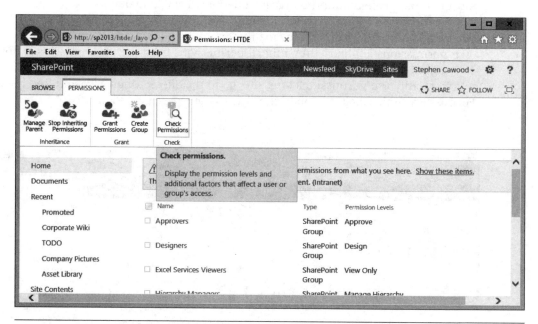

FIGURE 2-20 The Check Permissions option in the ribbon

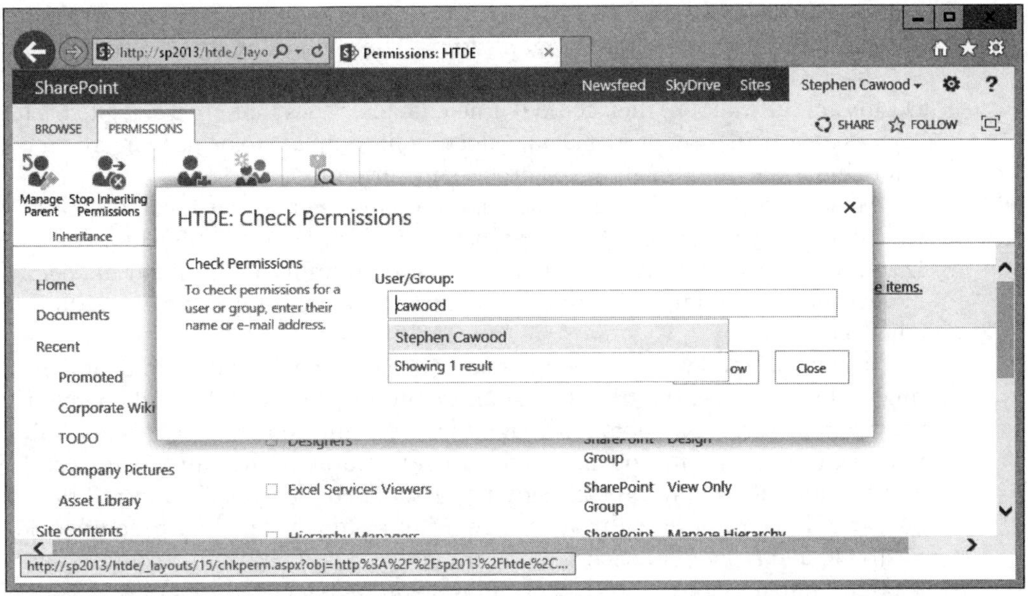

FIGURE 2-21   Check Permissions results

Content Types

The concept of content types has confused many a SharePoint user, but it doesn't have to be a confusing topic. A content type is simply a way to define a particular set of information. In the case of the document content type, this includes the actual file and some metadata such as the title and filename.

Here is the Microsoft definition of content types from the SharePoint 2010 section of the MSDN website (http://msdn.microsoft.com/en-us/library/ms472236.aspx):

> A *content type* is a reusable collection of metadata (columns), workflow, behavior, and other settings for a category of items or documents in a Microsoft SharePoint Foundation 2010 list or document library. Content types enable you to manage the settings for a category of information in a centralized, reusable way.

For example, imagine a business situation in which you have three different types of documents: expense reports, purchase orders, and invoices. All three types of documents have some characteristics in common; for one thing, they are all financial documents and contain data with values in currency. Yet each type of document has its own data requirements, its own document template, and its own workflow. One solution to this business problem is to create four content types. The first content type, Financial Document, could encapsulate data requirements that are common to all financial documents in the organization. The remaining three, Expense Report, Purchase Order, and Invoice, could inherit common elements from Financial Document. In addition, they could define characteristics that are unique to each type, such as a particular set of metadata, a document template to be used in creating a new item, and a specific workflow for processing an item.

Most users do not need to worry about content types. However, it's a good idea to understand that content types can have a parent/child relationship. For example, Document is a content type in SharePoint, but an unlimited number of specific types of documents could inherit from the Document content type and augment it to create a new content type.

If, for example, you wanted to create a Resumé content type in SharePoint, you might choose to use the base Document content type, and then add some useful information such as a photo (although that's not allowed in many places, but let's set that aside for a minute) or maybe the current status of the candidate's application. The Document content type already has associated columns for most of the metadata you would like to store with each resumé (for example, Title, Last Modified By, and so forth). To add a photo to each resumé in the list, you could add a column that provides a lookup into a picture library. This allows you to associate a photo with every resumé, and you could even make it a required field. You could view your resumés in the standard document library list template, or you could create your own custom template that shows the picture of the person associated with each resumé.

A Real-World Example

In this example, you'll be creating a new site and adding some functionality via the add web part option. The first step is to create a new site. Assuming your root site is using the default navigation, click the Subsites link, and then scroll to the bottom of the page to find the new subsite link. After you choose to create a new subsite, type in a name (such as ProjectX) and a description. Next, type something into the Web Site Address text box—this is what you'll actually type into a browser's address bar to get to the new site.

Note It is almost always a good idea to avoid using spaces in a URL. Spaces in URLs are nasty because browsers convert each space to "%20"—the ASCII representation of a space—which uses three characters instead of one, and also makes the URL far less human-readable.

The next step is to choose a template for the new site. In this case, select Team Site. By selecting this template, you're choosing the default functionality you'll find within your site. Of course, you are generally free to add or remove functionality after you've selected the template. You can leave the rest of the creation options at their default settings.

When you click the Create button, your site will be created, and you'll be taken to the home page of your new site. You'll see that the Team Site template includes adding a document library called Documents to the site.

In this example, you're going to be tracking the status of a project, so you'll need a tasks list. To add this list, click the Site Contents link in the quick launch navigation, and then click the add an app link. Choose the tasks list type, and give it a name (such as ProjectX Tasks). After you add the new list, you'll be back at the Site Contents page (see Figure 2-22). Click the new tasks list, and you can try out creating some task items.

Note that you can bulk edit the entries in a list more quickly by choosing the Quick Edit option from the List tab of the ribbon (see Figure 2-23).

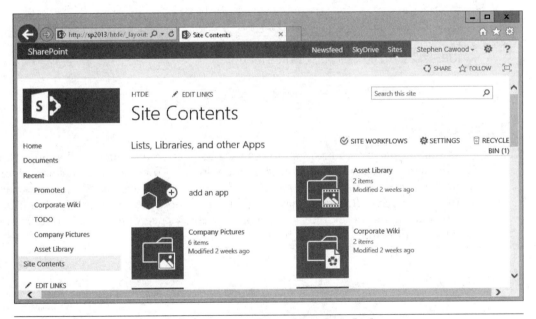

FIGURE 2-22 The Site Contents page after adding a tasks list

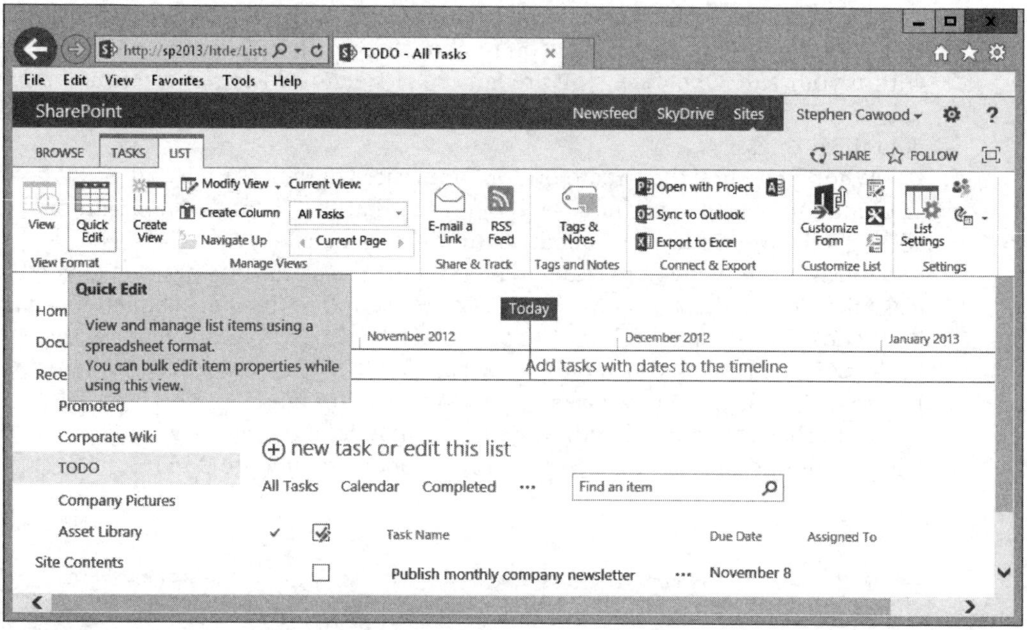

FIGURE 2-23 The List tab of the ribbon

Summary

This chapter has introduced you to the various SharePoint concepts that you'll be dealing with in your day-to-day interaction with your own SharePoint server. Working with sites, apps, lists, libraries, and items is clearly a skill that all SharePoint users will employ regularly. While you may never need to know the specifics of content types or how information is stored as metadata, it's always useful to have an understanding of what's happening under the hood.

3

Working with Documents

HOW TO...

- Use document libraries to manage your files
- Use the Fluent Ribbon UI
- Upload documents
- Add documents with Windows Explorer
- Create a new document from SharePoint
- Recover a document from the Recycle Bin
- View and edit document properties
- Work with document versioning features
- Use content approval features

In most offices, the ability to collaborate on documents is a daily necessity. However, many companies still do not have any proper document management software. When SharePoint was conceived, this was one of the primary problems it was designed to resolve. Instead of creating many copies of the same document—and often sending them over e-mail—the idea was to use a common repository that is authoritative and reliable, but also flexible enough to meet the users' needs.

At face value, collaborating on documents from a central store may seem like a simple system to build. But, as with many software problems, the devil is in the details. Offering users flexibility is often in conflict with facilitating features such as a structured content approval process, versioning, and publishing. The complexity of document management was summed up this way in the Microsoft TechNet document "SharePoint Portal Server 2001 Managing Content" (http://technet.microsoft.com/en-us/library/cc750859.aspx#XSLTsection123121120120):

> As an organization creates and collects information, employees spend valuable time searching, organizing, and managing that information. Microsoft® SharePoint™ Portal Server 2001 integrates document management and search functions with the tools you use every day.
>
> ...

Employees may find large and complex information sources, such as multiple file shares, difficult to organize and use because there is little or no organizational framework in place. The difficulty increases with the addition of information sources such as websites, e-mail servers, and databases.

Employees might also have difficulty collaborating with others on documents, controlling access to those documents, and publishing documents in their organization. Important documents can also be lost, overwritten, or hard to find. SharePoint Portal Server offers a number of features to help streamline your document development and avoid these common problems.

To help you manage documents, SharePoint Portal Server offers:

- Version tracking to record the history of documents
- Application of descriptive, searchable information to identify a document
- Document publishing control
- Automated routing of documents to reviewers
- Web discussions for online comments by multiple document reviewers
- Control of document access based on user roles

SharePoint Portal Server helps you collaborate with others, receive feedback from reviewers, identify the document with descriptive information such as keywords, and publish the document to a wide audience.

Looking at this text, it's clear that the document management goals have remained consistent throughout the many versions of SharePoint. It's also fair to say that, although SharePoint has included document management features since its first release, many end users would still agree that the ability to easily share documents with version control and content approval remains one of SharePoint's killer features.

The goal of this chapter is to cover the most important document management features available from within SharePoint document libraries and also some functionality available from Microsoft Office client applications. This will help you and your team members start collaborating on SharePoint documents right away.

Using Document Libraries

In SharePoint Server 2013, there are many types of libraries, but none are used as often as document libraries. This is not surprising, since one of the reasons organizations adopt SharePoint is frustration with managing electronic documents. Furthermore, document libraries are custom designed for addressing the complexity of collaboration.

 If you know that you'll be using certain document libraries, consider adding shortcuts to those libraries. You can do this by bookmarking the libraries in your web browser or by creating desktop shortcuts. Also, if you have rights to the Edit Links option, you could add them to the quick launch navigation within their parent SharePoint site. If you're not sure, check with your SharePoint administrator to see whether you can edit the navigation on your own. You can read more about customizing navigation in Chapter 9.

Opening a Document for Editing

Opening a document from within a SharePoint document library is as simple as clicking the name of the document. Once you click the link, SharePoint asks if you would like to open the document for editing (if you have rights to edit it) or open a read-only copy.

The exact behavior when you click a document will vary slightly based on the browser you're using and the SharePoint setup. For example, the first time you open a Microsoft Office document, you may see a warning that reminds you to open documents only from trusted sources.

Caution   When you open a document, SharePoint saves a copy in a temporary file location. This is akin to the way Internet Explorer handles a Microsoft Office document that you open from a website. This usually isn't a problem, because you generally don't want to save a SharePoint document to your local drive—it defeats many of the benefits of having the document managed by SharePoint. However, if you do want to save a copy, make sure that you save it to a location where you can find it later.

Using the SharePoint Ribbon

In SharePoint 2013, libraries continue to use the ribbon interface that was introduced in SharePoint 2010. The ribbon is part of the SharePoint Fluent UI, and you may recognize it from other Microsoft applications. The ribbon appears along the top of the window in Figure 3-1.

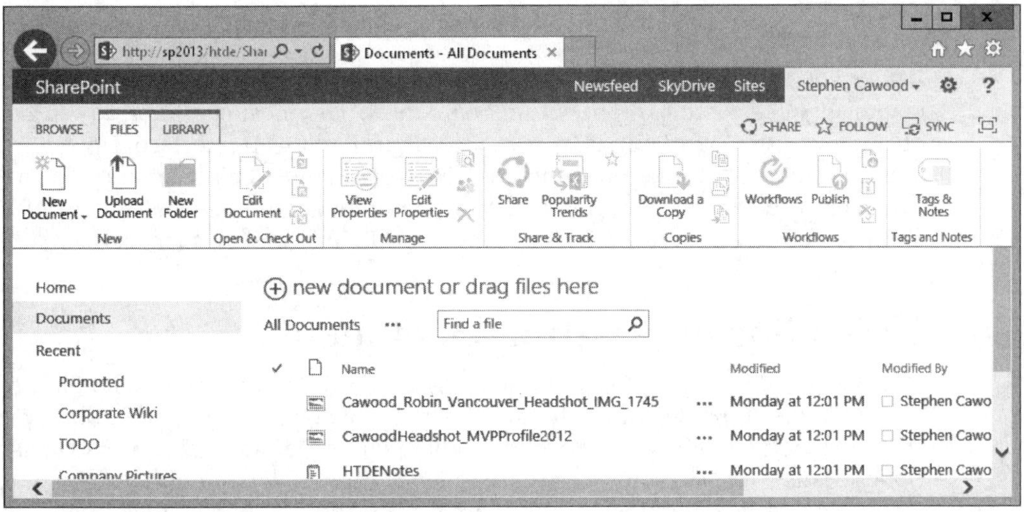

FIGURE 3-1   The SharePoint ribbon

You Can Be a Ribbon Hero

Microsoft Office applications (such as Microsoft Word and Excel) were the first to adopt the idea of showing menus in the new ribbon paradigm, but ribbon fever has swept across the Microsoft product teams in Redmond. There is even a Ribbon Hero game, which collects data while players earn points by using the ribbon interface or working through challenges. The game was popular enough that there is now a Ribbon Hero 2, Clippy's Second Chance (http://ribbonhero.com).

Many of the operations you'll want to perform within SharePoint libraries are offered on the ribbon, so it seems like a good idea to mention it up front. If you worked with older versions of SharePoint, you'll see the benefits right away. If you haven't, you'll need to imagine clicking through menus of links instead of using the new interface, or maybe you would prefer to blissfully stay in the present.

Tip If you're not planning on editing the document, opening it in read-only mode is a good idea because there won't be any chance of you accidentally making a change and then being asked by SharePoint if you would like to save your changes. This could be invaluable if you had opened the document days earlier and don't quite remember if you intended to make a change.

Adding Documents to SharePoint

Before you try some of the SharePoint document management features, you'll obviously need some content within SharePoint. The most common way to get documents into SharePoint is by using the SharePoint web interface. However, there are other methods for getting your stuff into SharePoint. This section covers a few ways that you can get your files into SharePoint and start taking advantage of all the management features, as well as general SharePoint benefits, such as regular backups.

Uploading an Existing Document

One way to add a single document to a document library is through the Files tab of the ribbon in the document library. First, navigate to the document library from within SharePoint. Once you're at the right document library, click the Files tab on the ribbon. This tab gives you access to the most common document library operations, including editing operations, content approval tasks, and publishing options. In this case, you're looking for the Upload Document option (see Figure 3-2).

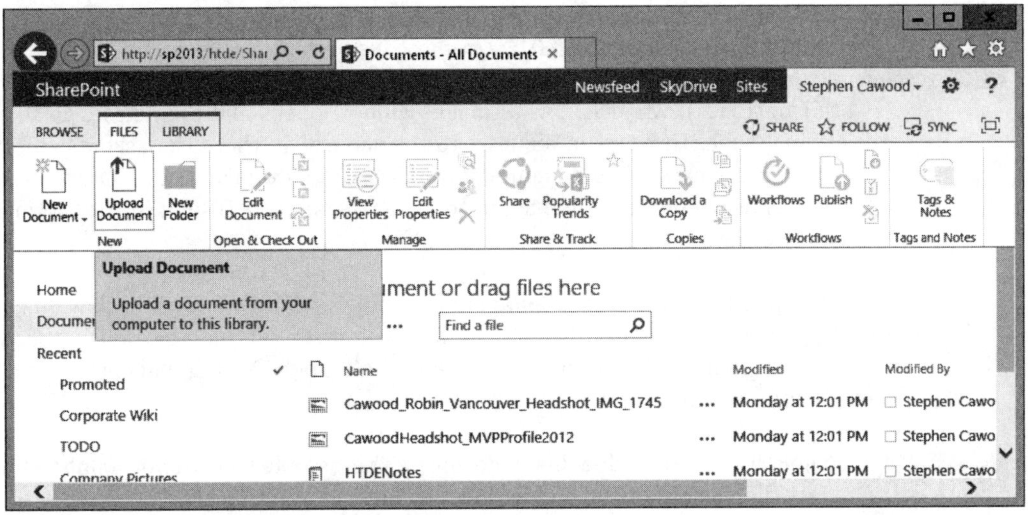

FIGURE 3-2   The Upload Document option in the ribbon

Clicking the Upload Document option launches a dialog that allows you to browse for the document you would like to upload (see Figure 3-3). At this point, you can click Browse to navigate through the file system and find your document. Note that you can get to the same Upload Document dialog by clicking the new document link at the top of the list view.

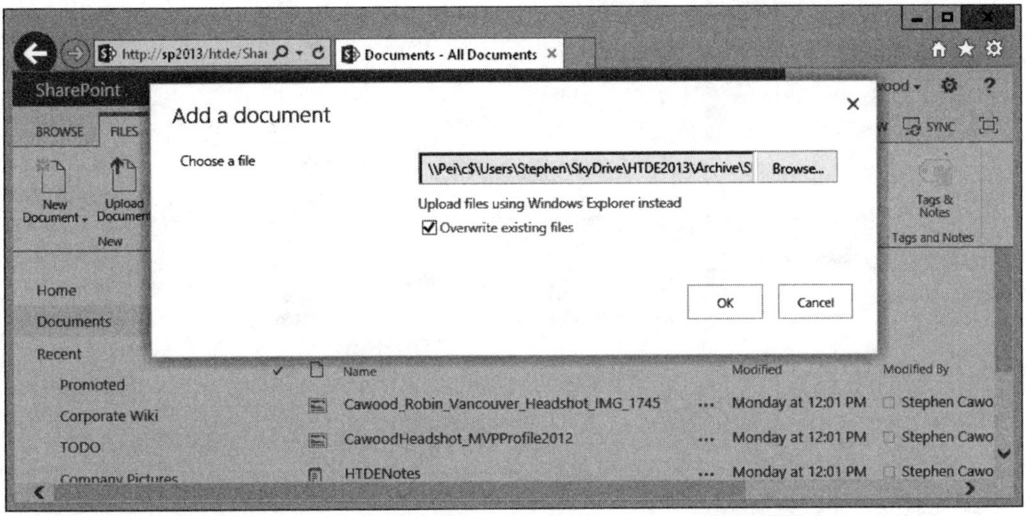

FIGURE 3-3   The Upload Document dialog

The Upload Document dialog is an example of a new type of dialog that was introduced in SharePoint 2010. In previous versions, this sort of operation required that the whole page be requested from the server (this is called an ASP .NET postback), whereas now a smaller window opens and then closes to show the original page. Those extra requests to the server—in this case, asking again for the list of documents—had a significant impact on performance. In SharePoint 2013, the UI has been overhauled again to introduce an Ajax UI and further performance improvements.

The Choose File to Upload dialog should look familiar to any Windows user (see Figure 3-4). Simply navigate through the folders on the left, select the file that you would like to upload to SharePoint, and then click Open. You can also skip the last step by double-clicking the file.

SharePoint will not allow blank documents to be uploaded. If you want to upload a test file, simply open the file and add some content to it before you try to add it to SharePoint. Filenames cannot contain any of these characters: \ / : * ? " <> | # { } % ~ &. Also, you cannot start or end a filename with a period or use two periods consecutively.

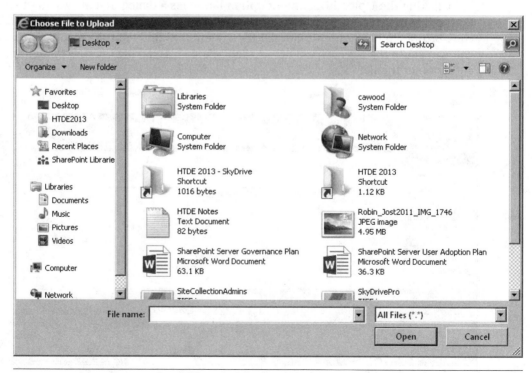

FIGURE 3-4   Browsing for a file to add to a SharePoint document library

After you select your file, you'll be returned to the Upload Document dialog with the path to your file included. Click OK to begin the upload.

| Tip | If you already have the file path for your file, you can simply enter or paste it into the Name field of the Windows Explorer–style dialog that opens when you choose to browse, and avoid the actual browsing altogether. |

It may take some time for large documents to upload. During the file transfer, you'll see a spinning animation to indicate that SharePoint is working on your request.

| Caution | SharePoint sites have a setting for the maximum file upload size. By default, the value is 250MB. If your file is larger than this setting, you'll need to either reduce the size of the file or change the setting in SharePoint Central Administration. This topic is discussed in Chapter 11. If you do not have sufficient rights to change the setting, you need to talk to your SharePoint administrator. |

When the upload is complete, you may be asked for some more information about the document that you are adding to the document library. However, the default document library list template will not ask you for any additional metadata. Optionally, you can provide a name and/or title, which does not need to match the filename. In fact, the Title field is specifically provided so that you can use a friendly name instead of a potentially cryptic filename. The title of the document can appear in the list of documents in the library.

After you click the Save button, you'll be returned to the document library, and the list will now include the document you uploaded.

Adding a document in this manner is a great illustration of a standard SharePoint task. Using the ribbon UI and dialogs, you'll be able to perform many similar operations and gain access to powerful document management functionality.

Of course, uploading files one at a time is not ideal if you want to import an entire directory into SharePoint. For that, you'll want to use the SharePoint features for uploading multiple documents.

Adding Documents with Windows Explorer

It may seem that SharePoint has already provided enough options for adding content to your server, but there are more. Here, we'll look at the option to add documents through Windows Explorer.

| Did You Know? | **You Can E-mail Documents to SharePoint** |

Document libraries and certain types of lists can be e-mail enabled to allow you to simply e-mail a document to them instead of uploading the files through the SharePoint web UI. Speak to your SharePoint administrator if this option is not enabled on your SharePoint server.

As you may know, SharePoint stores its content within a SQL Server database, so SharePoint files will not generally be accessible in your Windows folders. However, this doesn't mean that you can't use Windows Explorer to quickly get files into SharePoint and copy them out of SharePoint. To use this time-saving feature, go to the document library and, from the Library ribbon tab, choose Open with Explorer (see Figure 3-5).

 Note Open with Windows Explorer works only if you are using the Internet Explorer browser, and you must be using the 32-bit version. The 64-bit version of Internet Explorer (and other web browsers) will show the Open with Windows Explorer link grayed out.

SharePoint launches Windows Explorer and enables you to access your SharePoint content. Once you have the library open, you can drag-and-drop from your Windows folders into the document library, or vice versa (see Figure 3-6).

Caution If you copy a file out of SharePoint using Windows Explorer, you are doing just that: making a copy. The copy will not be bound by any workflow or management features enabled on the source SharePoint library. This is the same caution that applies to saving a copy of a document you opened from SharePoint.

You may be feeling flush with power after seeing how easy it is to copy your documents into SharePoint. Just bear in mind that uploading documents in Windows Explorer isn't the only way to add content.

FIGURE 3-5 The open with Explorer link in the upload file dialog

	HTDE - Documents	

Window chrome showing:

File   Home   Share   View

SharePoint ▸ HTDE - Documents | Search HTDE - Documents

Name	Date modified	Type	Size
⭐ Favorites			
■ Desktop			
Downloads			
Recent places			
HTDE2013			
SharePoint			
Libraries			
Documents			

Name	Date modified	Type	Size
01-ch01	11/21/2012 9:46 PM	Microsoft Word D...	
Cawood_Robin_Vancouver_Headshot_IM...	11/19/2012 12:01 ...	JPEG image	5
CawoodHeadshot_MVPProfile2012	11/19/2012 12:01 ...	JPEG image	1
connectToOffice	11/21/2012 9:21 PM	TIFF image	
HTDENotes	11/21/2012 9:32 PM	Text Document	

5 items

FIGURE 3-6   Dragging a file into SharePoint using Windows Explorer

Tip   A great time-saver is to add your SharePoint library or folder to the Favorites list in Windows Explorer. After you've done this, you can open Windows Explorer and go directly to the bookmarked list. To add SharePoint content to Favorites, simply drag the item into the Favorites area.

Uploading Multiple Documents with Drag-and-Drop

Although the Windows Explorer view is useful, you may want to quickly add some files into SharePoint without the bother of opening another window. SharePoint 2013 adds the option to simply drag-and-drop files into your browser (see Figure 3-7).

Clearly, the upload multiple document options are great time-savers. Don't waste your time and effort uploading a bunch of files individually; simply upload them in bulk.

Creating a New Document

If you have Microsoft Office installed, you'll also have the option of creating a new document from the document library ribbon. This is useful if you're starting a new Microsoft Office document and you know that you'll be uploading it to SharePoint eventually. Rather than going through multiple steps, you can simply create the file from within SharePoint.

First, go to the library where you want the document to be stored. Then find the New Document option on the trusty SharePoint ribbon (see Figure 3-8). This will create a new document using the document library's default document template. For example, if the default template is Microsoft Word 2013, Word will open and allow

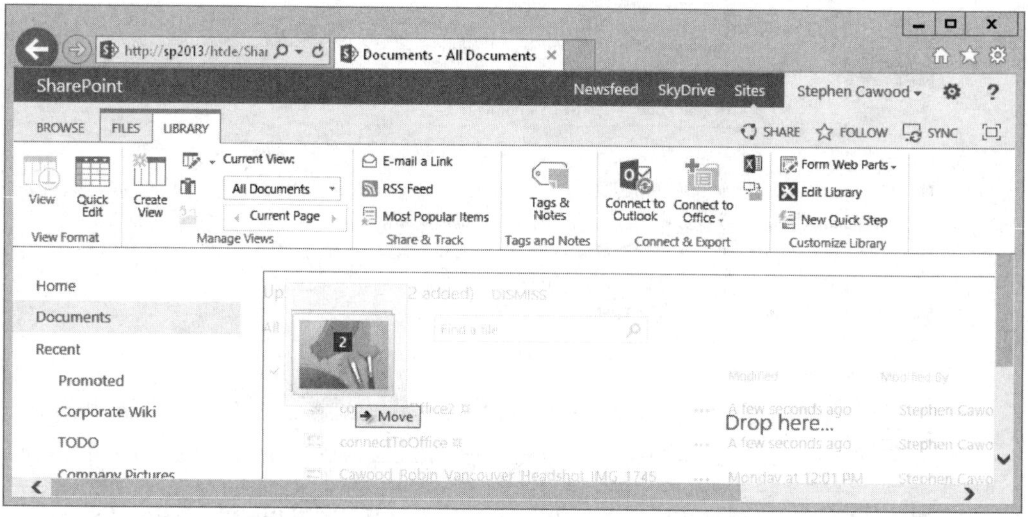

FIGURE 3-7 Dropping files into a document library

you to start creating your new document. You can work on the temporary copy of the document as long as you want, and when you choose to save the file, the client application will ask you to save it in SharePoint.

The choice of whether to first create new documents and then upload them to SharePoint or to begin the whole process within SharePoint is yours. Remember,

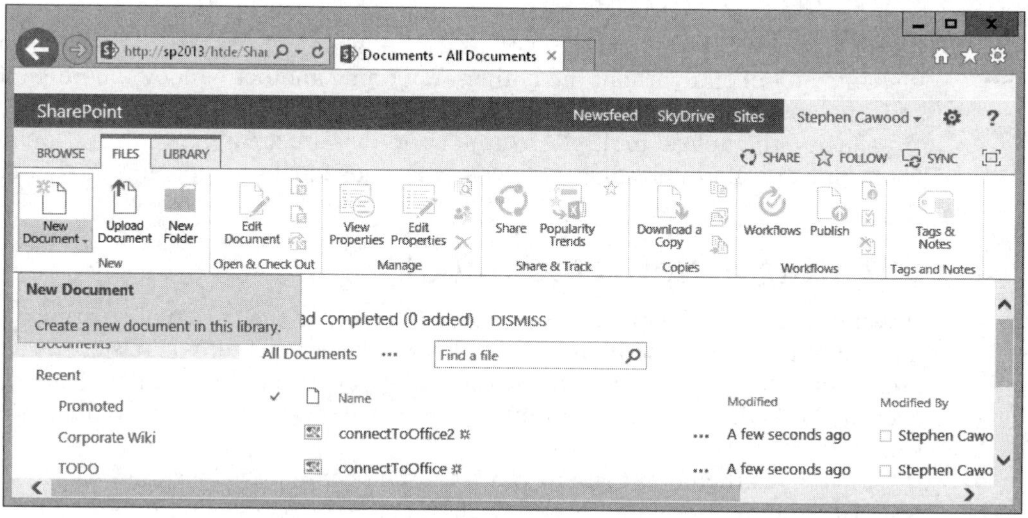

FIGURE 3-8 The New Document option in the ribbon

though, that getting your content into SharePoint as soon as possible often is the best plan, because it allows you to leverage features such as versioning, workflow, and possibly, regular backups as well.

Managing Documents

Now that you know how to get files into your SharePoint server, you're probably eager to learn what you can do with your content. With that in mind, this section introduces some common document management tasks. We'll begin with how to remove documents from SharePoint.

Deleting a Document

Although SharePoint does have a Recycle Bin, content in the bin will expire over time, so before you trash something, make sure that you really don't need it. After something has been completely removed from SharePoint, the only way to recover it is to get it from a database backup. Without a third-party restore tool, this can literally take an entire day, since it involves spinning up a new SharePoint server and then restoring the entire database—basically, not a fun time for the SharePoint administrator.

To delete a document, you can select its row by clicking an area of the row that does not contain a link. Clicking a field that contains a link simply opens that document, rather than selecting the row. If you want to delete more than one document, you can select those documents by checking their boxes in the documents list and then choosing Delete Document from the Files tab of the ribbon.

Another way to delete a document is to choose Delete from the drop-down menu that appears when you click the ellipses link next to the document's name (see Figure 3-9).

As you would expect, SharePoint then asks you to confirm the delete action via a dialog. You'll need to confirm that you do, in fact, want to delete the selected items from the list. After you confirm the delete action, you may see an indicator that SharePoint is removing the selected files, which appears on the far right of the screen.

Tip   You can also delete an item by selecting it and then pressing the DELETE key. Many more SharePoint keyboard shortcuts are available. Check online for a complete list. For example, http://office.microsoft.com/en-us/sharepoint-server-help/keyboard-shortcuts-HA010369395.aspx.

When the document has been removed, it may not be completely purged from the SharePoint server; as previously mentioned, it will usually end up in the site's Recycle Bin. This leads to the next topic. What if you want to recover a document that you or someone else has deleted?

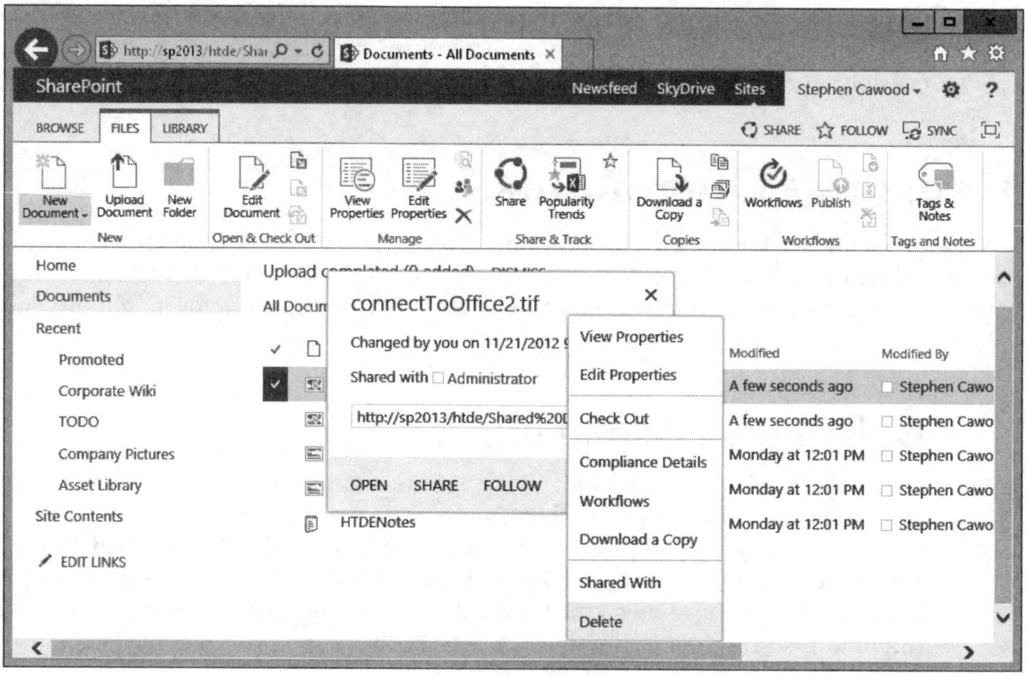

FIGURE 3-9   Selecting the option to delete a document from the list

Recovering a Document from the Recycle Bin

If you discover that you or someone else has deleted a file that you need to return to SharePoint, you should first check the Recycle Bin. If you check before the content expires, you'll be able to restore the file easily.

To check the Recycle Bin, navigate to the site that contained the deleted document and click the Site Contents option in the quick launch navigation. The Recycle Bin link is on the right-hand side. Click this link, and the site's Recycle Bin will open (see Figure 3-10).

In the site's Recycle Bin, you'll see a list of all the content that can be restored. Click the check box next to each item you need to restore, and then click Restore Selection. A dialog pops up and asks if you're really, truly sure that you want to restore the selected content.

The Recycle Bin is certainly a useful tool in SharePoint. However, it should be considered a last resort. Try to avoid making use of it on a regular basis.

FIGURE 3-10   The SharePoint Recycle Bin

> **Note**   SharePoint actually has a two-stage Recycle Bin system. If you cannot find your file, ask your administrator to check the site collection Recycle Bin. Neither of the bins is permanent, so eventually, deleted items will be removed from the SharePoint database. The first stage, the site Recycle Bin, can be set to expire after a certain number of days (30 days is the default setting). The second stage, the site collection Recycle Bin, can be set to expire when it reaches a certain storage capacity (50 percent of the site quota is the default setting). So, by default, deleted items stay in the site Recycle Bin for 30 days and then move to the site collection Recycle Bin, from which the administrator can still recover the items (subject to sufficient storage capacity). You can think of the second stage as the "global" Recycle Bin.

Viewing Document Properties

You'll often need to check into the finer details of your documents. This information is stored in the document's metadata. Metadata is basically data about data, and it is used for everything from search to sorting.

> **Note**   SharePoint supports a great number of metadata options. It is possible that your documents will already be loaded with useful information, but metadata doesn't necessarily get "automagically" populated by the system. Getting metadata into the system often relies on the diligence of users.

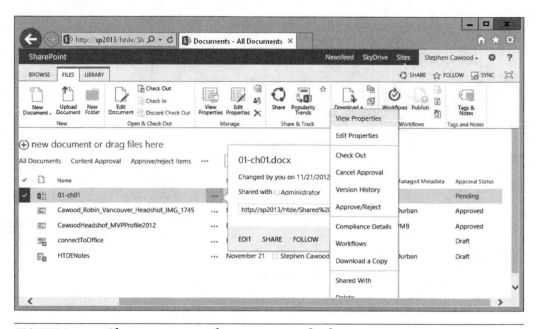

FIGURE 3-11 Choosing to view the properties of a document

The quickest way to look for metadata is to access the default document properties. What you'll find there will vary slightly, but information such as name and title is common. To see the properties of your documents, select a document from within a document library, click its ellipses link and the ellipses link on the callout menu, and then choose View Properties (see Figure 3-11). Alternatively, you can skip all that by using the View Properties option in the ribbon.

After you make your selection, the properties dialog opens, showing the properties of the document (see Figure 3-12). The properties you see for each document will vary based on the list template. For example, if you add a number of custom columns, you'll see that data appear by default in the properties dialog.

Along with viewing properties, if you have sufficient permissions, you'll also be able to make changes to the property settings.

Editing Document Properties

There are countless reasons why you might want to change the metadata associated with documents in SharePoint. For example, maybe the filenames used during the upload were the cryptic filename values from the file system, and now you want to make use of SharePoint's potential by assigning user-friendly titles.

To edit properties, first find your document. Then click the Edit Properties button on the ribbon or click the document's drop-down arrow and select the Edit Properties

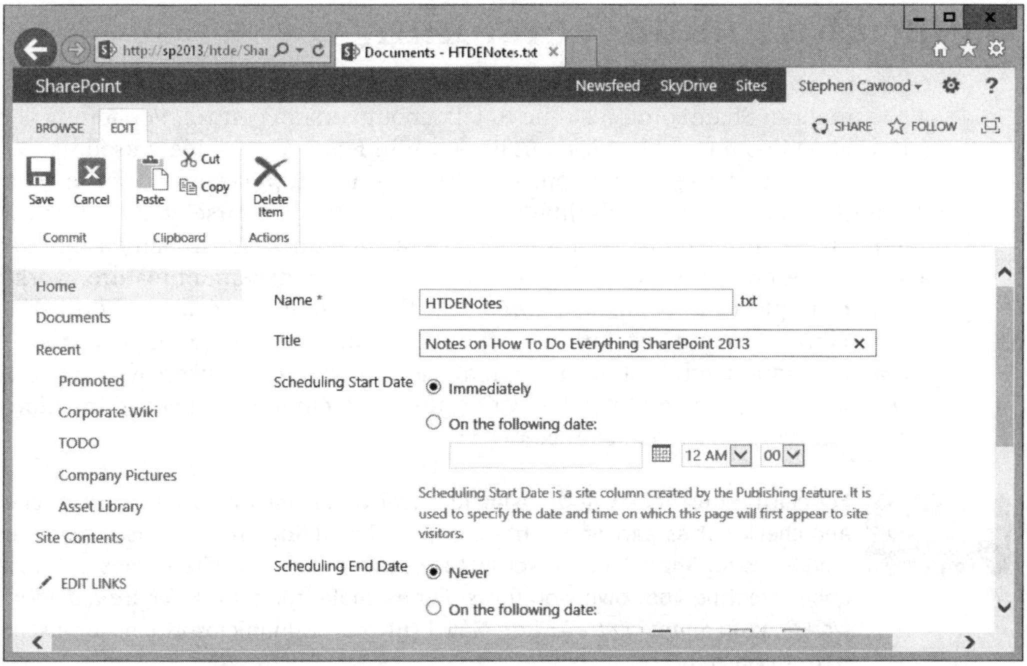

FIGURE 3-12 Viewing the properties of a document

option. When the dialog opens, you'll be able to alter any properties that you have rights to edit.

You will not be able to see every metadata value in the property edit dialog. You can think of each column of data in a list as a different metadata value. Not all of the columns are shown in the default list view, and they certainly are not all shown in the property edit dialog. If you are looking for information that does not show by default, you may need to create your own custom view. Creating your own list views is discussed in Chapter 9.

Tip   With the Enterprise Metadata Management (EMM) functionality in SharePoint, it's possible that you'll need to frequently edit document properties to tag them with taxonomy metadata. The information you add may seem unrelated to your daily tasks, but it will empower a number of use cases on your SharePoint server. For example, adding extra metadata will improve searches so that you can find content throughout the server. SharePoint taxonomy is discussed in Chapter 5. Since the underlying taxonomy service is called the Managed Metadata Service, many SharePoint folks refer to this functionality as MMS.

Using Document Versioning

Now that you have an understanding of how easy it is to add, remove, open, and edit a document in SharePoint, it's time to talk about version control. Versioning is not required on document libraries, but it's a useful feature and widely used.

Versioning gives you the ability to create a new copy—for a minor or major version—of a document each time you make an edit. Of course, you wouldn't want two people working on the same version of the document at the same time, so you also need another important SharePoint document management feature: workflow.

The simplest workflow in SharePoint is the content approval workflow that's included in the document library versioning settings. This requires that a user check out a document before that user can make a change. If other users want to edit the same document, they will need to wait until the document is checked in before they can check it out and make changes.

> **Note** For clarity, this book will occasionally refer to manual operations such as check-in and check-out as part of a content approval workflow. You can also create custom workflows for SharePoint Server 2013. Search online if you're interested in learning about creating your own workflows. For example, the article *Get started with workflows in SharePoint 2013* on MSDN (http://msdn.microsoft.com/en-us/library/jj163917.aspx).

Checking Out Documents

If a document library has been configured to require check-out before making changes, then you'll need to select the document by clicking its check box, and then click the Check Out option in the ribbon before you'll be allowed to open it for editing (see Figure 3-13).

After you choose Check Out, SharePoint opens a dialog that asks whether you would like to copy the file into your local drafts folder. If you choose Yes, you'll be able to disconnect from the SharePoint server (for example, to take your laptop home) and work on the document offline. Once you are finished with your edits, you can reconnect to the server and save your document back into its document library. If you choose not to copy a local version, you'll be able to save your changes only while you're connected to the SharePoint server.

> **Tip** When you choose to save a copy to your local drafts folder, a SharePoint Drafts folder will be created in your Documents folder in Windows.

If you're working on a desktop computer, you might choose not to save a local copy. This has the advantage in that any time you save that document, you'll be saving your work back to the server. However, if you are on a slow connection, this could slow down your productivity. Regardless of which option you choose, you simply need to remember to save your changes back to the server when you're finished.

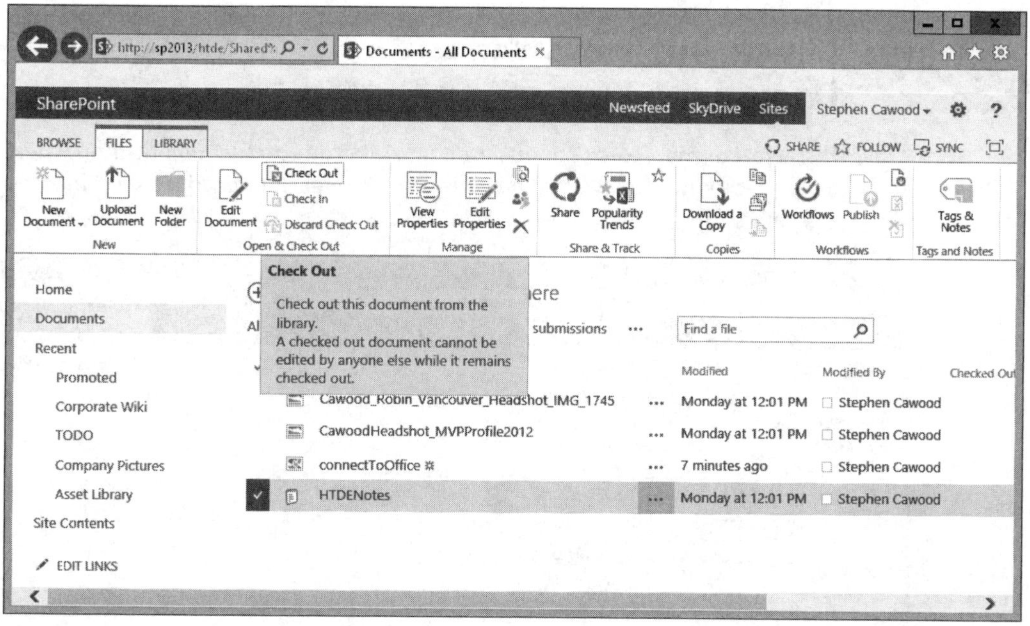

FIGURE 3-13   Using the ribbon to check out a document

After a file has been checked out, SharePoint will change the icon next to the document to a little green arrow.

Note If you choose to edit your document in the default editor assigned to the document type (for example, Microsoft Word), you will still be prompted to check out the file if check-out is required for that document library. Once the document is checked out, you will be able to edit and save your changes.

Checking In Documents

Naturally, the topic to cover after checking out a document is how to check in a document. In addition to the usual contextual menu (ellipses link) and ribbon options previously discussed, if you're using Microsoft Office clients, there's also a way to check in from the client.

Checking In with SharePoint

The first technique for checking in a document is to simply go to the library and use the ribbon. You might expect that SharePoint would simply check in the document and you would be finished, but that's not the case. When you check in, SharePoint

Check Out from the Document Properties Dialog

It's also possible to check out a document from the document properties dialog, as shown below. You may not use this feature, but just keep in mind that it's there.

asks if you want to retain the check-out status after the document has been checked in (see Figure 3-14).

This option may seem counterintuitive at first, but there is a logical reason for it. If you were working on a document and wanted to check it in to create a version, but you didn't want anyone altering the document before you made further changes, then you could retain the check-out status and not risk the chance that another user would check out the document before you remembered to check it out again.

In this dialog, you'll also be asked for a check-in comment. In the default content approval process, this comment is optional, but it can be very useful when you're looking through old versions of files and trying to figure out why a certain change was made.

Checking In with Microsoft Word

Another way to check in a SharePoint file is from one of the many clients that support SharePoint content approval workflow. If you're editing a file in Word, when you save and close the file, the client will ask if you want to check in (see Figure 3-15).

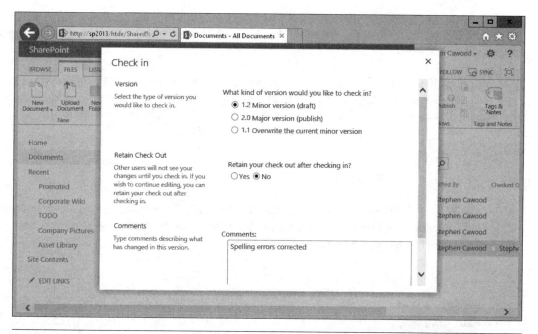

FIGURE 3-14   You can retain the check-out status after checking in a document.

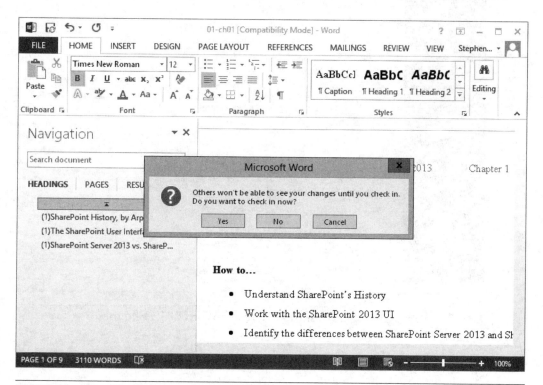

FIGURE 3-15   Check in from Microsoft Word 2013

If you want to check in a file from a client without closing the document, you can also choose File | Info, and then choose to check in from the available options (see Figure 3-16).

 The interface used for this example is part of the Microsoft Office Backstage view. Backstage offers a tighter integration between SharePoint and Microsoft applications, including Access, Excel, InfoPath, OneNote, PowerPoint, Project, Publisher, SharePoint Designer, Visio, and Word.

As with the other techniques, the client program will ask you to enter a check-in comment (see Figure 3-17).

 The client Info page shows all sorts of interesting information about SharePoint files. You'll be able to see properties of the document, as well as information about versions, permissions, and more.

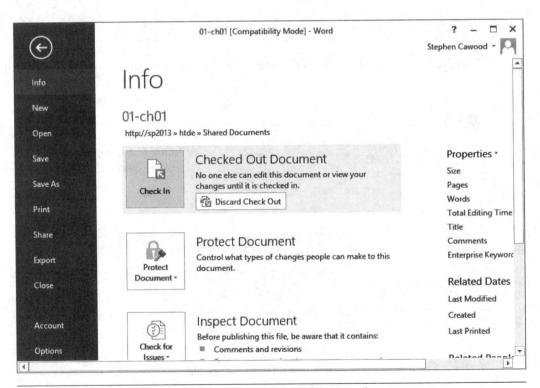

FIGURE 3-16   Check in from the Microsoft Word 2013 File menu

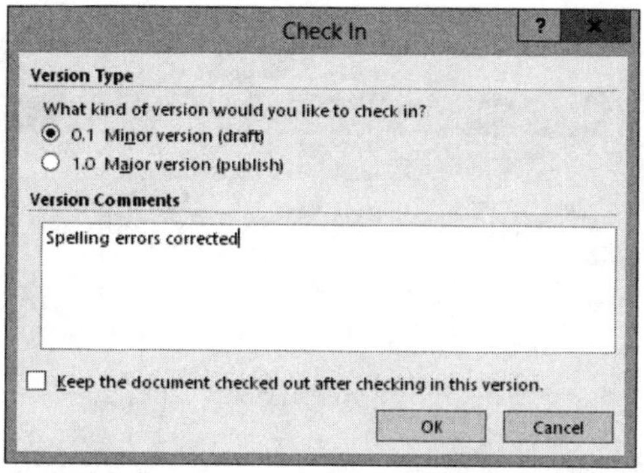

FIGURE 3-17   Adding a check-in comment from Microsoft Word

Approving a Document for Publishing

The subject of SharePoint workflow could easily fill a couple of books on its own. Topics include the default built-in content approval workflow associated with various list templates, designing workflows with the visual workflow designer, designing custom workflows in SharePoint Designer, and even developing custom workflows in Visual Studio. In this book, only the built-in SharePoint content approval workflow functionality will be discussed. This section provides just a few key examples.

Content approval requires that an item be approved before it is published in SharePoint. In fact, this simple type of workflow is so commonplace that there is an option to enable it in the library settings of document libraries. Once the option has been enabled, any document that is checked in will need to be approved before the changes are available. To approve the changes, a user with approval rights needs to select the Approve/Reject option from the ribbon (see Figure 3-18).

You probably noticed that the option Approve/Reject implies that there's more to this option than just approving an edit. In addition to the ability to approve any edits since the last approval, you also have the option to reject the changes, or you could select Pending to set the document so that it remains visible to just its creator and users who can see draft items (see Figure 3-19). In addition, there is a Comment text box that allows you to enter text that explains your choice or adds information for anyone who might be interested in the history of the document.

After you have selected the appropriate option, you'll be returned to the document library, and the change will be shown in the Approval Status column.

Tip   The Approval Status column appears only if the library has been set to require approval. In SharePoint 2013, there is a new Approve/reject Items link, which appears above the document library main area in libraries where content approval has been turned on by the library administrator. This is simply a filtered view of the main library that lets you quickly spot and review items up for review.

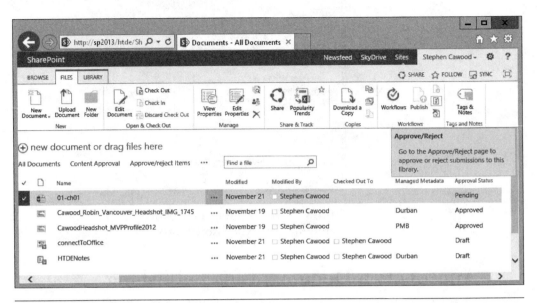

FIGURE 3-18 The Approve/Reject menu option

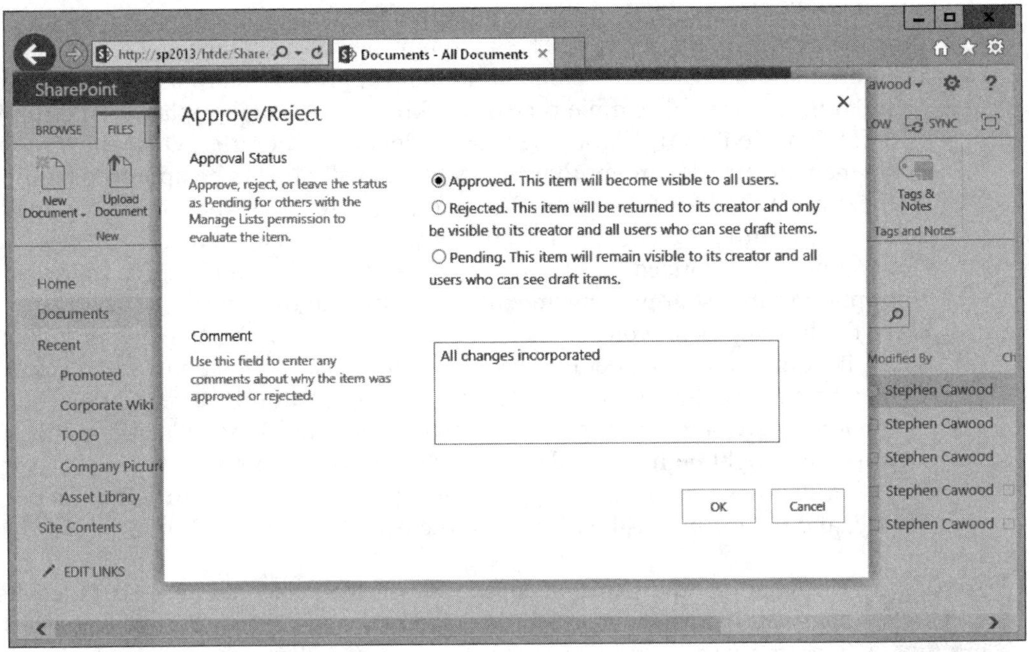

FIGURE 3-19 The Approve/Reject dialog

Having covered the straightforward options in basic content approval workflow, the next topics delve a little deeper into the document version options. For example, what if versioning isn't enabled on a library, or what if you needed to find previous versions of a document?

More About Versions

There are many reasons to take advantage of the document versioning features available in SharePoint. This section covers turning on versioning, setting versioning options, and working with version history.

Turning On Versioning

Suppose that your organization is legally required to keep all versions of documents. To make what might seem like a cumbersome task easy to enforce, simply enable SharePoint version control.

To turn on versioning in a document library, click the Library tab on the ribbon and then click Library Settings (see Figure 3-20). There are many options within the Document Library Settings page. Versioning Settings is the second link down in the General Settings section.

 Any settings page in SharePoint has a URL, so just as with any other page, you can bookmark a settings page for easy access in the future.

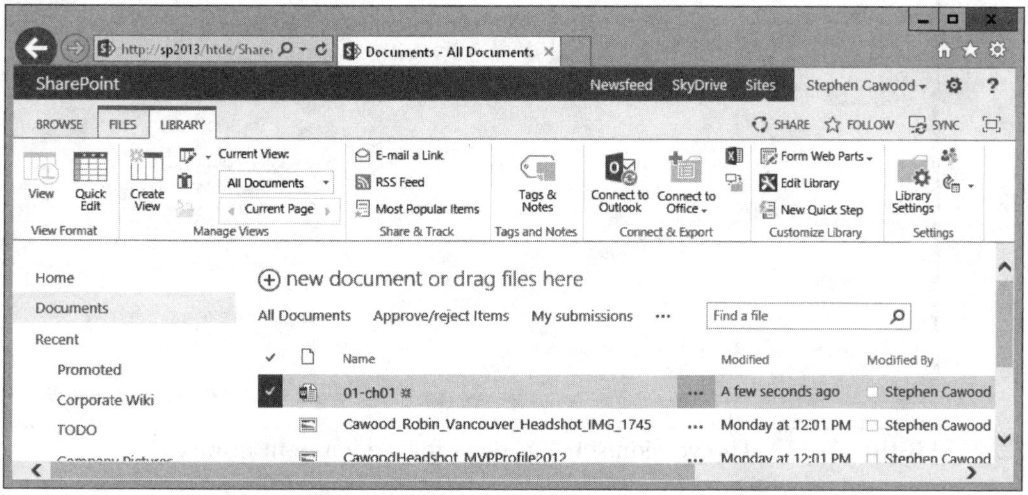

FIGURE 3-20 The library settings are accessible from the ribbon.

On the Document Library Versioning Settings page, you have a number of options (see Figure 3-21). The settings are divided into the following sections:

- **Content Approval** *Here, you can specify whether approval is required for items in the library. This is an example of using a simple out-of-the-box SharePoint workflow feature.*
- **Document Version History** *This section gives you options for how versions will be created. If you want, you can disable versioning, create just major versions, or create major versions and minor versions. In addition, you have the option to specify how many versions of the document SharePoint will retain. If storage is more important than retaining every copy of your documents, you may choose to limit the number of versions SharePoint keeps in its database. The decision of whether to create minor (draft) versions is more subtle; there may be many cases where the difference isn't important to you. However, if you want to be able to create multiple draft versions and then only "publish" by creating a major version, then you'll need to have both types of versions available.*
- **Draft Item Security** *This option allows you to restrict access to minor versions. As you would expect, this option is available only if both minor and major versions are enabled.*
- **Require Check Out** *This is another handy built-in workflow feature. If you want to enforce that only one person can be working on an item at a time, you can require users to check out the document before editing.*

FIGURE 3-21 The version settings page for a document library

Note The number of versions you decide to keep will be *N*+1. For example, if you chose to keep five versions, there could be six copies of a document in the library: the current "master" copy and five historical versions of it.

Working with Version History

Naturally, versions are useful only if you have an easy way to access the metadata for your versions, view old versions, and—in the worst case—restore an old version over the top of the current version. To see a list of the versions of a particular document that SharePoint has stored, select a document and choose the Version History option in the ribbon.

The version history dialog will open and show the versions that are stored in SharePoint (see Figure 3-22). This dialog shows both minor and major versions, as well as the modified date, who modified the version, the size of the particular version of the file, and any version comments that have been added.

If you click the date field in the Modified column, a drop-down menu appears with the options to View, Restore, or Delete that version (see Figure 3-23).

Choosing to view the information about a version will open a new dialog in which you can see all the metadata about the version in question. For the default document library list template, this includes the name, title, managed keywords, and approval status. You'll also see information that will be helpful if you need to figure out which

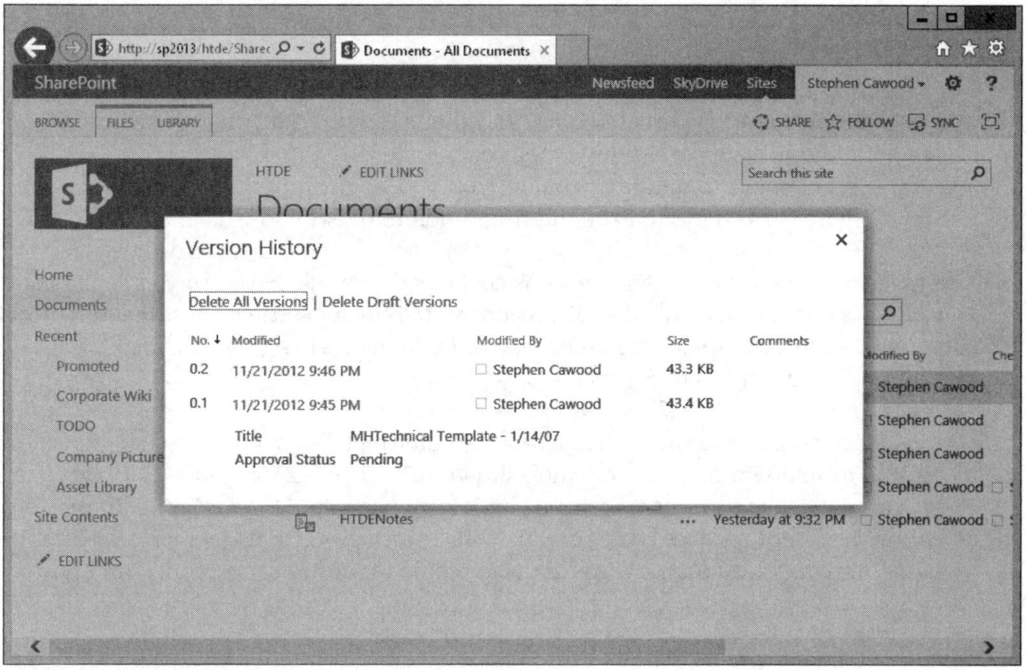

FIGURE 3-22 Version history dialog

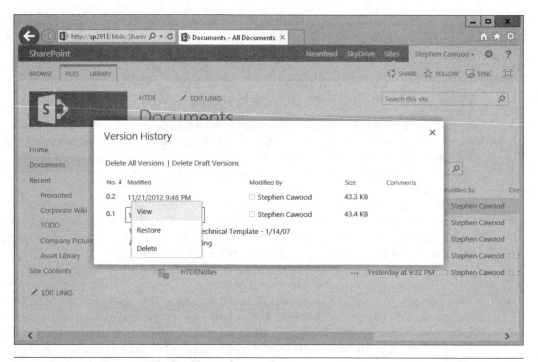

FIGURE 3-23 Version dialog drop-down menu

version contains some information that you need to view again. This includes the version numbers, the created date, and the last modified date—the latter two also include the user information for that data.

If you choose to delete a version, you will be prompted to confirm the operation (see Figure 3-24). One reason you might delete old versions is to save space.

 The default of infinite versions could lead to a full server, so you might want to set a maximum number of versions in the library settings. Just remember that after some time, there may be no way to easily recover the versions that are removed as a result of the policy you set.

Restoring a version is just as easy as deleting one. When you choose Restore in the drop-down menu, the dialog shown in Figure 3-25 appears. Restore could be particularly useful in cases where versioning has been enabled on a library, but approval is not required. If a team is collaborating on items in such a library, one user may make a change that isn't acceptable to another user. Since no approval was

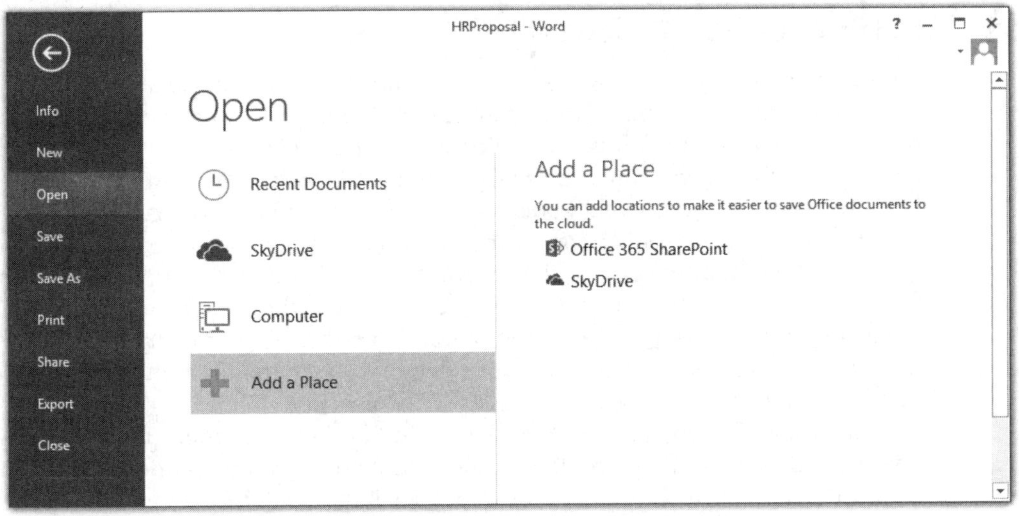

FIGURE 3-24   Deleting a document version

required when the item was checked in, the best way to undo the edits might be to restore one of the older versions.

> **Caution**   Restore makes the selected old version the current version. This means that the current version will get stored as an older version in the history. In other words, if you restore a version, you are putting it "in front of" the most recent version, thus demoting that newer version to an older version.

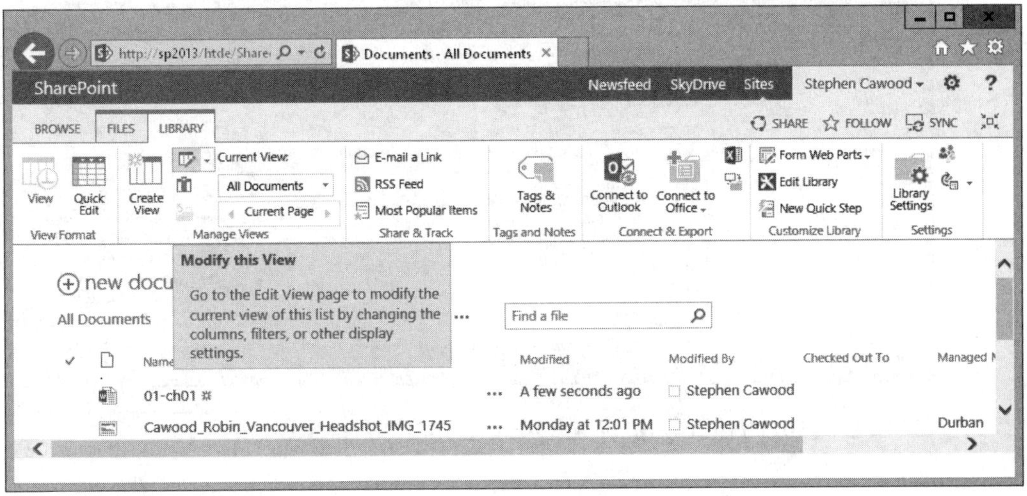

FIGURE 3-25   Restoring a version

A Real-World Example

Let's imagine that you're using a SharePoint document library to store project documents that are being edited by multiple members of your team. You're all fed up with the idea of e-mailing around copies of your documents and keeping track of versions by changing the name. No one wants to have a document called something like Proposal5_SC_Approved_LatestNew-FINALSeptember16.docx.

With the clear goal of streamlining your document management process, you've created a document library for the project files, and you've enabled the built-in workflow so that all files must be checked out before they can be edited. This is a great start, but it's not the end of the potential of SharePoint by any stretch. To easily keep track of what's going on with your documents, there are a number of handy features you can use.

You know that you can bookmark the URL of your document library in your favorite browser, but if you're going to be editing documents frequently, you might want to also create a shortcut inside Windows Explorer. The Connect to Office option in the document library ribbon is an easy way to do this (see Figure 3-26).

After choosing this option, Microsoft Office clients will show a shortcut to this SharePoint list (see Figure 3-27).

You may also want to easily see which of your team members is working on each document. For this, you can customize the default view to include a column for the name of the user who currently has the document checked out. To edit the current view, click the Modify this View link in the ribbon (see Figure 3-28).

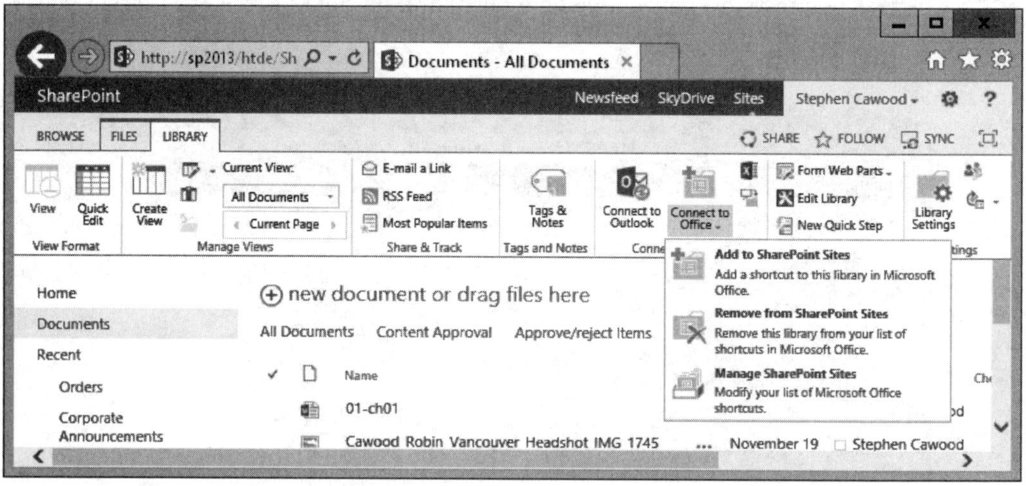

FIGURE 3-26 The Connect to Office option in the ribbon

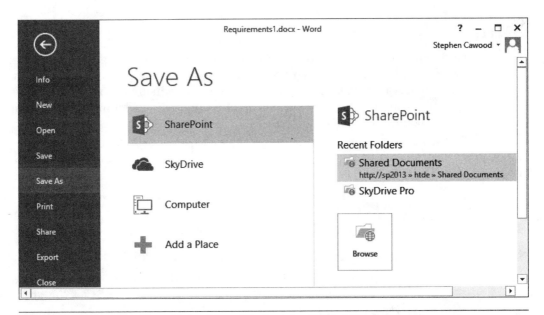

FIGURE 3-27 The SharePoint list added to the Office Backstage view

Once you have the Edit View page open, scroll down to the section that shows the current columns. You'll see that each has a numeric value next to it and a check box that indicates whether the column is visible. Check the box for the Checked out to column, and then click the drop-down and change it to the number 3.

With these changes in place, you'll be able to easily see who has checked out each document, and you'll be able to quickly open your SharePoint documents from within the Microsoft Office clients.

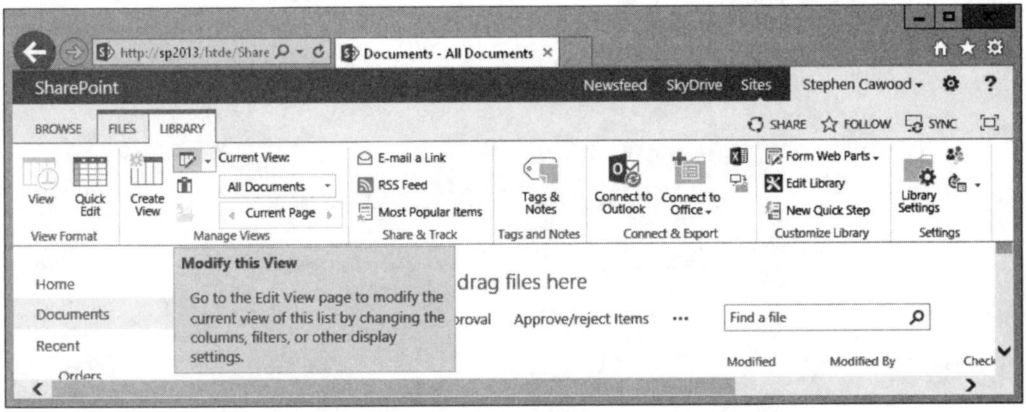

FIGURE 3-28 The Modify this View option in the ribbon

Summary

This chapter provided the information you need to start working efficiently with SharePoint documents. Whether you need to add documents, use the SharePoint content approval workflow, or work with document versions, the topics covered will help you quickly navigate the various options and choose what will work best for you and your team.

4

Collaboration

As the name "SharePoint" implies, collaboration has been at the core of SharePoint's functionality since its very conception. However, a great deal has happened in the domain of social networking since the release of SharePoint Portal Server 2001. The ever-increasing popularity of tools such as blogs, wikis, and other social media has significantly improved the way people collaborate.

In this chapter, we'll take a look at the various ways that SharePoint Server 2013 can grease the wheels of collaboration.

Discussion Boards

When talking about collaboration, back-and-forth conversation is the logical starting place. SharePoint provides discussion board lists exactly for this purpose.

Way back in 1980, a discussion board system called Usenet was launched. Usenet eventually became the world's most popular discussion system, and it retained that status until Internet forum sites came along to displace it as the most prominent technology for online discussions. Although the ability to access Usenet groups through a web browser makes them no more difficult to use than other types of Internet forums, Usenet's centralized system has been supplanted by the multitude of decentralized forums that have been spawned to cover virtually every topic imaginable. The main reason for the shift is that systems such as SharePoint discussion boards can provide both the usability of other technologies and the option to maintain complete control over data and security.

In this section, you'll learn how to create and use SharePoint discussion boards to enable conversations among your users.

Creating a New Discussion Board

As with most lists, the first thing you do when you want to create a discussion board is click the Site Contents link in the quick launch navigation, and then choose add an app (see Figure 4-1). This opens the Create dialog and allows you to choose what you would like to create.

Of course, there are other ways to create a list. For example, you could click the Settings gear icon, and then click the Add an app link (see Figure 4-1).

When you get to the Your Apps page, you'll see a list of the available apps that you can create (see Figure 4-2). Scroll down the page, and you'll find the Discussion Board app. If the app you're looking for isn't on the first page, you may need to scroll to the bottom of the page and click the next link to advance to the next page of apps.

Once you have the Adding Discussion Board dialog open, enter a name, and then click Create (see Figure 4-3). If you would like to give your discussion board a description, click the Advanced Options button before you create the board.

Now that you have created a discussion board, you'll obviously want to start using it.

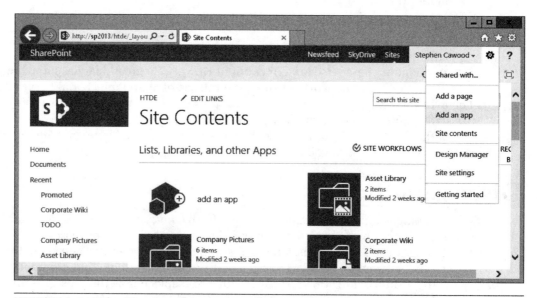

FIGURE 4-1 The Site Contents page and the Settings drop-down menu

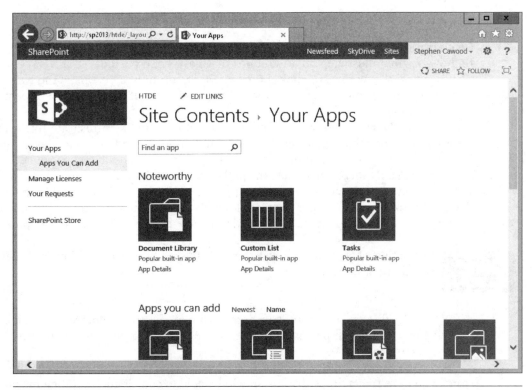

FIGURE 4-2   The Your Apps page

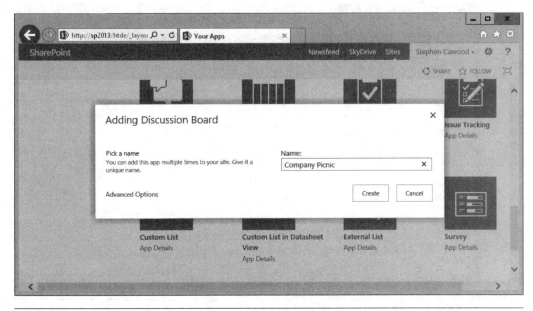

FIGURE 4-3   Creating a new discussion board

Using a Discussion Board

Conversations within discussion boards are divided into threads. Within threads, you'll find the original message and any replies that have been posted.

To create a new thread, click the new discussion link. This opens the New Item dialog and allows you to add the subject and body of your discussion post (see Figure 4-4).

In the Body section, you can use many text-formatting features. The Insert tab allows you to add tables, pictures, links, file attachments, and even video or audio files. These features are all provided to enable the richest possible experience in your discussions. Don't forget that you can spell-check your post before saving it. After you save your post, it will appear in the thread. In this example, a photo is added to the user's profile to give a more personal feel to SharePoint social interactions such as discussion board conversations. Personalizing your profile is covered in Chapter 7.

Note One option when creating a new thread is to specify that it's a "question" that you would like answered.

Naturally, discussions aren't very interesting unless they're more than one-sided. Replying to a discussion post is as simple as clicking the Reply link and writing a message (see Figure 4-5).

After submitting the reply, it will also appear in the discussion list (see Figure 4-6). Users who have rights to the discussion will be able to contribute by adding new replies.

FIGURE 4-4 Creating a new thread

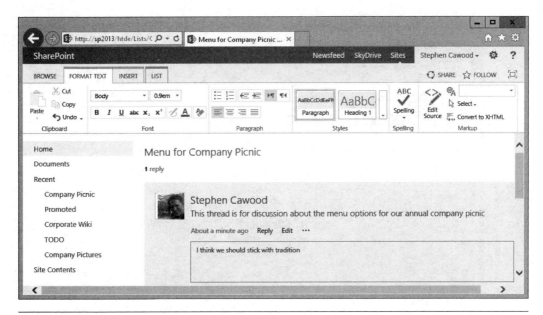

FIGURE 4-5   Replying to a thread

FIGURE 4-6   The thread view after a reply

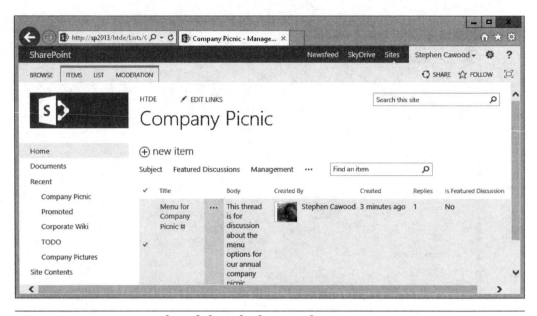

FIGURE 4-7 Discussion board threads shown in list view

To see each thread in the list view (see Figure 4-7), return to the main page for the discussion board, click the List tab on the ribbon, and then change the view to Management. In the list view, you can take advantage of the standard list management features, such as being able to delete multiple items in one operation.

Editing a Discussion Board Item

Although you generally won't need to take advantage of these options, it is possible to delete threads, individual posts, or the whole discussion board. Maybe an employee accidentally included sensitive information in a post, or you decided that an old thread should be deleted in favor of a brand-new conversation. In those cases, you'll be glad you have the list management options.

Whatever the reason you need to manage the discussion posts, viewing and editing a post is easy. First, choose the Edit Item option from the ellipses drop-down menu (see Figure 4-8) to open the properties view.

Once there, you'll also have options to edit the item, delete it, or run a spell-check (see Figure 4-9).

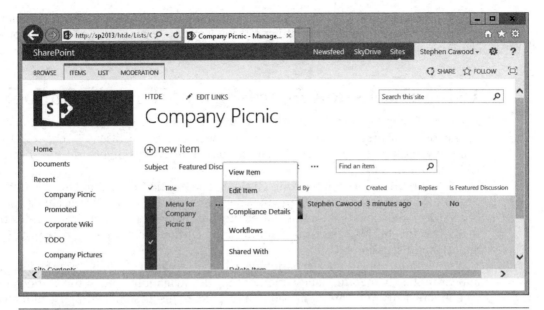

FIGURE 4-8   The context menu for a discussion board

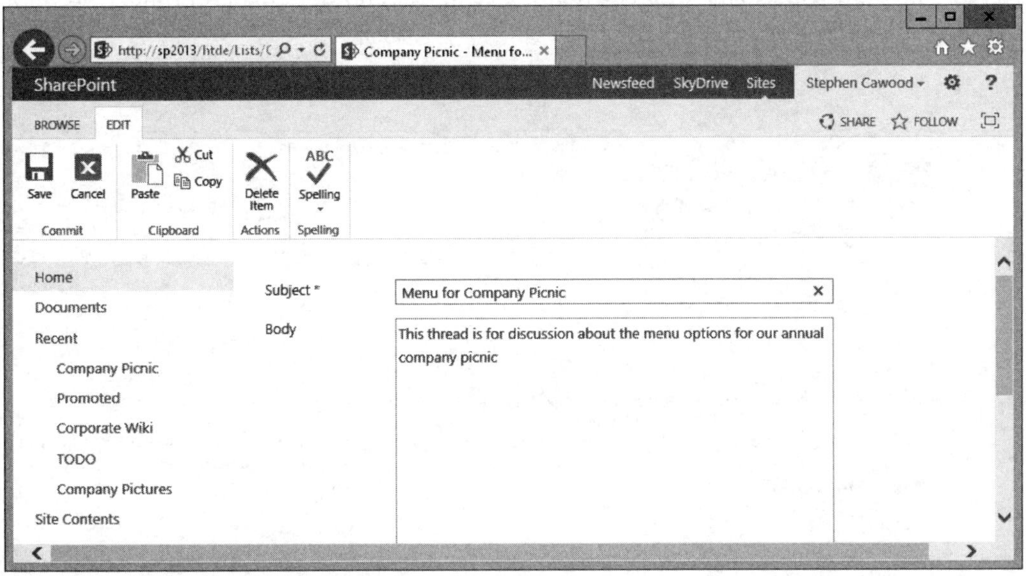

FIGURE 4-9   Editing the properties of a discussion board post

Like some other lists and apps, discussion boards can be set up to require approval. If you're worried about what information might be getting out, you can turn on this requirement.

Using Discussion Boards from Microsoft Outlook

If you are using Microsoft Outlook as your e-mail client, you have the option of connecting to SharePoint from Outlook. One such use case is discussion boards. Users can reply and carry on conversations in a SharePoint discussion board from within the Outlook interface.

To open the discussion board in Outlook, choose the Connect to Outlook option from the SharePoint ribbon. When you select this option, you need to accept a couple of security validations. These safeguards prevent malware programs from connecting to SharePoint. In this case, you're authorizing Outlook to read and write to your SharePoint discussion board.

After connecting your discussion board, you can open Outlook, and the list will appear in the SharePoint Lists section of the left navigation pane in the Outlook client (see Figure 4-10). You can then read and respond to discussion board posts directly from Outlook.

Accessing SharePoint content from Outlook can often help with SharePoint adoption by users who are hooked on e-mail. In the discussion board case, they will be able to converse in Outlook as they would in e-mail, but the content is stored in SharePoint, which means that it's available and searchable through the standard SharePoint interfaces.

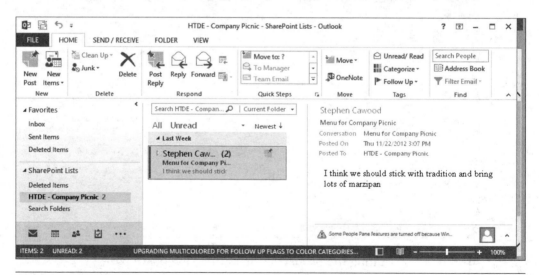

FIGURE 4-10 A discussion board open in Outlook 2013

Blogs

Discussion boards may be the best answer to your two-way conversation needs, but there's no doubt that web logs, commonly known as *blogs*, are the way to publish and share your writing. Many companies have started to use internal blogs as part of their knowledge management system. There's an old adage that much of the value of a company walks out the door at 5:00 P.M.; companies are looking for ways to mitigate this issue. For example, a blog can be used to create a knowledge base for frequently asked questions (FAQs). If an employee leaves for the day, or for good, her blog remains, and the company doesn't completely lose the value of that employee.

According to blog search engine Technorati, there are well over 110,000,000 web logs already on the Internet, and more are being added each day. Blogs are everywhere and cover every topic, ranging from gadget reviews (for example, www.gizmodo.com) to humorous stories (such as www.wiihaveaproblem.com, which records tales about damage caused while people play the Wii video game console).

In SharePoint Server 2013, blogs are a type of site template. As you've already seen, there are a few methods to create sites such as blogs. One option is to go to the Site Contents page and scroll down to the Subsites section and choose the new subsite option.

Once you've created your new blog site, you'll see that the first post is created for you (see Figure 4-11). You can choose to delete this welcome post or to modify it instead.

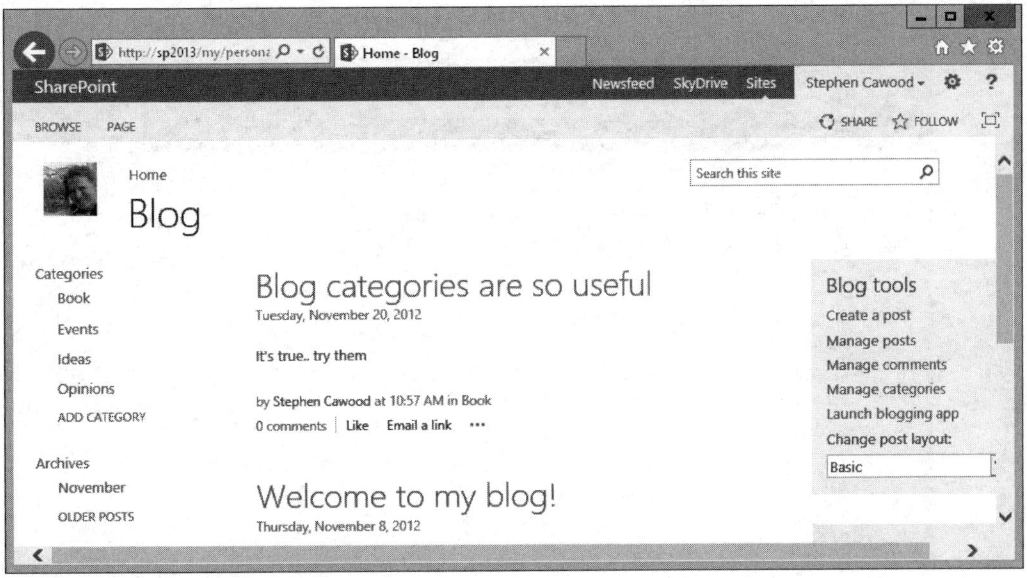

FIGURE 4-11   A new blog site

You can also use a blog on your personal site. Personal sites are discussed in more detail in Chapter 7.

To begin posting to your blog, choose the Create a post link on the right side of the page. The blog authoring dialog (see Figure 4-12) is similar to the dialog for discussion boards.

 Look for the RSS Feed link in the bottom-right area of the blog home page to get the URL for your blog feed. The feed allows others to be notified when a new post has been added. You can add Really Simple Syndication (RSS) feeds to your browser and to applications such as Microsoft Outlook or RSS readers.

The blog dialog also gives you the option of adding categories to your posts. Similar to other taxonomy features in SharePoint, these categories allow your readers to filter your blog for the posts that apply to certain topics. You can use the Manage categories link on the right side of the blog site to access the categories list and add new topics to the list, or you can click the Add Category link in the quick launch navigation.

When a blog is created, three blog categories are created out of the box: Events, Ideas, and Opinions. The simplest way to change the names of these categories is to click the Manage Categories link on the right side of the page, and then overwrite each name.

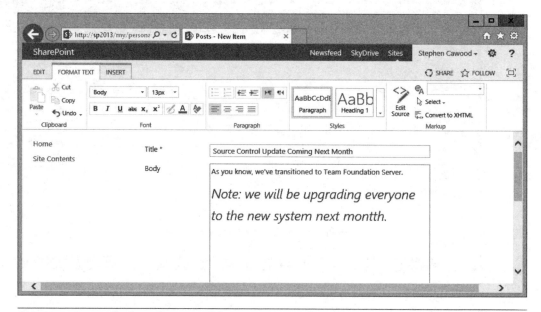

FIGURE 4-12 Authoring a new blog post using the SharePoint web interface

Posting Blog Comments

Blogs may not be as interactive as discussion boards, but that doesn't mean that they are only one-way. If you want to share your thoughts on someone's blog posts, you'll be able to post a blog comment (see Figure 4-13).

> **Note** On the main blog page, you'll see a summary of the most recent posts. At the bottom of each post, you'll see an E-mail a link option. This option will get you the permanent link, or "permalink," to the post. A permalink is a direct link to that post, unlike the link to the blog home page, which shows recent posts only. After other posts have been added, the postings in the summary view will eventually change, but the permalink will always point directly to the posting. So, if you want someone to read a particular post, or reference the post on some other page, you should use the permalink URL. When you click the E-mail a link option, your e-mail client will open, but you can simply copy the URL and paste it wherever you want.

Managing Blog Posts

When viewing a blog site—as a user with sufficient privileges, of course—you will notice that there is an Edit link next to each post. Clicking this link allows you to make changes to the post. If, for example, you notice a spelling mistake or other typo, you can use the edit option to quickly correct the mistake. However, if you would like to work with the blog items in the usual SharePoint list view (see Figure 4-14), click the Manage posts link on the right side of the blog page.

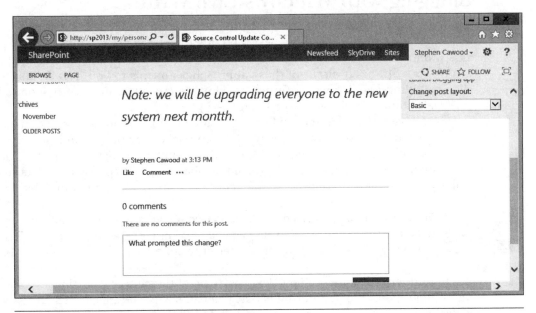

FIGURE 4-13   Adding a blog comment

FIGURE 4-14 Managing blog posts

Note If you would like to use Microsoft Word to write your blog posts, and you're using Internet Explorer, click the Launch blogging app link (under Tools for blog owners). Some people prefer to blog in Microsoft Word because they can take advantage of Word features such as SmartArt.

Blogging with Windows Live Writer

If you're a fan of Windows client applications, you may not want to use the SharePoint web interface to record your deepest thoughts in your SharePoint blogs. And you may want to have a "what you see is what you get" (WYSIWYG) editor that allows you to work offline. If either of these approaches appeals to you, you should try Microsoft Windows Live Writer (http://windows.microsoft.com/en-US/windows-live/essentials-home) for blogging (see Figure 4-15).

Since Live Writer is a free application included with Windows Live Essentials, you can download it and try it quite easily. Once you have the application installed, you can choose Tools | Accounts and add your blog accounts (see Figure 4-16). Many of the most popular blogging applications, including SharePoint, of course, are supported. While you're in there, you might wish to check out some of the other options.

Tip One of the options provided by Windows Live Writer is to automatically upload to an FTP server any images you drag and drop (or paste) into your posts. This is useful if you're already using an FTP server to store files.

To start writing, choose File | New Post. One of the benefits of using a Windows client program for blog authoring is that you can easily add images wherever you want them and size them to match your needs—all without needing to know anything

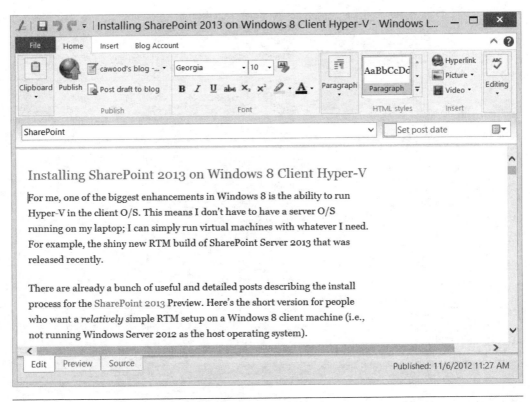

FIGURE 4-15   Windows Live Writer

about the underlying HTML code. Simply drag and drop or copy and paste to add an image, and then use the mouse to size the picture.

The blog page is actually a web part page, so if you switch to edit mode, you'll be able to add web parts.

Now, instead of waiting until your flight lands, you'll be able to blog away at 30,000 feet.

By default, site owners and approvers (designers) are the only users who can directly publish blog posts. Everyone else submits a post as a draft that needs to be approved. To change this behavior, navigate to your blog site and choose Site Actions | View All Site Content | Posts | List Settings | Versioning Settings. In the Content Approval settings, the first option is Require Content Approval for Submitted Items. If you turn off this option, no one will need their posts to be approved.

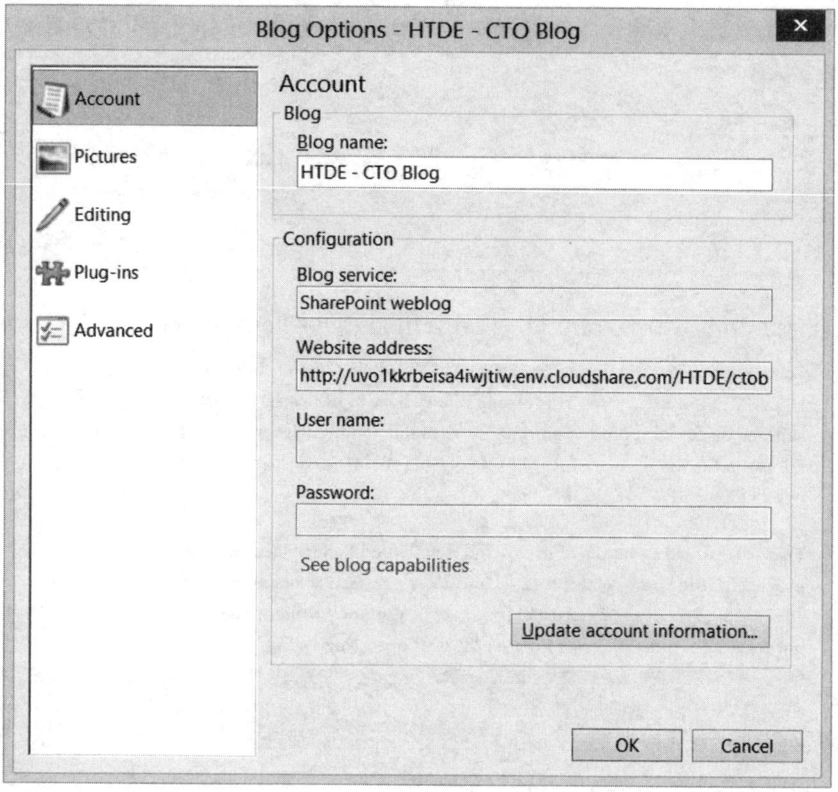

FIGURE 4-16 Opening a SharePoint blog with Windows Live Writer

Wikis

If you've ever used Wikipedia.com, then you've benefited from the potential of wiki sites. The name *wiki* comes from the Hawaiian word for quick. The creators of the wiki realized that the best way to create a lasting and shared store of knowledge was to make contributing and editing quick and easy.

SharePoint Server 2013 offers a couple of options for creating wikis: the wiki page library and the Enterprise Wiki site template. The wiki page library is closer to what most people would think of as a traditional wiki website, providing the ability to quickly create and edit pages. The wiki page library is commonly used on intranets to publish web-accessible, living documents that need to be edited frequently. SharePoint Enterprise wikis combine wiki functionality with other features such as project management.

Note The Enterprise Wiki site template is available only after the SharePoint Server Publishing feature has been activated. Furthermore, the site-level feature can't be activated until the publishing infrastructure has been activated at the site-collection level. If you do not have access to SharePoint Central Administration, you'll need to ask an administrator to turn on the feature.

In this section, you'll get an introduction to wikis, but first you'll need to create a wiki to experiment with.

Creating a Wiki

As you would expect, the process for creating a wiki page library is the same as for creating other types of lists: click the Site Contents link in the quick launch navigation and select add an app. After you choose the wiki page library, SharePoint will create the library and fill in the first page with some welcome content—just as when you create a blog.

Of course, the benefit of a wiki is collaborative editing. Unless you and your fellow SharePoint users are making edits, there won't be much combined value to your wikis. To start editing, click the Page tab at the top of the page, and then click the Edit button. Many users choose to remove the sample content as their first edit.

One of the ease-of-use features built in to wiki libraries is shorthand syntax for adding links and creating new wiki pages. The syntax for a link is [[*Link Text*]]. While in edit mode, simply type [[, and you'll be offered a choice of pages to link to (see Figure 4-17).

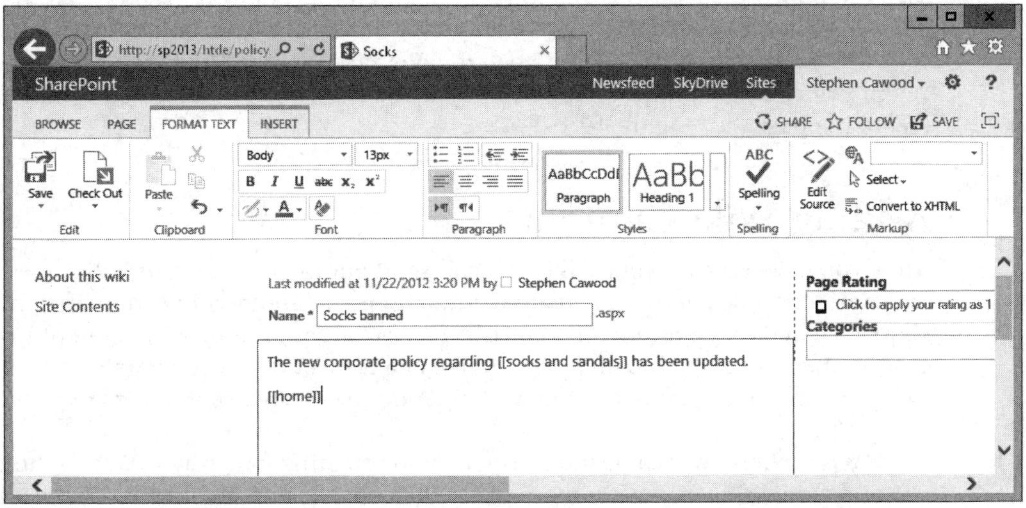

FIGURE 4-17   Adding a new link to a wiki page

FIGURE 4-18 A wiki link to a page that doesn't exist yet

 This page link functionality works on any SharePoint dashboard page.

To add a new wiki page, create a link in the same way that you create one for an existing page: type the name of the page you want in square brackets. After you save the page, you'll see that the link has a dotted line below it to show that the page doesn't exist yet (see Figure 4-18).

After adding the link, all you need to do is save the page and then click the link. When you click the link, a dialog will pop up and ask you whether you would like to create the page (see Figure 4-19).

Adding Wiki Content

After you have created your wiki, you can send out the URL to your colleagues and start working together to create content. Some content will need to be tightly controlled and may require an editorial process, but other topics can benefit from groups of users being able to quickly make changes and correct errors.

Here are some examples of how SharePoint users have been leveraging wikis:

- **FAQs** Wikis are a fantastic technology for creating FAQ pages. Due to the ease of team editing, users are more likely to keep wikis updated with the most recent information.
- **Checklists** Document a particular process that has a tendency to change and could be updated by multiple people.

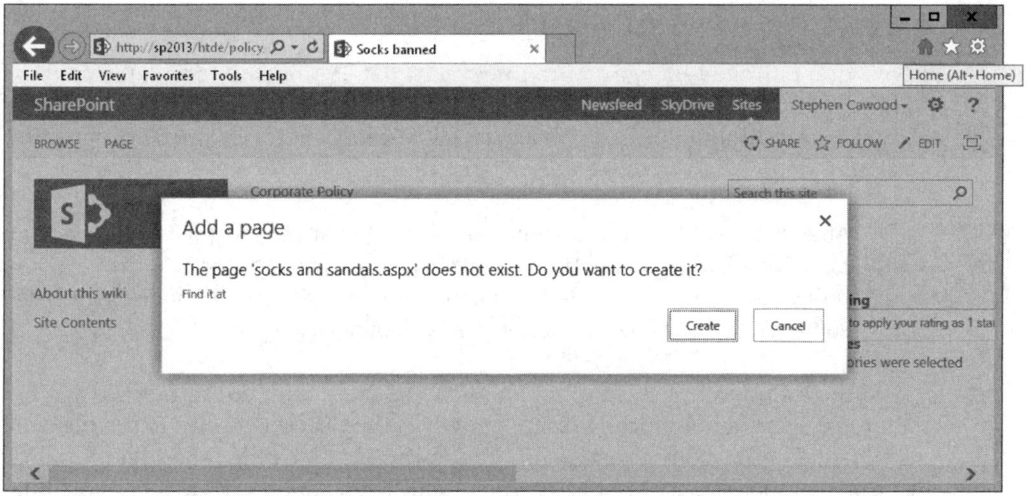

FIGURE 4-19   Adding a wiki page

- **Contacts**   If you share a detailed contact list with a group, a wiki can be a great way to manage the content.
- **Reference**   When most people think of a wiki, Wikipedia.com comes to mind. Wikipedia is an encyclopedia and an excellent demonstration of one way to use a wiki.
- **Event planning**   If you're working with a group to plan an event, a wiki can help make collaboration easier.
- **Notes**   If you're looking for a way to quickly store information that you can access from a browser, and you're not using a solution such as Microsoft OneNote, a wiki might help.

Announcements

If you've been asked to get the word out about the company picnic or notify people about a new press release, one way to go is to e-mail everyone who is interested. However, what if you don't know exactly who might be interested? In that case, it's probably best not to spam your entire company, but rather let people check your SharePoint site for news on the topic.

Another way to notify your colleagues of news is to use SharePoint to post an announcement. The announcement can not only let your colleagues know about something interesting that has happened or is about to happen, but it also can provide links or other helpful information for your fellow SharePoint users.

Creating an Announcement

If you don't already have an announcement list—some site templates come with one—you can go to the Site Contents page and click add an app to create a new one. To add a new announcement to the list, click the Add New Announcement link and complete the New Item dialog (see Figure 4-20).

 Announcement lists can be e-mail enabled. E-mail–enabled lists must be configured by a SharePoint administrator, however. If you are able to use them, instead of going to the SharePoint UI, you can simply e-mail the announcement list; the subject line and body will become the announcement.

Since announcements are all about news, you can choose to have your announcements automatically disappear when they become stale. To do this, choose an expiry date for your announcements in the Expires field (see Figure 4-21). For example, suppose you want to advertise that there will be cake for Sue's birthday on Friday. You could set the announcement to expire on Saturday so that it drops off the radar once the event has passed.

 You can set the expiry date when you create the item, or you can retroactively edit the announcements item and add an expiry date later.

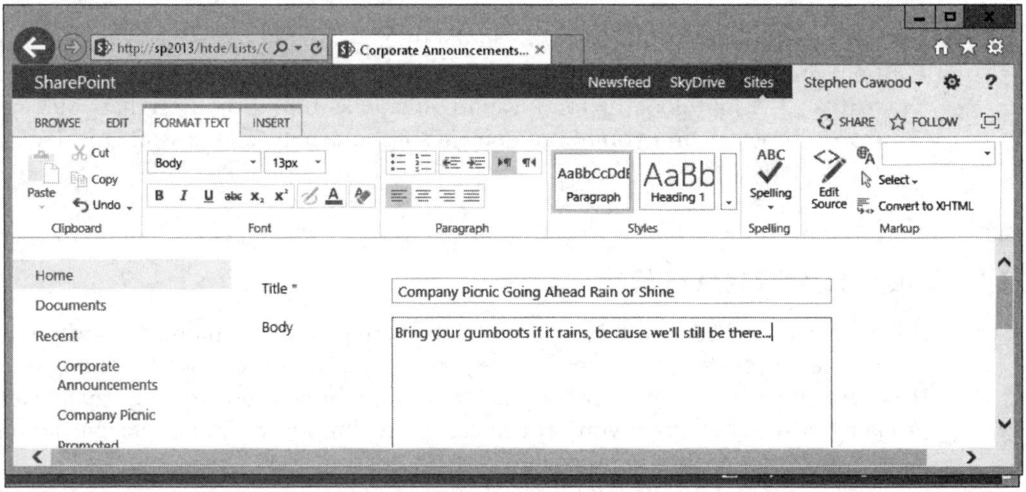

FIGURE 4-20   Adding a new announcement

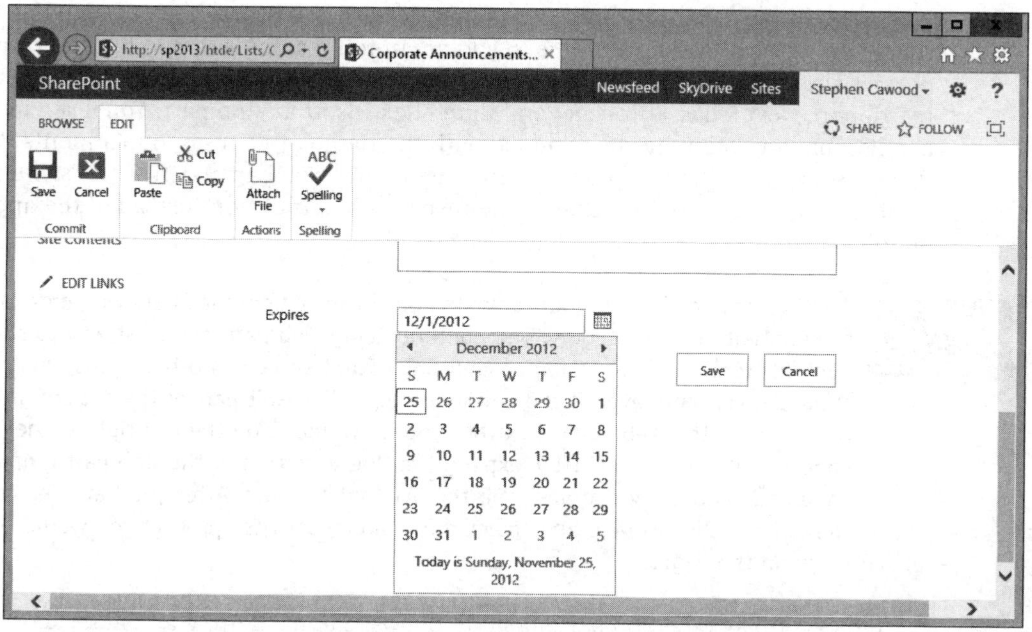

FIGURE 4-21   Setting an expiry date on a new announcement

A Real-World Example: Announcements to Aid User Adoption

One thing I quickly found when I spun up the SharePoint intranet for Metalogix Software is that it's pretty tough to have a full-time job and also keep an intranet site looking and feeling fresh. The problem is that keeping the site up to date is a key component of user adoption. In other words, a user may visit your intranet a few times, but if that user doesn't see any continuing value, she is not going to keep coming back. There are other ways to keep users' interest, such as great content or something on the intranet that's integral to their work process, but there is still value to keeping a fresh feeling on the main pages, and announcements can help tremendously.

Obviously, announcements are meant to get out the word about interesting things that have happened or events that are coming up. They can also have great value as a quick way to keep your site looking fresh.

As you'll learn in Chapter 8, you can create announcements in an announcements web part. One way to keep your sites fresh is to add an announcements app part to the main pages. Each time a new announcement is posted, the page will show the fresh content. This is an especially effective technique if you use images in your announcements.

For example, let's say you're managing the main site for your intranet. The first thing you do is go to Site Contents to add an announcements app to the site (if one doesn't already exist). Then go to the home page for the site and click the Page tab on the ribbon. Next, click Edit page, and then click insert an app part. You'll see in the app list that an option has been added with the name of your announcements list. In this example, it's called Corporate Announcements. You can also find the same part in the Apps category, if you choose the insert web part option instead of the app part option.

Note Another way to show announcements is to insert a Content Query web part from the Content Rollup category. The Content Query web part is a great way to show content from another section of your SharePoint server. In other words, you can show the contents even if the announcements list isn't part of the current site. After adding the web part, click the drop-down menu on the top-right corner and choose Edit Web Part. Finally, expand the Query section of the web part properties pane and choose Show items from the list that appears. After you have selected the option, click Browse and select the announcements app that you would like to show on the page.

Once you have the app part added to the page and set up, you will be showing your users a slightly new look whenever they visit the home page (see Figure 4-23).

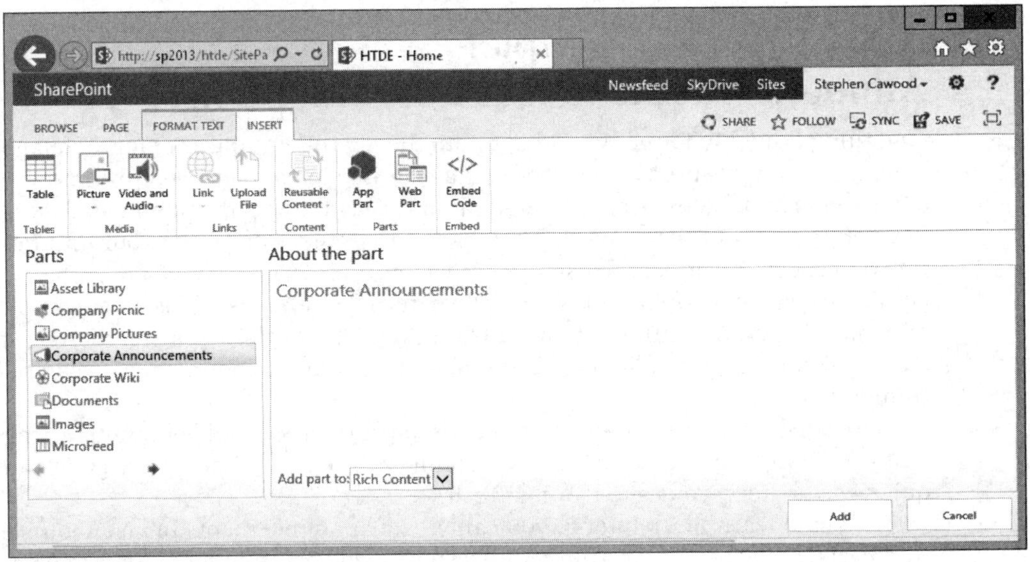

FIGURE 4-22 Adding the announcements app part

FIGURE 4-23 The home page showing dynamic announcement content

Calendars

After finding out about an event via an announcement, the next thing SharePoint users will want to do is mark it on their calendars. SharePoint calendars are the best way to keep track of events, meetings, and other types of appointments.

Creating a Calendar Event

Some site templates, such as the project site template, come with a calendar. But if you don't have a calendar, simply use one of the app creation options and choose to create a calendar. When the calendar is created, you'll see the option to create a new event on the left side of the Events tab on the ribbon (see Figure 4-24).

The New Item dialog allows you to specify details of the event (see Figure 4-25). These entries are typical of those for calendar applications, such as location, start time, and description.

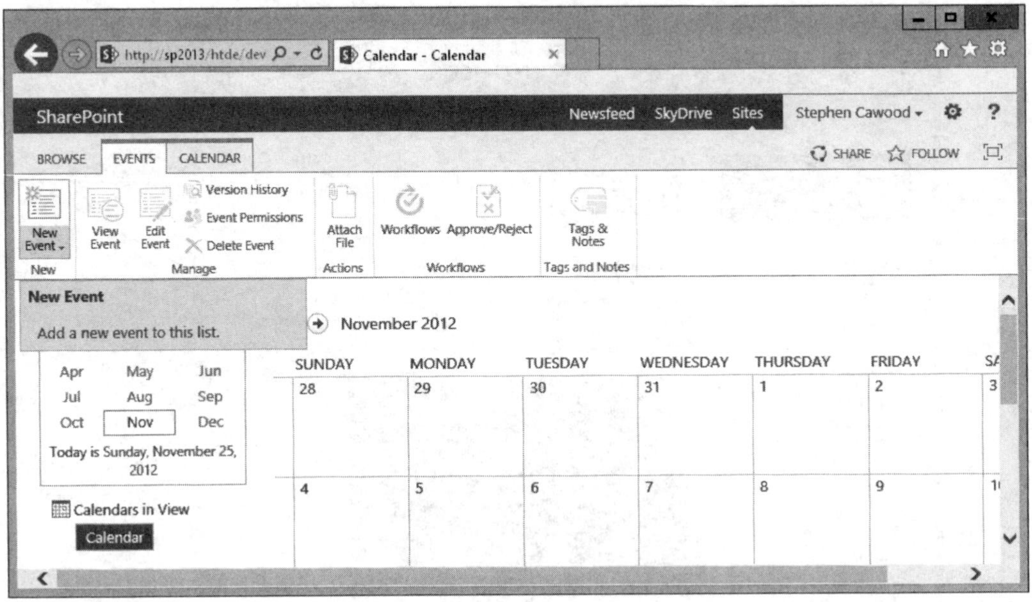

FIGURE 4-24 A SharePoint calendar

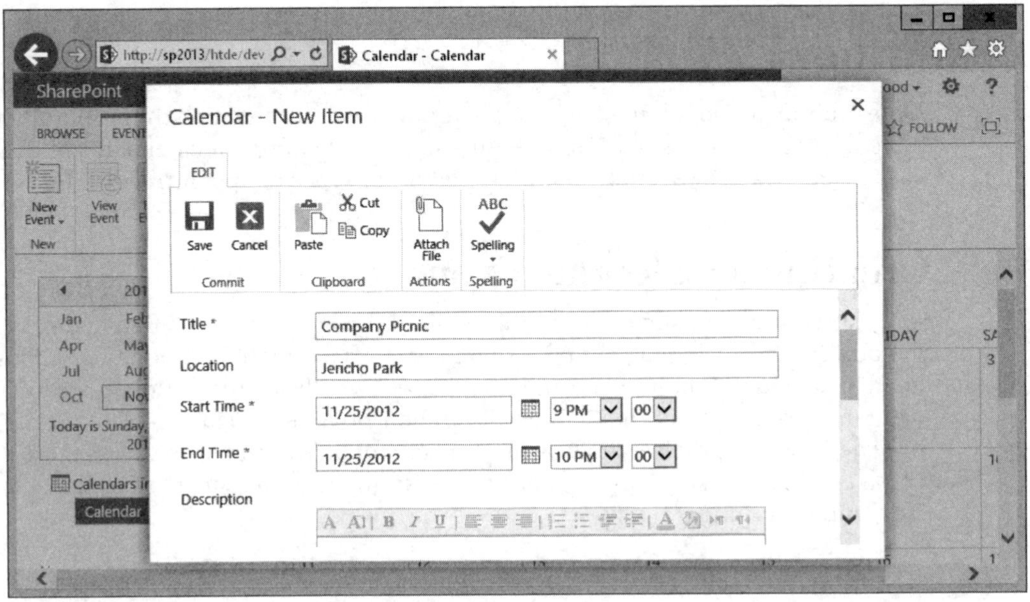

FIGURE 4-25 Adding a new event item

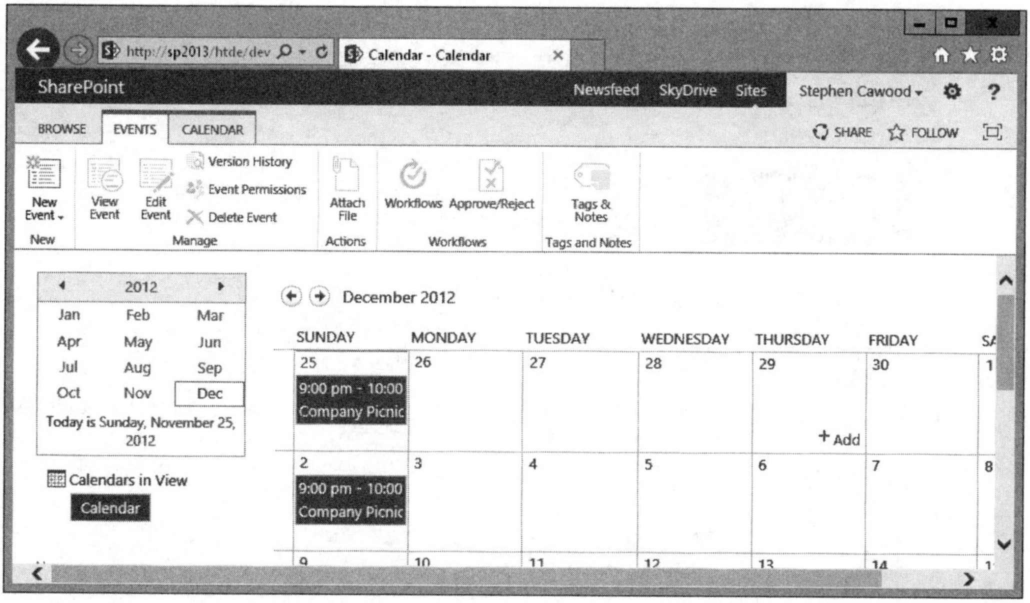

FIGURE 4-26   The recurring event in the calendar

An important aspect of SharePoint events is that they can be one-time or recurring. When you check the box labeled "Make this a repeating event," the recurrence options will appear. If you're familiar with Microsoft Outlook or other calendar applications, you've likely used recurring events before.

You can specify for your event to occur regularly based on time between occurrences, or you can even choose particular days or weeks to determine the recurring pattern. After you add a recurring event, you'll see that it appears multiple times in your calendar (see Figure 4-26).

Note   You can overlay up to ten calendars in one view. To add more calendars to the current view, click the Calendars in View link on the left side of the calendar page.

Calendar Views

Just as with other lists, when you create a calendar, SharePoint will offer some different views of the list data. If you would rather see an existing calendar in a different view, you can simply choose a view from the Scope section of the Calendar tab on the ribbon. For example, you could switch to the All Events view (see Figure 4-27).

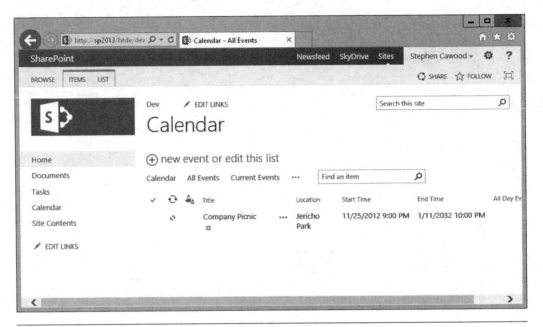

FIGURE 4-27 The same calendar in the All Events view

It's easy to change between the available views, but suppose that none of the existing views shows the calendar in the format you need. If you find yourself in that position, you'll want to create a custom view.

Creating a Custom Calendar View

If you find that the out-of-the-box views don't show the data you need to see or don't show the data in the format you prefer, you can create your own view. Creating a new view is not difficult. The first step is to choose the Create View option in the ribbon (see Figure 4-28).

The options on the Create View page are not just specific to calendar lists. You can use the Create View options with many SharePoint list types (see Figure 4-29).

For this example, choose the Calendar View type (see Figure 4-30). In the view options, you can choose a URL for your new view. Remember that you can bookmark the URL for easy access in the future.

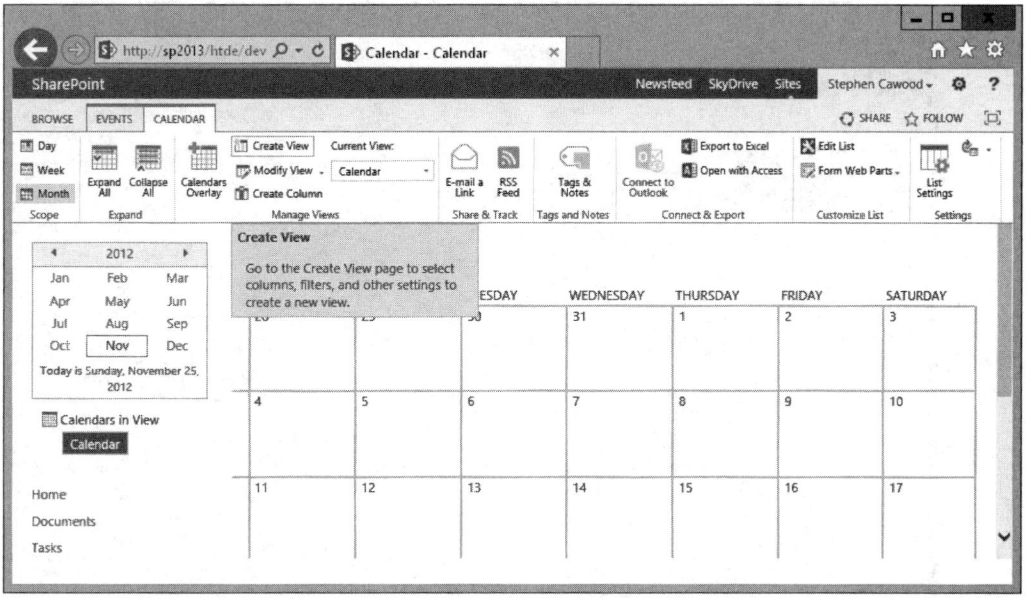

FIGURE 4-28   The Create View option for a SharePoint calendar

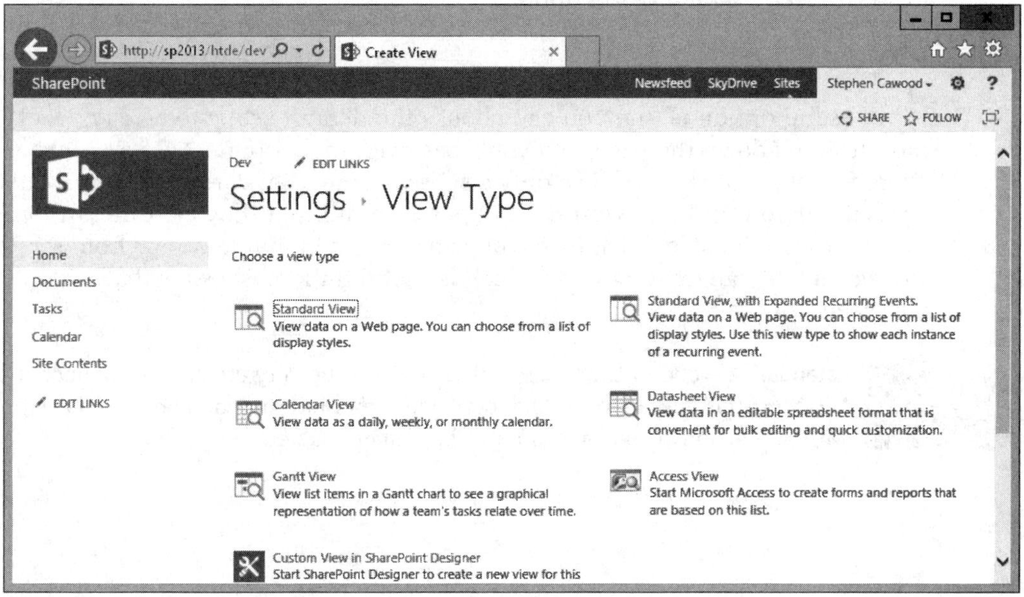

FIGURE 4-29   Create View options

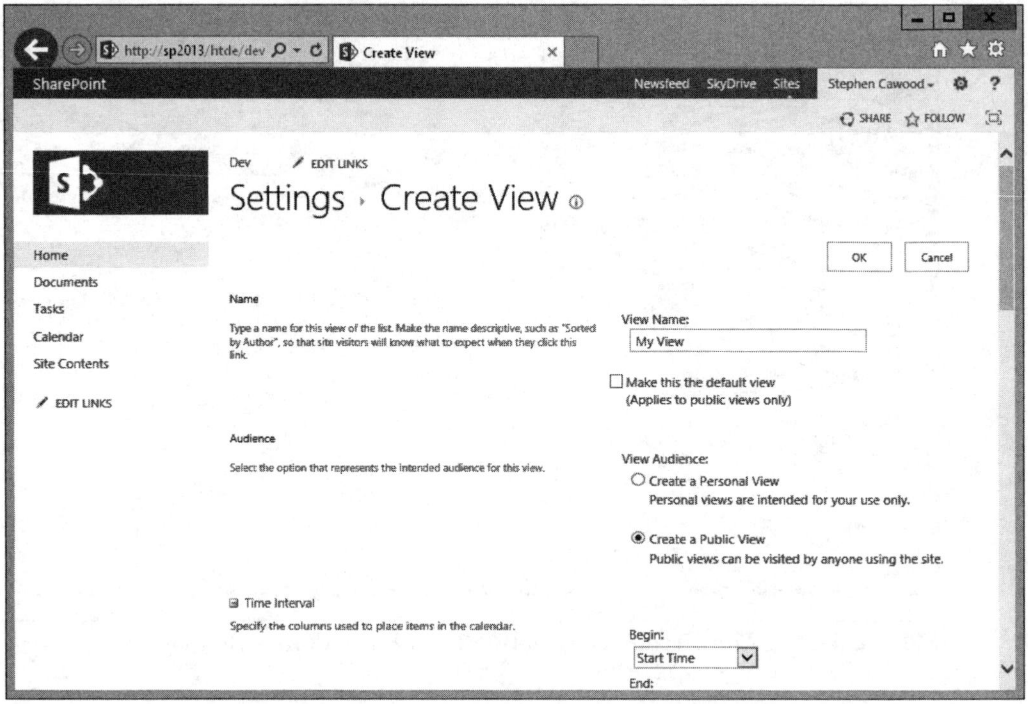

FIGURE 4-30 Calendar view options

A useful option is that you can choose the default scope to be day, week, or month. Scroll down the page, and you'll see even more options. For example, you can choose to filter the data to show only a subset of the calendar information. This can be useful if you find that your calendars are so full that they are difficult to read.

If these options do not suffice, you can create a brand-new view from scratch. You can also modify an existing view, which is useful if there is a view that's close to what you need.

> **Note** Calendars are one of the types of lists that can be very effectively connected to Microsoft Outlook. Refer to Chapter 10 for more information about using Outlook with SharePoint. Calendars can also be e-mail enabled.

Surveys

"How do you like SharePoint Server 2013?" "Are there enough staplers in the office?" "Are you finding this chapter useful?" These are just some of the questions you might like to ask your coworkers. Discussion boards and blog comments are one way to get feedback, but if you're looking for answers to a number of questions—and possibly anonymous responses—then a survey is the way to go. As you would expect, the first step is to create a new app with the Survey template.

Creating a Survey

Once you have selected the Survey template, you can specify options such as whether the respondents' names will appear and whether multiple responses will be allowed from the same user (see Figure 4-31).

After you have selected your options and SharePoint has created the list, you can start to write your questions by choosing the Add questions option from the Settings drop-down menu. SharePoint allows you to pick from a wide variety of response types (see Figure 4-32), including the following:

- Single line of text
- Multiple lines of text
- Choice

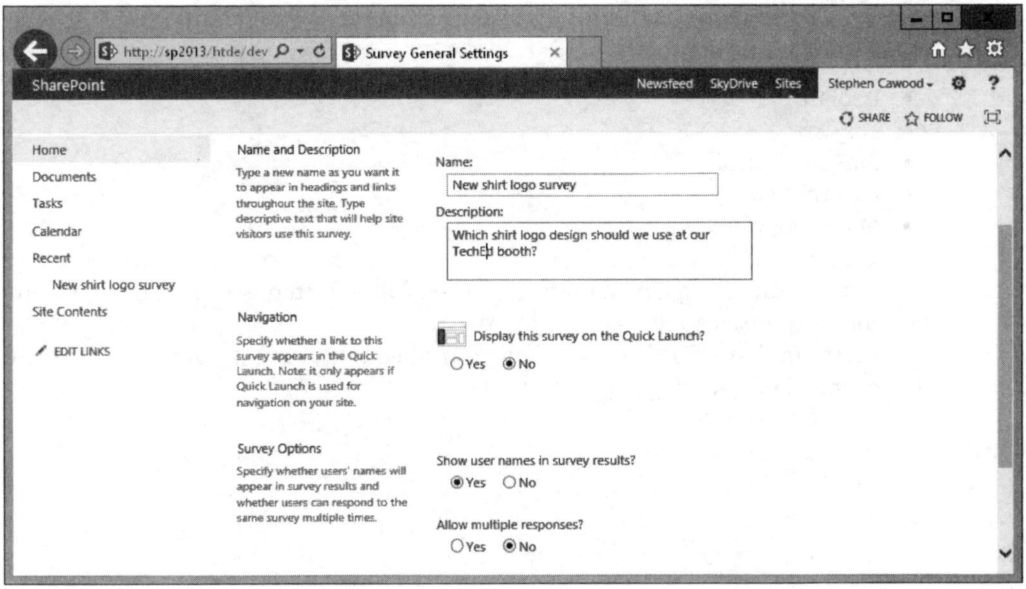

FIGURE 4-31   Survey options

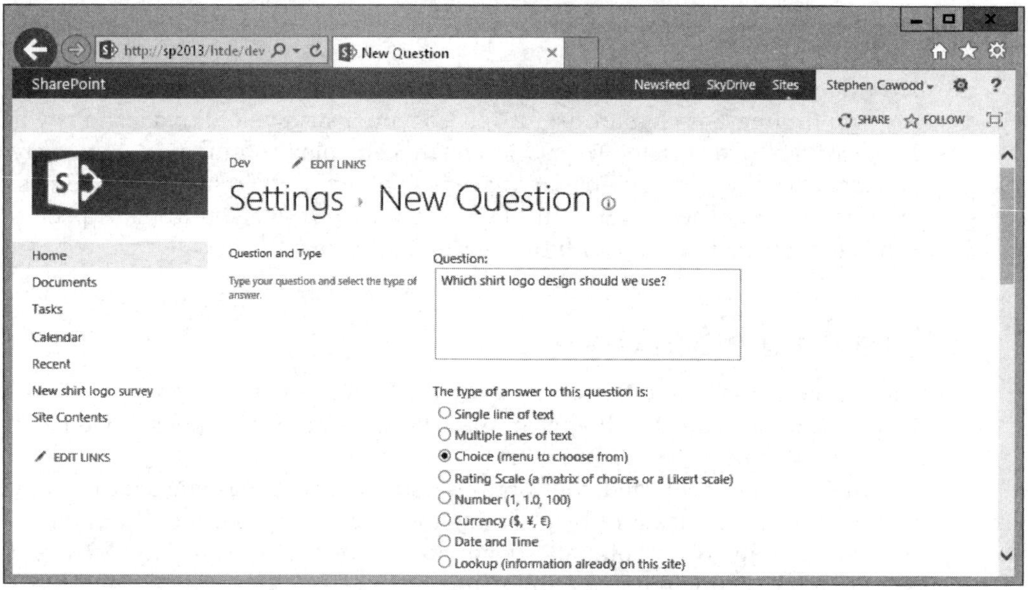

FIGURE 4-32 Creating the first survey question

- Rating Scale
- Number
- Currency
- Date and Time
- Lookup
- Yes/No
- Person or Group
- External Data
- Managed Metadata

In this example, a Choice question type was selected, so a text box for entering the possible responses appears (see Figure 4-33).

After you have finished entering your questions, your survey item is ready to gather feedback (see Figure 4-34).

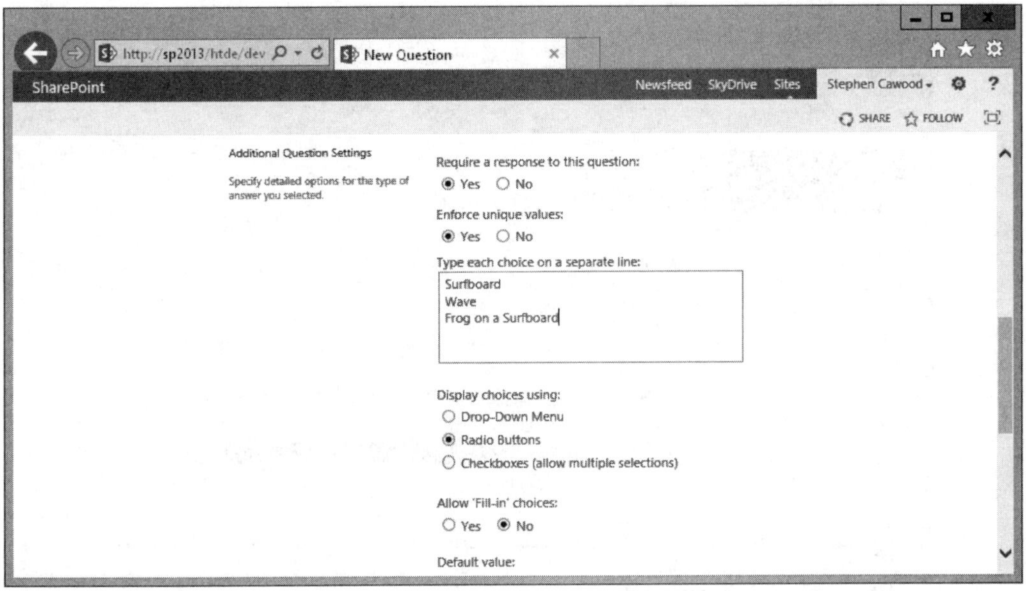

FIGURE 4-33 Specifying choices

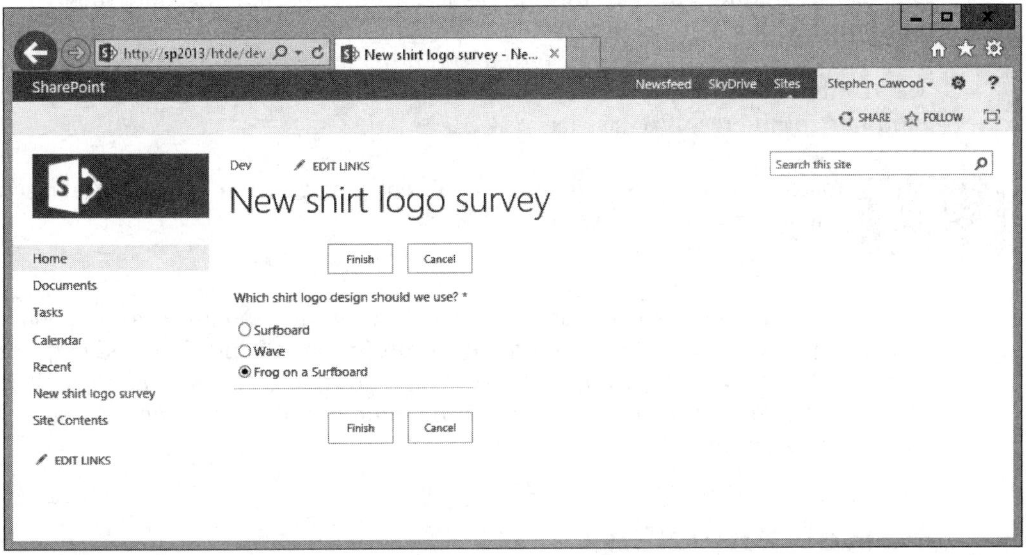

FIGURE 4-34 The survey item

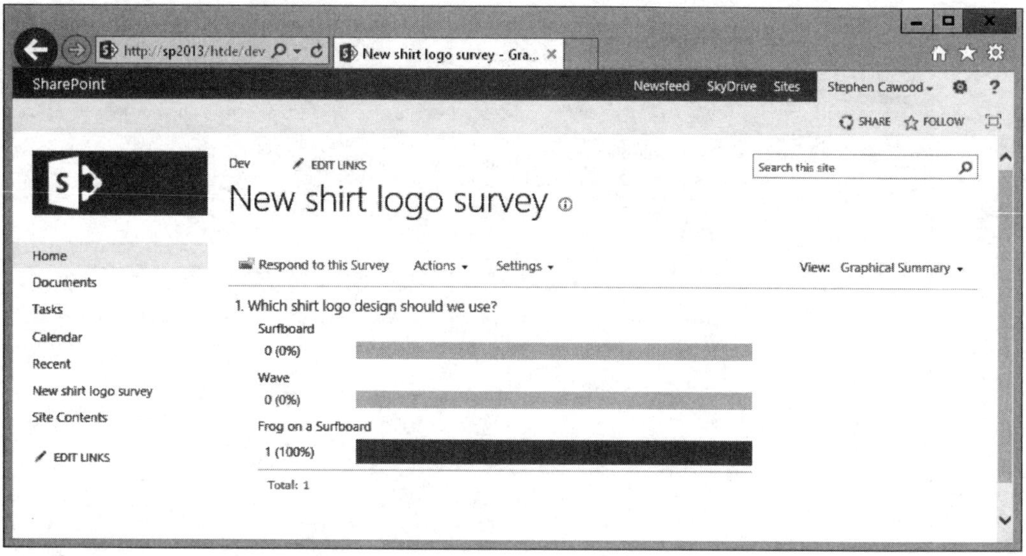

FIGURE 4-35 Viewing graphical survey results

To get the news out that you have a survey ready, you might choose to send an e-mail with a link to the survey page. When users choose to respond, they will be prompted with a dialog containing the survey questions.

Once your responses have started to roll in, you will undoubtedly want to view the results. Your options are to view a list of all the results or to see a graphical summary of the results (see Figure 4-35).

> **Tip** You can use the survey actions drop-down menu to set an alert when someone responds to your survey.

One point to note about surveys is that you can make changes as you go along. For example, you might like to send out a draft to a small audience and gather some feedback before sending out the survey link to your target audience. As you receive suggestions, you can make edits to accommodate them, such as reordering, adding, or removing questions.

Survey Branching

You may find that you would like to dynamically change your survey questions based on the respondents' answers. SharePoint enables this functionality with *survey branching*. Branching allows you to jump to a specified question based on the answer to a different question. For example, if you're asking for opinions about dogs and cats,

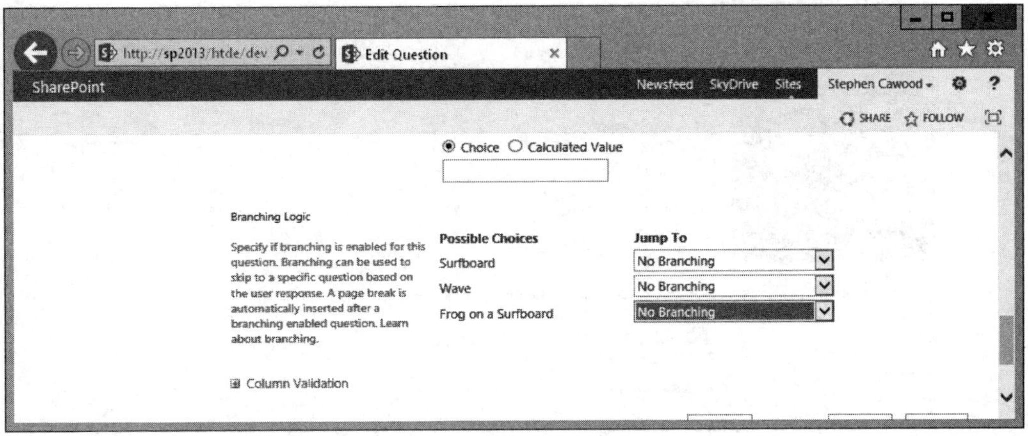

FIGURE 4-36   Choosing branching logic for a survey question

you can first ask which type of pet the user has at home. If the user responds that she has a cat, you can jump to a question about cats, whereas if the user says that she has a dog, you can jump to a question about dogs.

To enable branching, first enter your questions, and then go to the survey settings, choose the question that will determine the branching, and select the target for the branch (see Figure 4-36).

Newsfeeds and Microblogging

Social features are clearly one of the areas of improvement in SharePoint 2013. One such feature that SharePoint users have been requesting is microblogging. Most people know this functionality as "tweeting" because Twitter is by far the most popular microblogging platform.

In SharePoint 2013, you can write short messages (1 to 512 characters) and post them to the newsfeed. You can choose who you would like to share the messages with, and you can also use some of the same conventions as Twitter to get your messages noticed. For example, you can use the @ character in front of an account alias to have your message show up in that users Mentions feed. Also, you can use the hashtag (#) symbol for keywords that you want to track. For example, if someone wanted to start a conversation with me about the company picnic, she would write something like, "@cawood what are you bringing to the #picnic?" This message would show up in my Mentions feed, and it would also appear in the Tag Cloud for the term #picnic. To see all posts that contain the #picnic tag, you simply click that tag and the about page for the tag will open (see Figure 4-37).

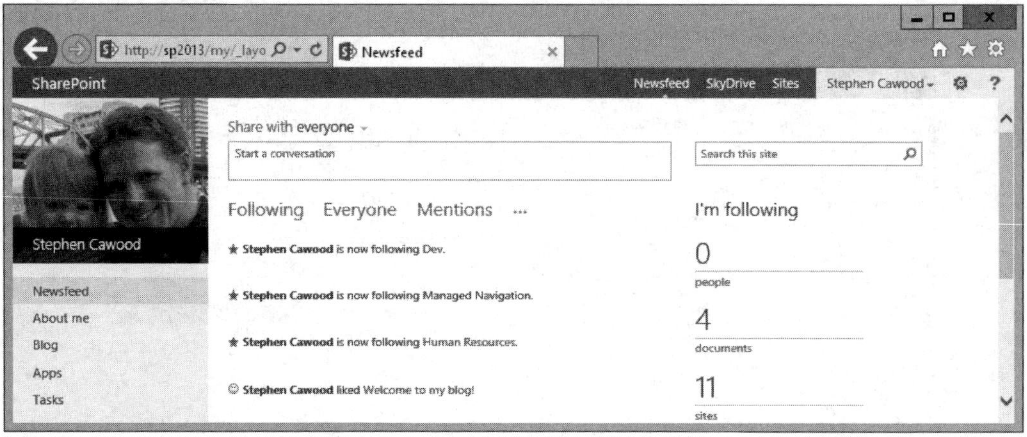

FIGURE 4-37 The SharePoint newsfeed

Sharing Files

SharePoint 2013 introduces a new way to share files that are stored within SharePoint. Previous versions of SharePoint required that users have rights in SharePoint before they could access any files you wanted to share. This is not the case in SharePoint 2013. It is now possible to share a link with anyone. All you need to supply is an e-mail address (see Figure 4-38).

FIGURE 4-38 Sharing a file via an e-mail address

Another improvement in SharePoint 2013 is that the SharePoint Workspace client is no longer required to synchronize files in SharePoint with a folder on your local computer.

Note Many people use Microsoft's personal SkyDrive service for keeping files in cloud storage. This service has been available for a few years. By using the SkyDrive Pro branding in SharePoint, Microsoft is saying that SharePoint is your online storage destination for business use. Or as Microsoft explains it, "SkyDrive Pro is your professional library—the place to keep your work documents. You can think of SkyDrive Pro as your SkyDrive for business. When you store your files on SkyDrive Pro, only you can see them, but you can easily share them with co-workers and access them on your mobile devices. Your files are safely kept in the cloud with SharePoint Online or on your company's SharePoint Server 2013 servers, depending on what your company has set up." http://office.microsoft.com/en-us/sharepoint-server-help/what-is-skydrive-pro-HA102822076.aspx. If you would like to read more about SkyDrive Pro, refer to this helpful blog post: http://sharepoint.microsoft.com/blog/Pages/BlogPost.aspx?pID=1033.

Summary

SharePoint Server 2013 clearly has numerous features that facilitate collaboration. This chapter covered some of that functionality. Combined with the document management features introduced in Chapter 3, these features allow you to take full advantage of SharePoint's collaboration functionality—it's all about teamwork.

5

Tagging and Taxonomy

HOW TO...

- Use social tagging to follow and rate items in SharePoint
- Use the Newsfeed and About Me pages to keep track of your activity
- Enable a folksonomy in SharePoint and add personal notes
- Use enterprise keywords
- Use enterprise managed metadata
- Tag items with managed metadata terms

Enterprise Metadata Management (EMM), or SharePoint taxonomy, is a relatively new feature. It was added in SharePoint 2010—and even later than that for Office 365—so there is still a lot of talk about how the functionality should be used.

What's all the fuss about EMM? Why is taxonomy arguably the most important feature added in SharePoint 2010? Hasn't SharePoint always had metadata? As you'll see in this chapter, the new EMM functionality enables a number of features, including better social computing capabilities.

Note In SharePoint Central Administration, the taxonomy service is called the Enterprise Metadata Service, so some people refer to SharePoint taxonomy as EMS or MMS, for Managed Metadata Service.

Facebook and Twitter have propelled social computing into mainstream acceptance, and it's not surprising that many businesses would like to be able to use social computing to accelerate collaboration and enhance knowledge management within their staff. With many social computing features already available in SharePoint and more coming with each release, a relevant question to consider is that posed by Edward Cone in the title of his 2007 article for *CIO Insight* magazine, "Will Microsoft Become Facebook for the Enterprise?" (www.cioinsight.com/c/a/Past-News/Will-Microsoft-Become-Facebook-for-the-Enterprise/). This chapter will give you a sense of why the question was asked, and as you'll see, SharePoint is well on the way.

Note SharePoint personal sites (previously called My Sites), which were offered in SharePoint Portal Server 2003, were available before Facebook was launched in 2004.

Two types of taxonomy are available in SharePoint Server:

- **Managed** This is a centrally managed and controlled tagging system. The benefit is that the tags can be guaranteed to fit into a rigid taxonomy. However, this type of system needs to be properly planned and built before users can start applying tags.
- **Social tagging (aka folksonomy)** This is a loose system that can lead to varied results. On the positive side, people are free to use a taxonomy that makes sense to them, and because people define their own terms, they may be able to find items easier. However, issues are likely to arise where slightly different terms are used to tag items that really should all have the same tags. For example, some people might use the tag EU to refer to the European Union, but others could use the tag Europe.

This chapter discusses both types of taxonomy and how they are used in SharePoint Server.

Social Tagging

One aspect of social computing that SharePoint lacked in the past is social tagging. SharePoint Server 2013 comes with a few improvements in this area. The first of these that you might notice are the Follow and Tags & Notes options that appear in the ribbon for document libraries and in other contexts. These options allow you to bubble up content that is interesting in some way, as well as classify it for easier retrieval down the line.

In Chapter 4, you saw how you can create discussion boards to carry on conversations with other SharePoint users. Now suppose that you've come across an interesting thread, and you would like to not only share it with your coworkers, but also make it easier for you to find in the future.

Follow

The first option for SharePoint social tagging is the simple-to-use Follow option. All you need to do is go to any SharePoint item that you would like to tag, select it from the list, and follow it. For example, when you're looking at a document library, select an item, click the ellipse link, and then click Follow from the hover card options—it's that simple (see Figure 5-1).

Once you're following something, you will be able to find it more easily, and you'll see activity for that item in your newsfeed.

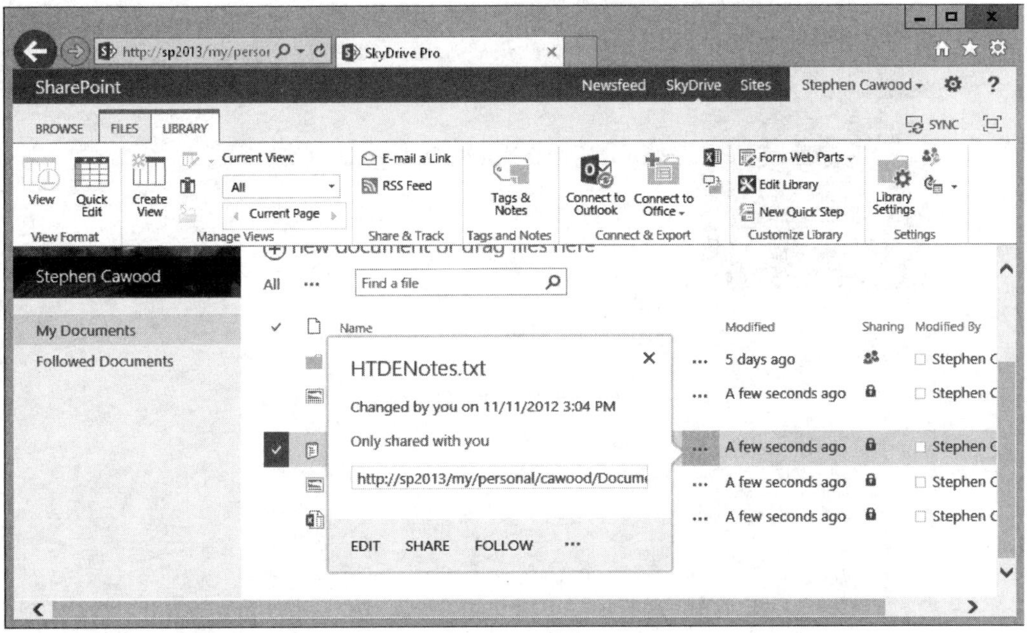

FIGURE 5-1 Using the Follow tag

Ratings

There may be times when you would like to gather feedback about which documents are the most useful or the best suited for a particular purpose. SharePoint ratings can help you gather this data.

If you would like to allow users to assign a value to items in a list, you can enable the ratings option. To turn ratings on for a list, go to the list settings, and under General Settings, click Rating Settings. Once you have navigated to the Rating Settings page, you can simply click the radio buttons to enable or disable the rating option. You can also choose between Star Ratings, which allow users to give the item a value from one to five stars, or you can use Likes. Likes work similar to Facebook likes in that users can choose to like something to give it an "up vote," and therefore show that they prefer that item to other choices.

Whether you use likes or stars is up to you. One way to differentiate the two options is to use stars as a measure of quality and use likes when you simply need an A/B choice or you want to know which items are more popular.

About Me and Newsfeed

When you have tagged something with the Follow option, the action will appear in the newsfeed for your profile (if this option is enabled). In this way, you can share your choices, and your social network will benefit from your tagging activities.

FIGURE 5-2 The SharePoint About Me page

You can also add information to your About Me profile page, both to make your SharePoint experience more personal and to help other people in your organization figure out your expertise and interests. Microsoft uses this information internally to allow employees to track down subject matter experts when they have questions. For example, someone with a SharePoint question can use the profile information to find a SharePoint expert. The profile also includes an organization browser so that you can see who works on specific teams.

Other actions, such as adding notes, can also appear in your newsfeed. To view what you've tagged and see your newsfeed, go to the top right of a SharePoint web page and click the Newsfeed link. To view your profile, go to the same area and expand the drop-down menu under your username. From there, choose About Me to view or edit your profile page (see Figure 5-2).

Tags and Notes

Similar to choosing the Follow tag, you can also make up your own tags and apply those to SharePoint items. These types of tags aren't predetermined, so you can make up tags for whatever you need. This open taxonomy is referred to as a *folksonomy*, and you'll learn more about it in the "Managed Keywords" section later in this chapter. For now, you can think of Tags & Notes as another open taxonomy option.

To apply your own custom tags to an item, select the item, and then click Tags & Notes on the ribbon (in the File tab) to open the dialog shown in Figure 5-3. You

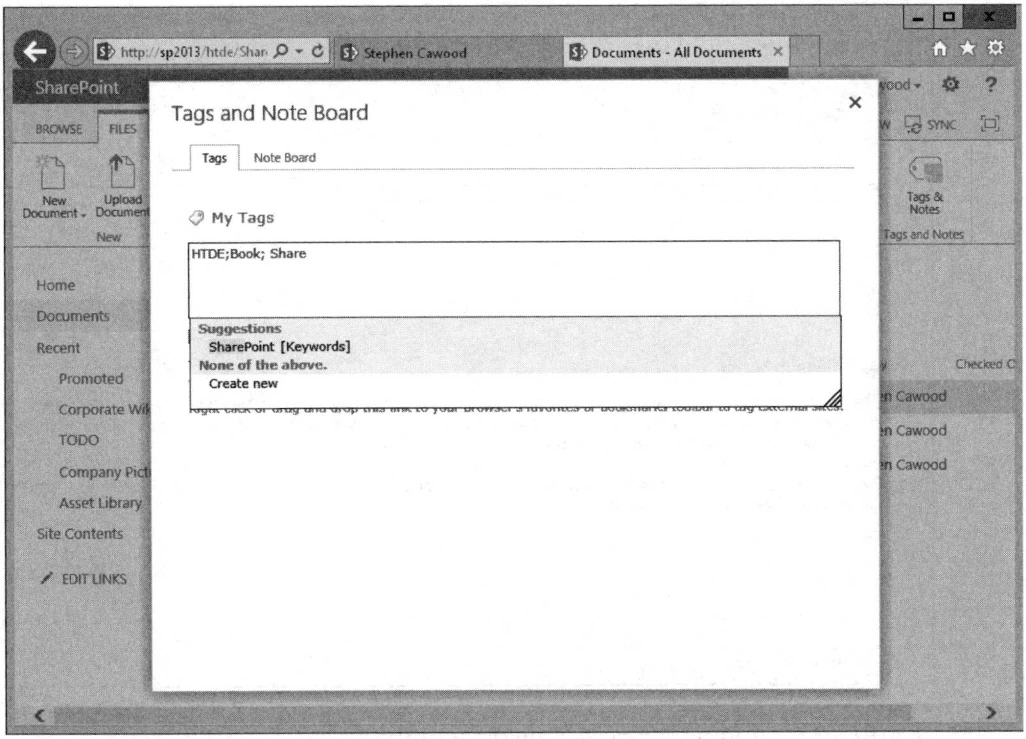

FIGURE 5-3 Tagging an item with a personal tag

can then start typing keywords to tag the item. After you have tagged some things, go back to your profile page and check what appears in your newsfeed and under the Tags & Notes section. You'll notice that there are actually two options for tags, Public and Private, so that you can choose whether you want your tags to be publicly visible. Another interesting feature is that you can use the Note Board to write about links that are external to SharePoint.

As with tags, you can add notes by selecting your target item and choosing Tags & Notes. When the dialog opens, click the Note Board tab to enter your notes (see Figure 5-4). Notes allow you to store more information about an item than you can with tags. Instead of a word or phrase, you'll be able to write up to 250 characters and store that information with the item. You may want to do this to keep track of your thoughts, or you may want to keep track of related information by pasting in a link. What you do with notes is up to you.

As previously mentioned, you have the option of making your notes public or private. If you make them private, you will be able to view them in your profile, but no one else will be able to read them. If you make them public, they will appear in your newsfeed, and everyone will be able to benefit from your insights.

Documents - All Documents   ✕

| Tags | Note Board |

This is a useful document. I appreciate the level of detail. |

Post

‹Previous | Next›

There are no notes posted yet. You can use notes to comment on a page, document, or external
site. When you create notes they will appear here and under your profile for easy retrieval. Other
people can also view the notes you post.

Right click or drag and drop this link to your browser's favorites or bookmarks toolbar to use notes
to comment on external sites.

FIGURE 5-4   Adding notes to a SharePoint item

 Personal sites and profiles are SharePoint Server features. They are not available in
SharePoint Foundation.

Enterprise Managed Metadata

The Microsoft TechNet Library article "Overview of managed metadata in SharePoint
Server 2013" (http://technet.microsoft.com/en-us/library/ee424402.aspx) defines
managed metadata as follows: "*Managed metadata* is a hierarchical collection of
centrally managed terms that you can define, and then use as attributes for items
in Microsoft SharePoint Server 2013." Managed terms and keywords can be used
to enhance or enable a number of features within SharePoint. For example, using
the taxonomy created by managed terms, users can have a more powerful search
experience and navigation can be partly based on metadata terms.

SharePoint Taxonomy

While it's true that SharePoint has always provided the option to associate metadata
with the data stored in SharePoint, before managed metadata, organizations using
SharePoint would need to either build their own taxonomy solution or rely on

business rules for how their users should add metadata. This meant that different users could tag items with slightly different terms, thereby eliminating most of the value of taxonomy.

Technical constraints also prevented creation of a custom solution. For example, the logical place to store terms would be in a list, but lists couldn't be shared across site collection boundaries, so the taxonomy would need to be duplicated if you wanted to share terms. There was also no concept of hierarchical metadata, and no way to share a collection of terms with delegated permissions.

All of these issues were resolved in SharePoint Server 2010. If you want to understand the impact of the changes, SharePoint MVP Chris O'Brien (www .sharepointnutsandbolts.com) wrote a whole post, "Managed Metadata in SharePoint 2010—some notes on the why," about why SharePoint taxonomy is important. Also, the Microsoft TechNet Library article quoted at the beginning of this section includes a "Benefits of Using Managed Metadata" section, which lists and describes the following benefits:

More consistent use of terminology

Managed metadata makes it easier to use terms and enterprise keywords more consistently. You can predefine terms, and allow only authorized users to add new terms. You can also prevent users from adding their own enterprise keywords to items, and require them to use existing enterprise keywords. Managed metadata also provides greater accuracy by presenting only a list of correct terms from which users can select values. Because enterprise keywords are also a type of managed metadata, even the enterprise keywords that users apply to items can be more consistent.

Because metadata is used more consistently, you can have more confidence that it is correct. When you use metadata to automate business processes—for example, putting documents in different files in the record center based on the value of their department attribute—you can be confident that the metadata was created by authorized users, and that the value of the department attribute is always one of the valid values.

Better search results

A simple search can provide more relevant results if items have consistent attributes.

As users apply managed terms and enterprise keywords to items, they are guided to terms that have already been used. In some cases, users might not even be able to enter a new value. Because users are focused on a specific set of terms, those terms—and not synonyms—are more likely to be applied to items. Searching for a managed term or an enterprise keyword is therefore likely to retrieve more relevant results.

Dynamic

In earlier versions of SharePoint Server, to restrict the value of an attribute to being one of a set of values, you would have created a column whose type is "choice," and then provided a list of valid values. When you needed to add a new value to [the] set of choices, you would have to change every column that used the same set of values.

By using managed metadata, you can separate the set of valid values from the columns whose value must be one of the set of valid values. When you have to add a new value, you add a term to the term set, and all columns that map to that term set would use the updated set of choices.

Using terms can help you keep SharePoint items in sync with the business as the business changes. For example, assume that your company's new product had a code name early in its development, and was given an official name shortly before the product launched. You included a term for the code name in the "product" term set, and users were identifying all documents related to the product by using the term. When the product name changed, you could edit the term and change its name to the product's official name. The term is still applied to the same items, but its name is now updated.

To borrow a joke from Dan Kogan, Microsoft SharePoint Program Manager, delivered during his SharePoint Conference 2009 talk, "When we talk about terms, we need to first define our terms." The following definitions are adapted from the same TechNet Library article about managed metadata:

- **Term** *A word or phrase that can be associated with an item in SharePoint Server 2013*
- **Term set** *A collection of related terms*

Note According to the MSDN article "Managed metadata and navigation in SharePoint 2013" (http://msdn.microsoft.com/en-us/library/jj163949.aspx#SP15_ ManagedMetadataAndNav_ManagedNav), "If you want to make your term set available to other site collections connected to the managed metadata service, create a global term set. If you want to create a private term set that is available only to a specific site collection when it is stored in the managed metadata service, create a local term set."

- **Managed terms** *Terms that can be created only by users with the appropriate permissions, and are often organized into a hierarchy. Managed terms are usually predefined.*
- **Enterprise keywords** *Words or phrases that have been added to SharePoint Server items. All managed keywords (also called enterprise keywords) are part of a single, non-hierarchical term set called the keyword set.*
- **Term store** *A database that stores both managed terms and managed keywords. The Term Store Management Tool is available in Central Administration (and Site Settings). This tool manages terms centrally for the whole farm and can be used to create, copy, reuse, move, duplicate (for polyhierarchy), deprecate, delete, and merge terms (see Figure 5-5). The Term Store Management Tool is also used to manage permissions on term stores.*

Note A polyhierarchy-enabled tree can include leaves (nodes) that have more than one branch (parent node). In SharePoint Server, you can create a polyhierarchical structure with the Reuse Terms action in the Term Store Management Tool. For example, imagine that you have a taxonomy of people terms, and the term sets define teams to which they belong. A person could be on more than one team, and therefore, you might want to reuse terms rather than copy them (and potentially have them become out of sync if edits occur down the line).

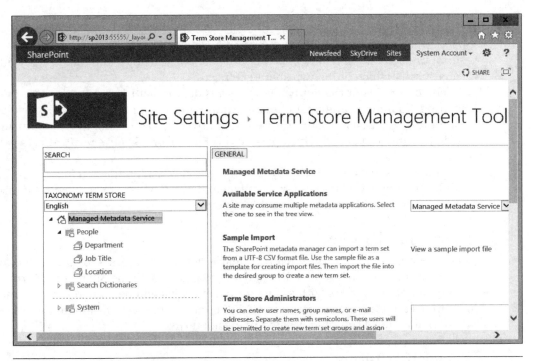

FIGURE 5-5 The Term Store Management Tool

Also, here's another important definition that isn't clear in the article:

- **Group** In the term store, all term sets are created within groups. In other words, *group* is the parent container for term sets. Groups can be used to define security boundaries.

A Taxonomy Primer

Before you set out to use the SharePoint EMM functionality, it's important to have an understanding of taxonomy at a higher level. In case you aren't a library scientist or a taxonomist, this section offers a quick introduction to some taxonomy concepts. Taxonomy relationships are commonly divided into three types:

- Equivalent (synonyms: "LOL" is equivalent to "laughing out loud")
- Hierarchical (parent/child: "sports equipment" is the parent node of "ball")
- Associative (concept/concept: "bouncy things" is related to "ball")

SharePoint provides SharePoint users, administrators, and developers with the UI and application programming interface (API) required for the first two types of relationships. This means that faculties such as centrally managed terms, folksonomy, and Tag Clouds (social tagging) are enabled. The third type—which SharePoint does not offer—is associative relationships. Let's quickly review each type.

Equivalent Terms

SharePoint taxonomy allows synonyms and preferred terms. Synonyms allow a central understanding that LOL is the same as "laughing out loud," and preferred terms specify which of the two should be used.

The other side of the equivalence coin is dealing with words with more than one meaning. To help disambiguate terms, SharePoint term descriptions are displayed in a tooltip so that users can differentiate between *G-Force* (the movie featuring a specially trained squad of guinea pigs) and G-Force from *Battle of the Planets* (a cartoon from the 1980s).

Another aspect of equivalency is multilingual considerations. If you are tagging in different languages, there's a good chance that you'll want to create a relationship between words that actually mean the same thing.

Hierarchical Terms

A central repository of terms enables consistency across users. Providing a hierarchy allows for information architecture and organization. With the SharePoint Term Store Management Tool, users with sufficient permissions will be able to perform many operations on terms in the hierarchy. The hierarchy has a term store at the top, then a group, then term sets, and, finally, managed terms.

Associative Terms

Associative terms are used to create ontologies. There are endless possibilities for these types of relationships. For example, you could have a hierarchy of terms that includes the terms "ball" and "bat" as children of the term "sports equipment." An ontology would allow you to also create a relationship between "bouncy things" and "ball" because they are conceptually related.

Note Why didn't the SharePoint team add ontologies? That's a reasonable question, but the fact is that tackling such a specialized function simply might not have been worth the effort when the team was already trying to build an ambitious feature. Also, I've heard people wonder aloud whether anyone but a library scientist or a taxonomist will complain.

Enterprise Keywords

The SharePoint EMM system has two types of tags: enterprise keywords (sometimes called *managed keywords*) and managed terms. You have already seen managed keywords in action in the "Social Tagging" section earlier in this chapter. Now you'll see how those tags fit in with the overall taxonomy strategy in SharePoint. This section shows examples of how users can take advantage of the various features that each type of tagging enables. Managed terms are covered in the next section.

Enterprise keywords (or just *keywords*) are used for user-focused tagging. Users decide which keywords they want to add to the system and what needs to be tagged.

This type of open tagging is called a *folksonomy* because it's created by people instead of laid out by the organization. In this way, keywords are used to informally tag content within SharePoint.

Note Unlike managed terms, enterprise keywords do not have a hierarchical structure.

You've already seen one way to add keywords to a SharePoint item by using the Tags & Notes dialog. Another way to add keywords is to edit the properties of an item. In Chapter 11, you'll see how this is done in an example of adding an enterprise keyword to a document in a document library.

Enabling Keywords

If keywords have not been enabled for the document library, you need to click the Library tab in the ribbon, and then click Library Settings. Once you are at the Document Library Settings page, look for the Enterprise Metadata and Keywords Settings link under the Permissions and Management settings category. Click the link, and you'll be offered the choice to enable enterprise keywords (see Figure 5-6).

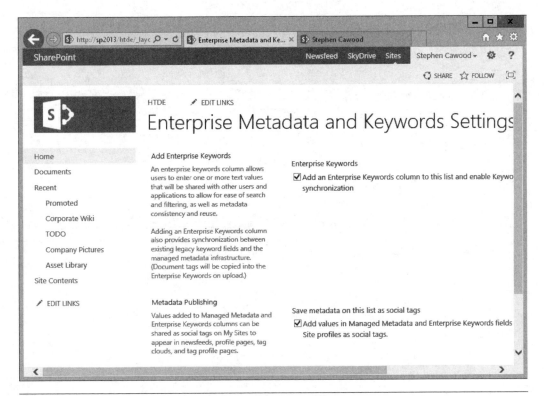

FIGURE 5-6   Enabling keywords for a document library

In this dialog, you also are given the option to add the keywords and terms that are associated with the items in this library to personal site profiles. If you select this option, that data will appear in Tag Cloud web parts and on profile pages. To add a managed term to a document, select the document in the document library, and then select Edit Properties from the drop-down menu (see Figure 5-7).

Once you have the edit document properties dialog open, find the Enterprise Keywords field and start typing either an existing keyword (in which case, you will be prompted with suggestions as you type) or a new keyword (see Figure 5-8).

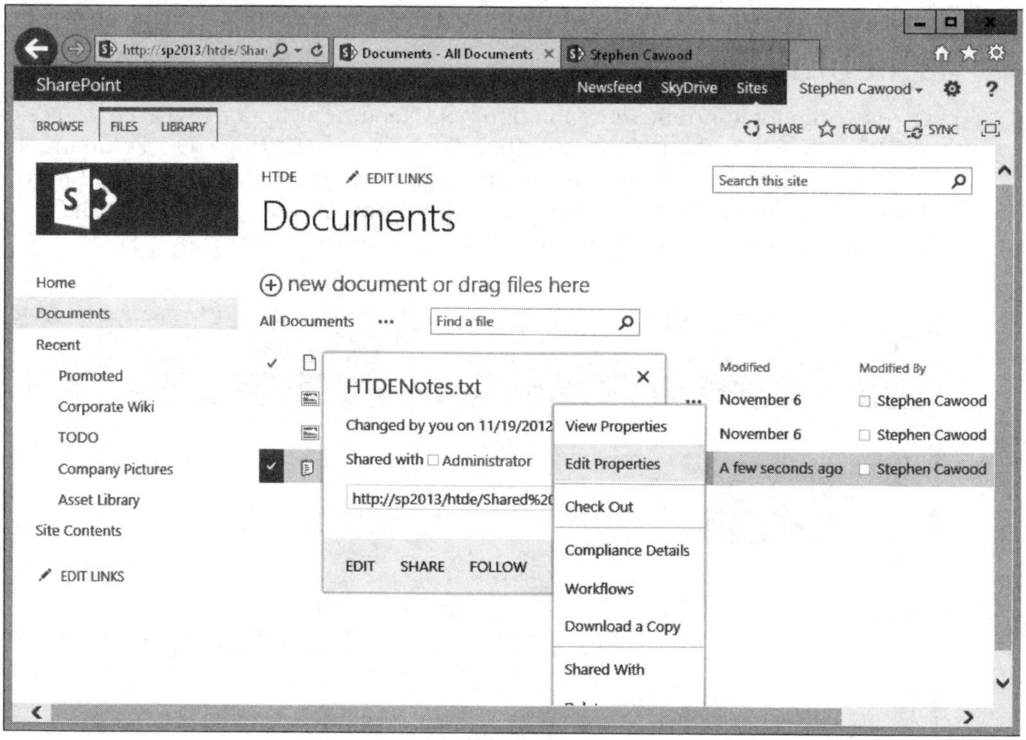

FIGURE 5-7 Selecting to edit a document's properties

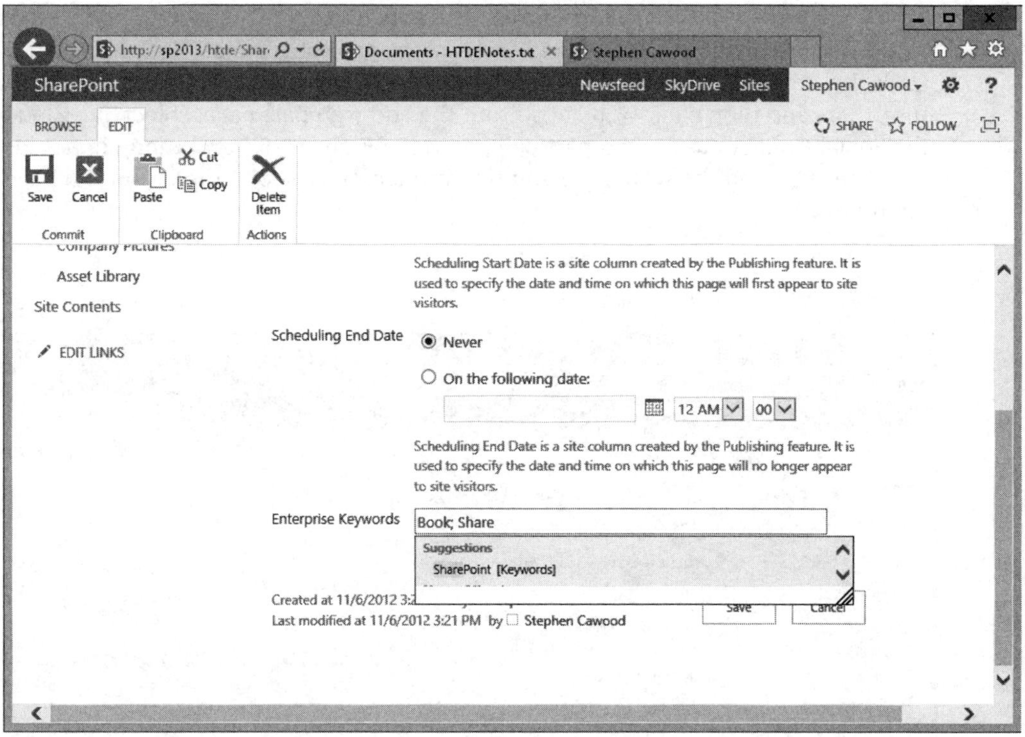

FIGURE 5-8   Adding a keyword to a document

Managed keywords can also be promoted to managed terms using the Term Store Management Tool, as discussed in Chapter 11.

Using the Tag Cloud Web Part

Once you've begun tagging things, you'll probably want to be able to use that data in convenient ways. The Tag Cloud web part is a quick way to view the folksonomy being created on your SharePoint server.

If you have sufficient permissions to create a web part page and add web parts, you'll be able to add the Tag Cloud web part to web part pages. To add the web part, click the Edit Page button on the ribbon or the Edit icon in the top right, click the Insert tab, and then click Web Part. From the add web part page, select Tag Cloud from the Social Collaboration web part category (see Figure 5-9), and then click Add.

After you add the web part, you will immediately see it appear on the page (see Figure 5-10).

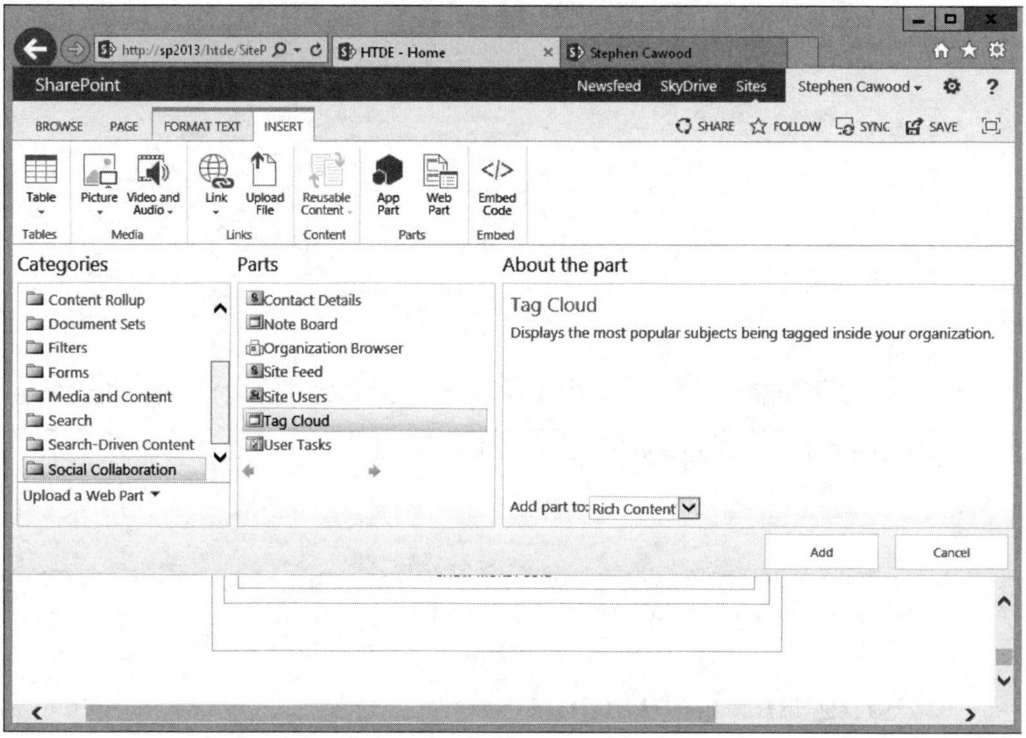

FIGURE 5-9 Choosing to add the Tag Cloud web part to a page

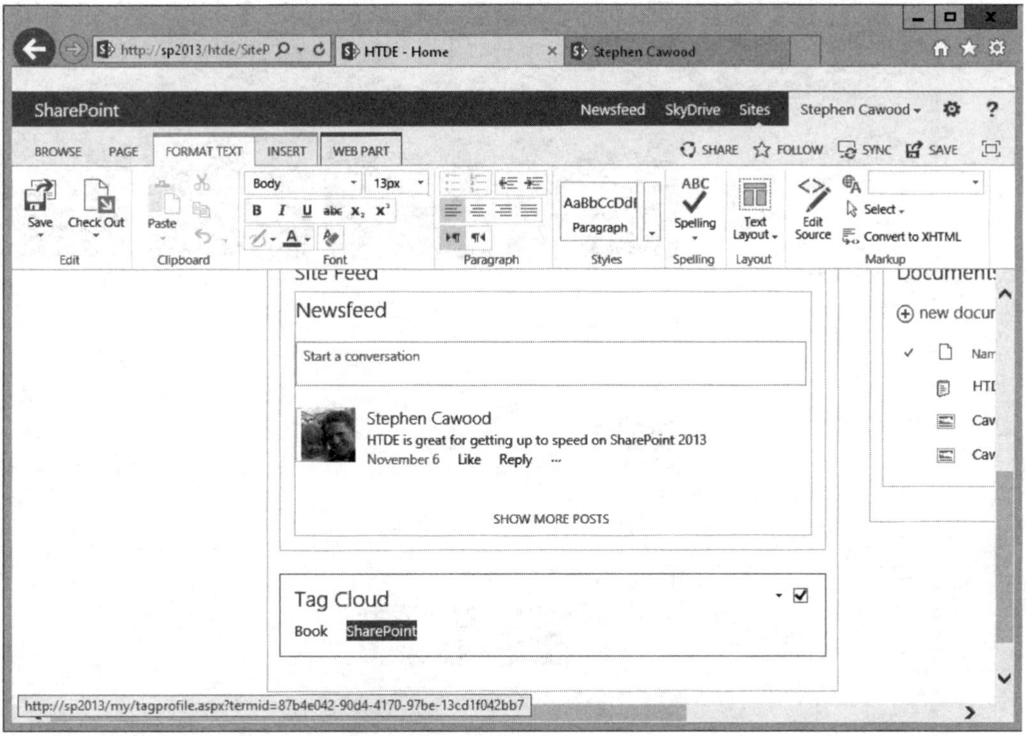

FIGURE 5-10   A Tag Cloud web part in edit page mode

The relative sizes of the terms indicate how popular they are on the server. In the example in Figure 5-11, the "SharePoint" term has been added more than the others.

If you choose to edit the web part, you will find a number of options in the Tag Cloud settings. For example, you can choose to show only your tags or to show tags from all users.

> **Tip** Many features can be deactivated at the site collection level. If you find that you're not offered the Tag Cloud web part or some other out-of-the-box web part, ask your SharePoint administrator to investigate. Also, we noted earlier, these features aren't available in SharePoint Foundation.

FIGURE 5-11 The Tag Cloud web part in action

Managed Terms

Managed terms are the other type of tags in SharePoint EMM. Unlike managed keywords, managed terms are placed in a controlled central repository. This enables consistency across users, provides hierarchical organization, and allows for strict information architecture. In the SharePoint Term Store Management Tool, users with sufficient permissions are able to perform many operations on terms in the hierarchy. However, most users will simply use the terms from the central store.

As with keywords, terms can be added to many types of content within SharePoint. The following example will show you how to add a term to a document within a document library that has already been enabled for tagging with terms.

 To enable this functionality, someone with sufficient rights must first add a managed metadata column to the document library. It's important to remember that the column could have any name—managed metadata is the type of data it will contain, not the name required for the column.

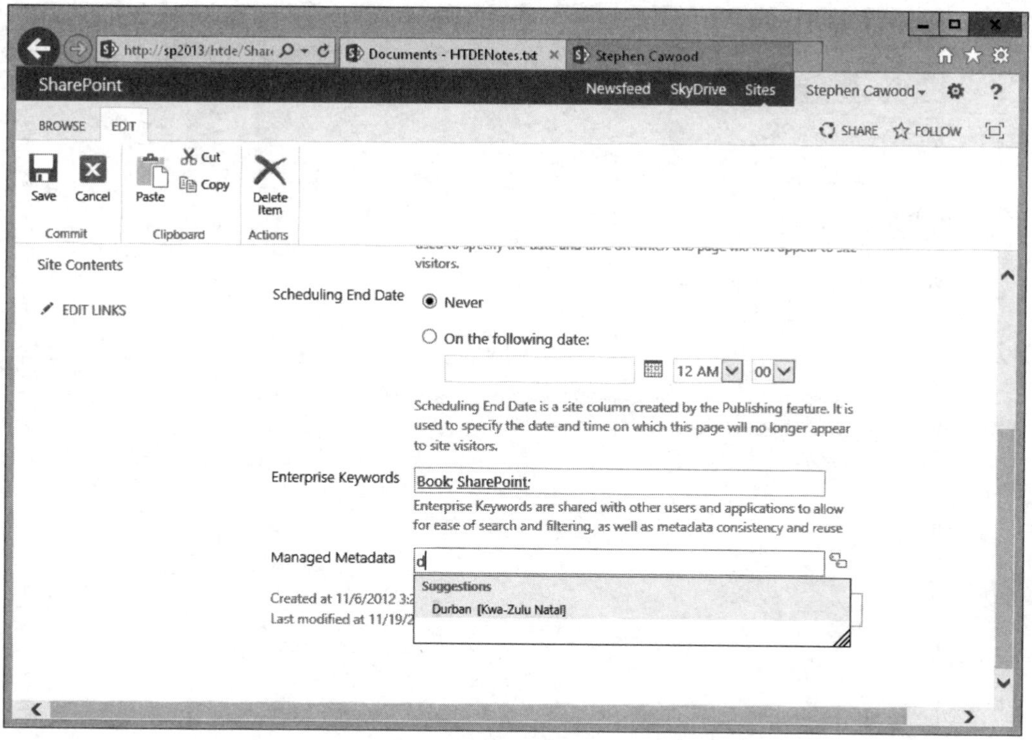

FIGURE 5-12   Browsing for a term to add to a document

To add a managed term to a document, first select the document in the document library, click the ellipses icon, and then select Edit Properties from the drop-down menu. In the edit document properties dialog, find the Managed Metadata field and either start typing a term or click Browse for a valid choice icon on the right. This will open the Select Managed Metadata dialog (see Figure 5-12).

> **Tip**   Terms can be labeled with a description that helps users figure out which term to use.

Filtering Lists Using Taxonomy

It can be difficult to convince people that SharePoint taxonomy is a cool and exciting addition to the platform. The problem is that taxonomy is infrastructure—it's an enabling technology, or a means to an end. The real value is the features that are built on this infrastructure. Filtering lists via managed metadata is one of the out-of-the-box features that are powered by managed metadata.

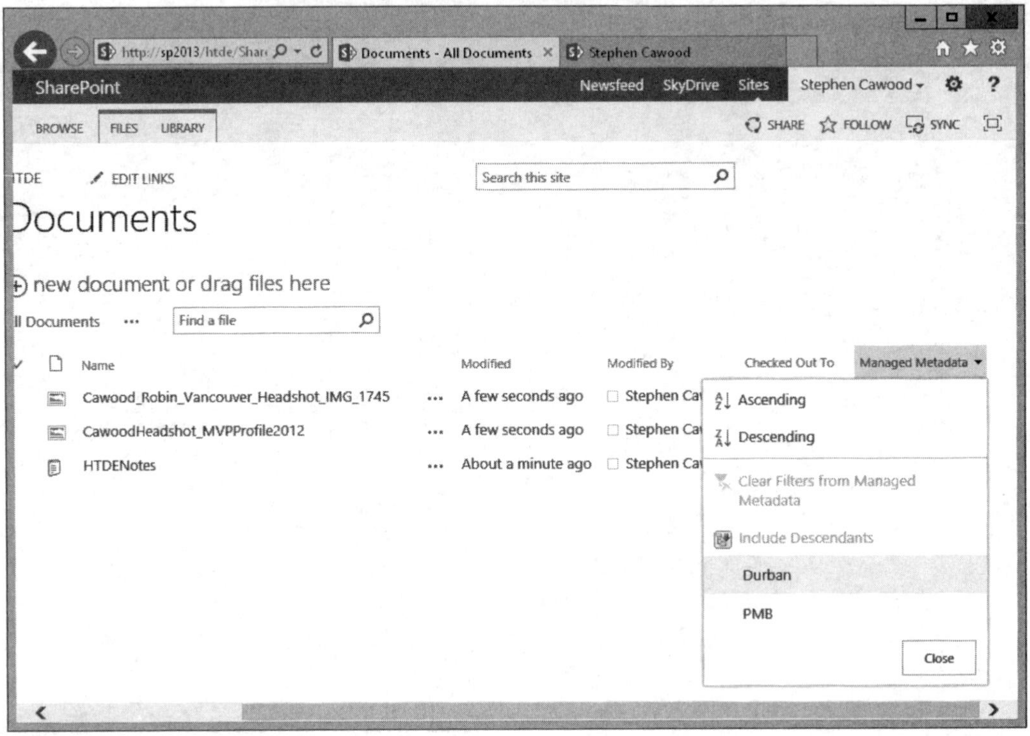

FIGURE 5-13 Filtering a document library using the managed metadata term "Durban"

Managed metadata can be used to help manage, organize, and present items within SharePoint. If you go to a list that has a managed metadata column, you'll be able to filter the view by simply selecting one of the terms being used in the list (see Figure 5-13). This enables the end user to instantly filter lists without needing to create a custom view. Once you apply the filter, the column heading will show a funnel icon to indicate that you're not seeing the full list.

This feature is extremely powerful because it eliminates (in most cases) the need to organize items into folders. Not using folders allows users to find what they're looking for without navigating through a potentially complicated hierarchy. This is similar to the move toward using search to find files on your computer, rather than asking you to remember which directory contains each item.

How Is SharePoint Taxonomy Used in the Real World?

Obviously, the most popular end-user application of EMM will be building a taxonomy to fulfill business needs and social tagging. If enterprise keyword tagging and managed term tagging are enabled, users will be able to tag their list items, documents, and so forth with open keywords or centrally managed terms. This end-user associated metadata will then be used to classify, organize, find, and share information within SharePoint. By tagging external pages, users have a way to add links to their favorite browser's bookmarks.

However, another aspect of the new managed metadata functionality is how it can be used for enhanced navigation and searches. For example, terms can be used to enable more advanced parametric search features, filtering, and targeted search. For sure, customers and partners will find interesting ways to use the taxonomy framework.

In terms of navigation, the ability to alter the way you navigate your data based on tags is also referred to as *faceted navigation*. When I was working on Microsoft Office SharePoint Server 2007 navigation, faceted navigation was nicknamed, "navigation goggles," the idea being that you could choose different types of navigation the same way you can shift between song view, albums, or artists on many MP3 players.

The Term Store Management Tool available in Central Administration (and Site Settings) enables administrators to manage a central vocabulary of terms for the whole farm. Operations that administrators can perform on the term hierarchy include copying, reusing, moving, duplicating, deprecating, and merging. Furthermore, having a managed repository enforces consistency across users.

The SharePoint EMM functionality is exciting and provides options for centrally managed taxonomies, as well as social tagging and improved search. Through managed metadata, SharePoint users gain access to functionality such as folksonomy, Tag Clouds, list filtering, metadata-driven navigation, and more powerful search options.

Summary

Tagging and taxonomy are fundamental features in SharePoint. This chapter introduced the topics with a look at how tagging can make SharePoint more social, and Managed Metadata enables use cases, such as creating a folksonomy and metadata filtering.

6

Publishing Sites

HOW TO...

- Use publishing sites to create interesting pages
- Work with page layouts
- Change the site master page
- Create a publishing site with workflow
- Create and format a publishing page

It's no secret that SharePoint was originally targeted at internal websites (that is, intranets). However, Microsoft has been working for many releases to break SharePoint out of the internal server box. SharePoint publishing sites allow you to create and edit pages that are more akin to the web pages that people associate with their favorite Internet sites. Many companies have chosen to use the SharePoint for Internet Sites license option to create public-facing websites in SharePoint. For example, the impressive-looking Ferrari website runs on SharePoint (www.ferrari.com).

As well as allowing you to create web pages, publishing sites offer many useful features that are enabled by the SharePoint framework. For example, you'll be able to use content approval workflow or require users to check out pages before they can be edited. All of these features help to maintain a consistent publishing process.

Note The publishing site functionality is a feature that can be enabled in SharePoint Server. Publishing features aren't available in SharePoint Foundation.

Publishing Site Template

The publishing templates are a big part of WCM with SharePoint. WCM is such a huge topic that an entire book could be written about SharePoint WCM; in fact, a couple of books have been written specifically about SharePoint ECM and WCM. In this section, we'll take a look at the publishing site templates and some of the options they enable.

Naturally, the first step for this exercise is to create a publishing site, and you'll need to have sufficient rights to create a new site. If you've read the previous chapters, you know that you can access the Site Contents page from the gear icon menu or the quick launch navigation. From there, click the new subsite option to create a new site and choose the Publishing Site template (see Figure 6-1).

Once you have selected the Publishing Site template and given your new site a name and URL address, you can click the Create button. SharePoint will provision a site that you can use to try the examples in this section. The reason you are given a chance to enter both a name and a URL is that you may want to use an abbreviation for the URL. For example, spaces will be converted to "%20" in a URL, so many users choose to eliminate the spaces that appear in the name.

 The Quick Launch setting option will change to Navigation once you have publishing enabled. And you won't find Quick Launch in the Site Settings options after publishing is enabled.

Before you can make changes to your publishing pages, you need to switch to edit mode, and that leads right into the next topic.

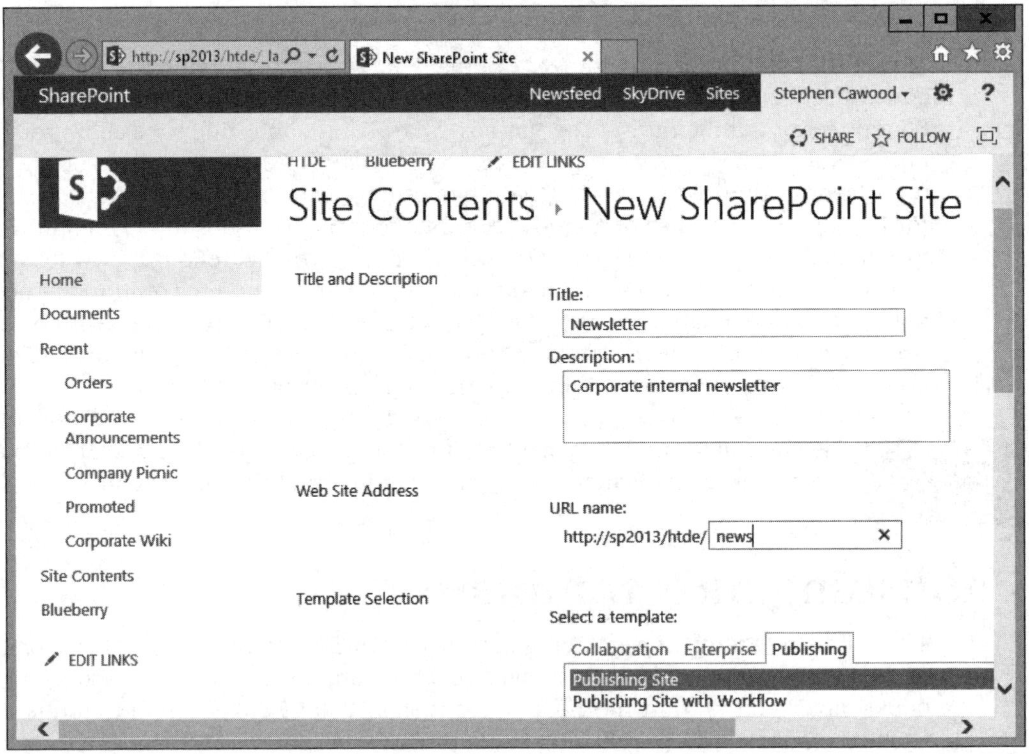

FIGURE 6-1 Creating a new publishing site

Editing a Page

To enter edit mode from the publishing site home page, click the little edit icon in the top right of the page—it looks like a pencil. You can also click the Page tab on the ribbon, and then click Edit. When you switch to edit mode, you will see that a wealth of functionality is available for your publishing pages (see Figure 6-2).

The most obvious edits that you might want to make would be in the Page Content section of the page (where the cursor is located in Figure 6-2). You'll be able to use various editing features, such as spell check and markup styles.

You also have quick access to the Title and Page Image areas. For example, you can simply click the link to set the page image, and then browse your SharePoint server for the link to use as the page image (see Figure 6-3).

When you have the page in edit mode, you can use the Insert tab options. These include options to add tables, pictures, audio, video, links, files, app parts, and web parts. You can also add items from the Reusable Content list. For example, you might want to have a standard copyright notice or signature that can be easily reused. If you choose the More Choices option from the Reusable Content menu, you'll be shown the current content in the list, and also be able to open the list to add more (see Figure 6-4).

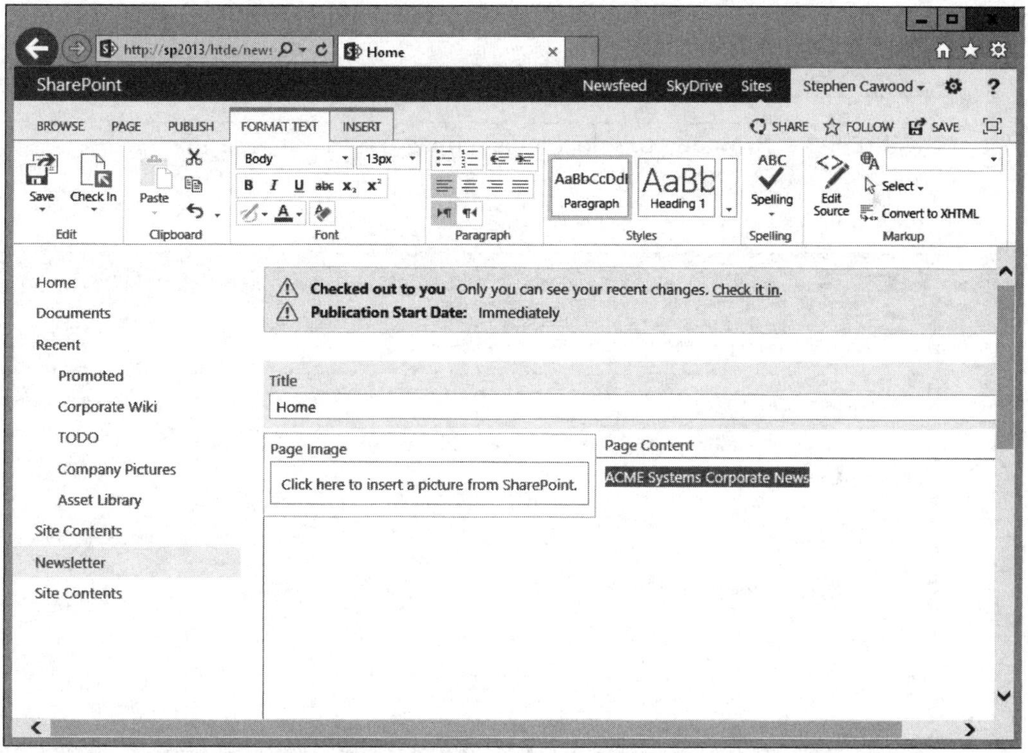

FIGURE 6-2 A publishing page in edit mode

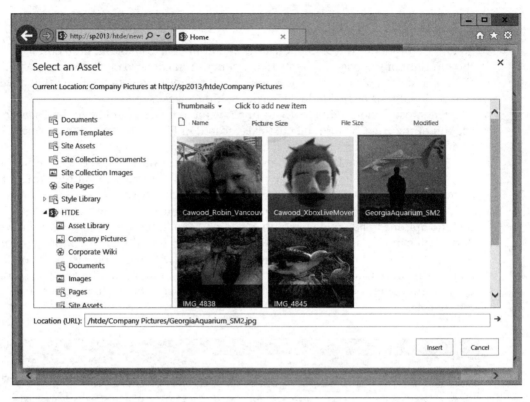

FIGURE 6-3 Browsing to select a page image

Select Reusable Content -- Webpage Dialog

Choose an item to insert into the web page. An item with automatic update will be inserted as a read-only reference to the original item and will be automatically updated whenever a new version of the original item is published. An item without automatic updates is inserted as a copy which you can then modify. Help

Open List | Refresh   Views: Content Preview ▾

	Title	Show in drop-down menu	Automatic Update	Comments	Reusable Content
Content Category : None					
	Byline	Yes	Yes		**By Rich Haddock**
	Copyright	Yes	Yes		Copyright© 2009 Contoso Corporation - All Rights Reserved
	Quote	Yes	Yes		*"Example quotation"*

OK   Cancel

FIGURE 6-4 The default Reusable Content options

After you've edited your page, don't forget to click Save. If the page requires check-in, you'll also need to check it in before it can be published. Your changes won't be visible to users who have only read access until you have published the page. Use the Publish tab in the ribbon to access the available publishing options.

Summary Links

Near the bottom of the default home page, you'll find a section for summary links. When you want to add a link, switch to edit mode and click the New Link option under Summary Links. When you choose to add a link, you'll be presented with a New Link dialog that provides you with many options (see Figure 6-5).

Web Parts and App Parts

Directly below the summary links, you'll find some web part zones (see Figure 6-6). As you may have guessed, web part zones are containers for web parts and app parts.

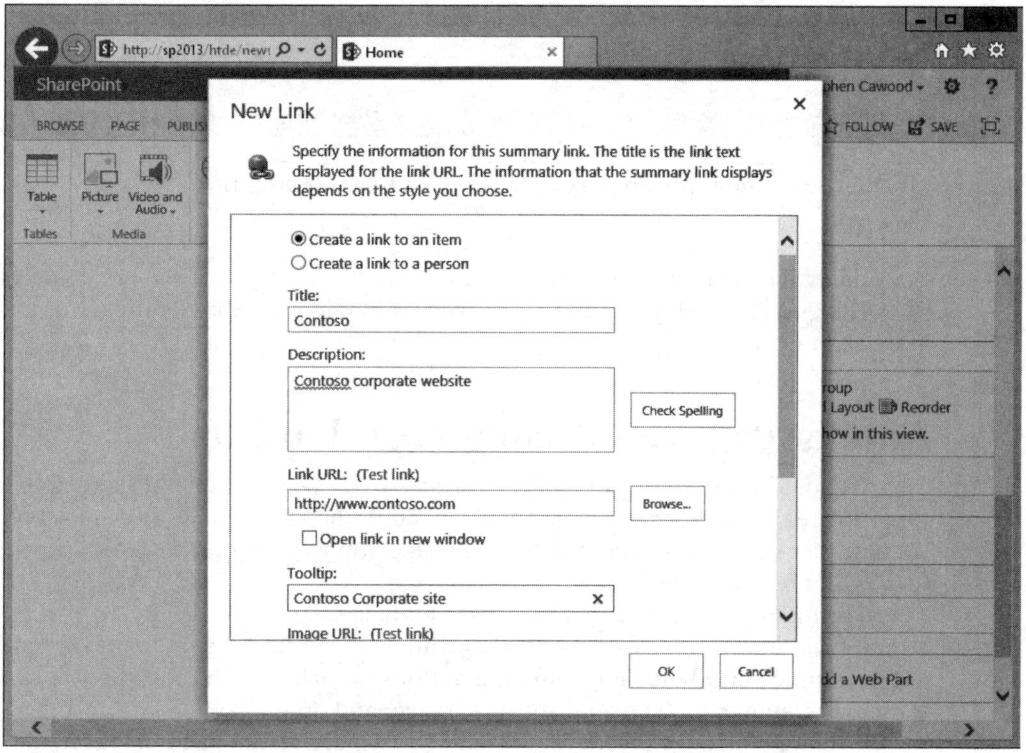

FIGURE 6-5   Adding a new link

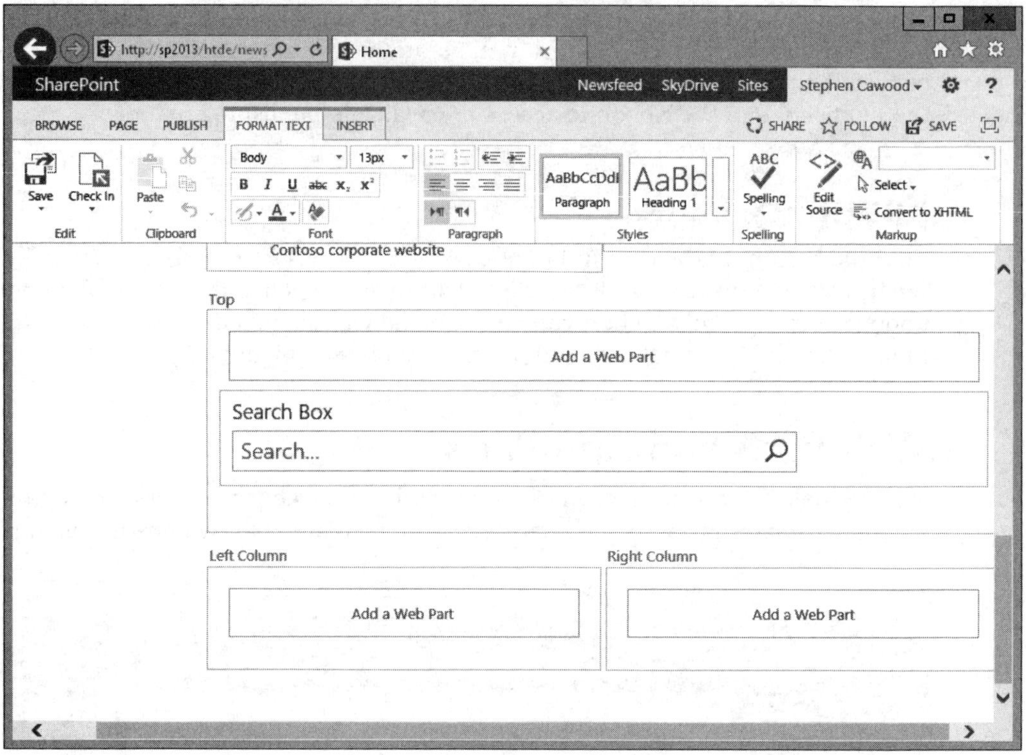

FIGURE 6-6 The top web part zone after adding a search box

Adding web parts to your pages is as easy as clicking one of the Add a Web Part links. The various web parts and app parts that come with SharePoint are discussed in Chapter 8.

Adding Pages and Using Page Layouts

Clearly, you'll need to create your own pages if you want to fully utilize publishing sites. To create a new page, select the Page tab in the ribbon, and then click New Page. You'll be asked to supply the name of the page you want to create. When you click Create, the new page will open.

Most likely, the first thing you'll want to do is select the page layout that will be used for the new page. Page layouts determine the position of elements on publishing pages, but they also help determine the options available within the page. For example, some page layouts include a prominent image, and others do not.

To change the page layout, make sure that you have the page in edit mode, and then click the Page tab on the ribbon and click the Page Layout drop-down button to show the available page layouts (see Figure 6-7).

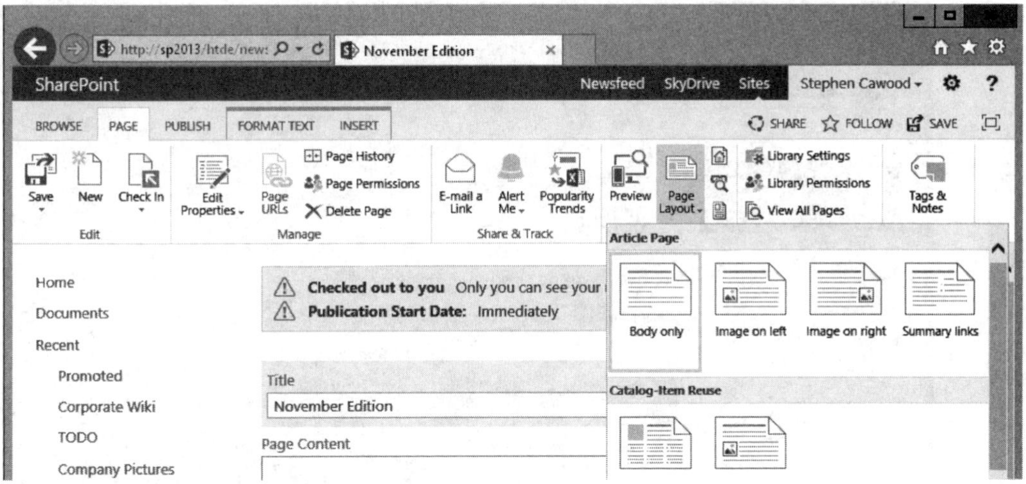

FIGURE 6-7   Choosing a page layout

The Pages List

While it's true that you could navigate to each page when you have page tasks to complete, you might also want to be able to apply actions to multiples pages at the same time. Since the pages within a publishing site are stored within a pages list, you can navigate to the list and view the pages in SharePoint's famous list view.

To find the pages list, choose Site Contents, and then scroll down a bit to find the Pages library. Once you have navigated to the Pages library, you'll see the regular list view showing all the pages in the publishing site. If you expand the drop-down menu next to one of the page names, you'll see the options available (see Figure 6-8). The options include Check In, Check Out, Discard Check Out, Version History, Manage Permissions, Send To, Compliance Details, and Delete. Of course, some options are contextual, so not all of these options will appear in all cases.

Remember that you have the option of choosing multiple pages by clicking the check box next to the items you want to select. You can select all items by checking the box next to the Type column.

The Gear Menu

Like the item options, the gear menu's options (top-right corner of the page) are also contextual. As you navigate from one type of site to another, you'll find that you see different options. Publishing sites offer these choices:

- **Shared with...**   Allows you to grant user's permission to view the site.
- **Edit Page**   Puts the current page in edit mode.
- **Add a Page**   Creates a new page in the site.

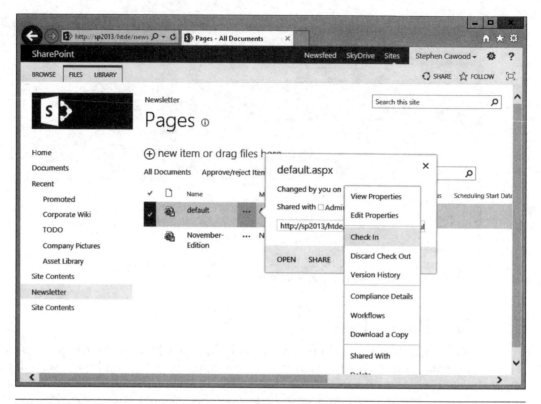

FIGURE 6-8 Selecting the actions menu for a page list item

- **Add an App**   Adds a new app to the site.
- **Site Contents**   Shows the contents of the current site. If you're trying to find an app or subsite, this view can be very useful.
- **Design Manager**   Allows web designers to use their favorite HTML editor to design SharePoint pages, and then upload those designs into SharePoint. This feature is new to SharePoint 2013.
- **Site Settings**   Allows you to set the options for the current site.

Master Pages

Page layouts are useful, but if you really want to change the look and feel of your site, you need to switch or customize the master page. Master pages define the underlying structure of SharePoint pages.

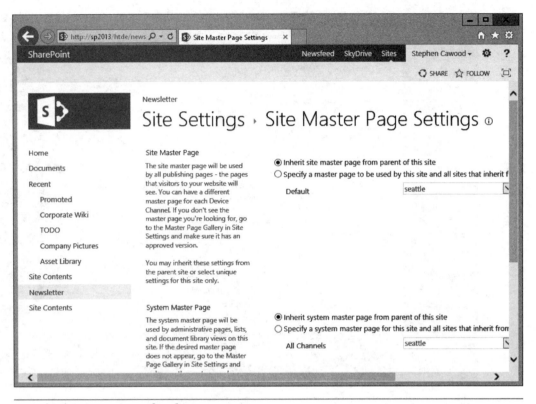

FIGURE 6-9   Settings for the master page

To change the master page, you'll need to have publishing enabled. Go to the Site Settings page and, under the Look and Feel section, click Master Page. The Site Master Page Settings page will open and let you customize the master page settings (see Figure 6-9).

Publishing Site with Workflow

If you would like to add some more structure to your publishing experience, you might want to create a publishing site with workflow instead of a regular publishing site. As the name implies, edits under this type of site need to be approved by a user who has sufficient rights.

One thing you'll notice about the Publishing Site with Workflow template is that you'll have another option in the Publish tab of the ribbon: Schedule. The scheduling feature allows you to set a time frame for publishing the page (see Figure 6-10). Using the Publish tab on the ribbon, you can open the scheduling window and set both start and end dates for the page to be live.

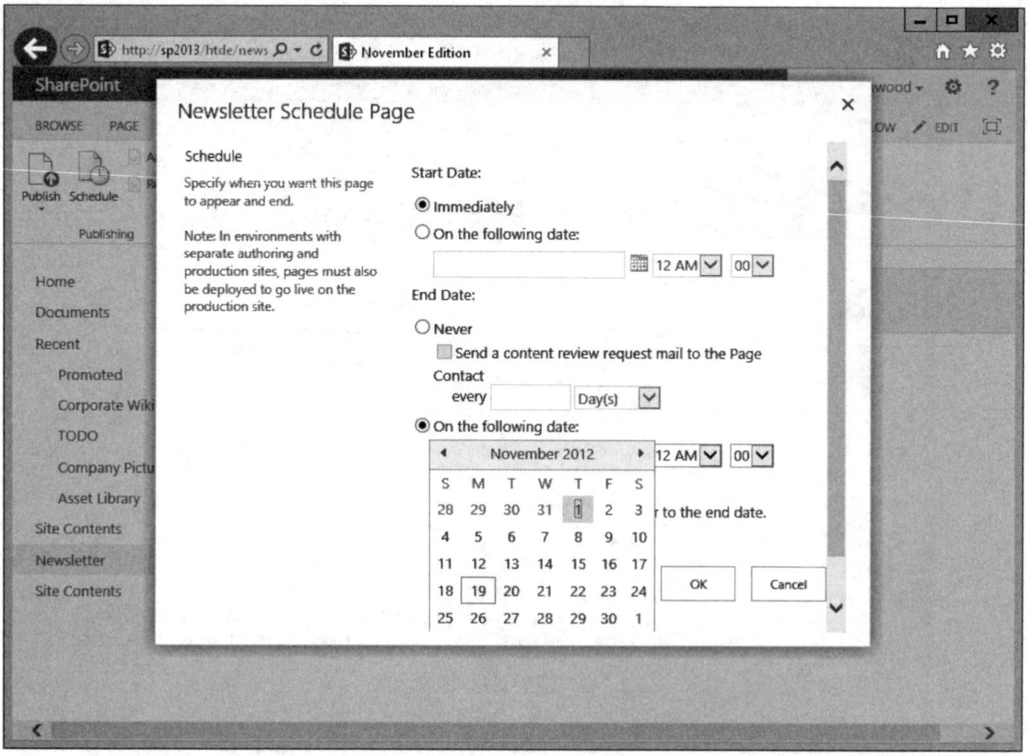

FIGURE 6-10 Setting the start and end dates for a page to be published

The other options you'll see in the Publish tab are for the content approval workflow. If you are logged in as a user who has permission to edit changes but not approve them, you'll find that your edits will not go live until a user with sufficient permissions approves the changes. Of course, it is also possible that your changes can be rejected. Content approval workflow is discussed in more detail in Chapter 3.

Real-World Publishing Site Exercise

This quick review exercise will walk you through the process of creating a new SharePoint publishing site and give you a chance to try some of the formatting features available in SharePoint publishing site pages. For this exercise, you'll be creating a publishing site with workflow. At the end of the exercise, you'll have a publishing site with a home page that looks something like Figure 6-11. The example shown here is a site advertising a company charity drive.

FIGURE 6-11   The final result

Creating the Site

The first thing you'll want to do is create the site and add some content to the main page.

1. Navigate to the site that will be the parent site of the new publishing site.
2. Choose Site Content | New subsite.
3. When the Create dialog opens, choose the Publishing category.
4. Select Publishing Site with Workflow, and then enter a name and URL.
5. When the new site has been provisioned, click the Edit button in the ribbon.
6. Now that you're in the site and have the home page open in edit mode, enter some text in the Page Content section. Here, you can try some of the formatting features, such as the following:
   - Add a heading line to the top of your page content and use the Markup Styles option in the ribbon to assign the Heading 1 (H1) style.
   - Add some color and other formatting, such as bold and italics.
   - Change the name of your home page. For example, in this case, the home page name has been changed to Charity Drive Home.

Adding an Image

Next, you'll add an image to the home page.

1. If you already have your image in SharePoint, you can skip the upload step. Otherwise, you'll need to upload your home page image before you can select it. Make sure you've saved the changes to your home page. You'll find a little Save & Close icon where the Edit button used to be.
2. After you've saved the page, go to Site Contents. As you saw in previous chapters, this will bring up a listing of everything under the current site. In this case, you'll add your image from your computer to the Images library for the charity site.
3. Under Document Libraries, click Images.
4. Click Add New Item.
5. Click Browse. Find your image from your computer, and then click OK to add the image to the Images library. Since there is content approval on this site, you may need to choose to check in the image.
6. From the breadcrumb navigation, click the link to the home page of your site. In the example, it's called Corporate Charity Drive.

 You can also navigate to the site's home page by clicking the site image in the top-left corner of the page. Since you have not changed it yet, it will look like an orange box with three people in it.

7. You should be back to the site home page. Once again, click Edit to get the home page in edit mode.
8. You are now ready to add your page image, so click the link that reads Click Here to Insert a Picture from SharePoint.
9. Next to Selected Image, click the Browse button, find your image in the Images library, select it, and click OK.
10. In the Edit Image Properties dialog, you'll find a number of choices, including the alt text that appears when someone hovers over the image and some useful layout options, such as the image alignment. Once you've set your options, click OK to add the image to the page.

 If the image is not the right size, you can change how it is displayed by dragging the anchors around the border. This action does not actually resize the original image, but simply changes how it is displayed.

Adding a New Page

Next, you'll add a new page where you can provide directions to the event. As you've seen throughout this book, there are generally multiple methods to complete actions in SharePoint. To create a new page, you could use the Site Actions menu, or you could even navigate to the Pages library and add a new item from there. However, since you're already on the home page, for this example, you will use the wiki-style page creation shortcut.

1. Type the name of the page you wish to create in square brackets (for this example, **[Directions]**), and then save the page
2. Click the Directions link to create the new page.
3. Choose Create, and you'll be taken to the new publishing page.
4. At this time, you don't need to make any changes to the Directions page, so click the home page icon or the home page breadcrumb link to get back to the main page.

Publishing Your New Page

Finally, you will publish your new page so that others can enjoy it.

1. From the home page, switch to the Publish tab in the ribbon and choose to Publish your page. If you did not have rights to publish, you might only be able to submit the changes for approval by someone who has approval rights on the page.
2. You'll be asked for a comment so that a history of each modification will be maintained.

Congratulations, you have created your publishing site!

Summary

This chapter introduced publishing sites and some of the features that will help you create your own masterful pages. You also learned how you can customize your pages by using app parts, web parts, text formatting, and images.

The chapter also covered master pages and page layouts, which help present your pages in a style that suits your audience and subject matter. You learned that a publishing site with a workflow template is available if you require an approval process in your organization. The chapter concluded with a simple example for you to try.

This chapter has given you the information you need to wade into publishing sites. It's up to you how deep you choose to dive.

7

Personal Sites and Personalization

HOW TO...

- Use your personal site to share information
- Use your personal blog and newsfeed
- Make changes to your SharePoint profile
- Change the look of SharePoint pages

In Chapter 1, you learned that Microsoft CEO Steve Ballmer described SharePoint as "a general-purpose platform for connecting people with information." This chapter focuses on the "connecting people" part of that statement by exploring SharePoint personal sites and personal profiles.

 Personal sites are a SharePoint Server feature. You won't have all of the options described in this chapter if you are using SharePoint Foundation.

Personal Sites

In previous versions of SharePoint, the term used for a personal site was My Site. This was true for end users and administrators alike. However, in SharePoint 2013, the branding of My Site has been removed, and only administrators will commonly use that term (although many SharePoint veterans will surely continue to use the term, and some screens still reference My Sites).

Many people like to use the analogy that SharePoint personal sites are Microsoft's version of Facebook pages for business. However, as mentioned in Chapter 5, SharePoint My Sites, which were available in SharePoint Portal Server 2003, actually preceded Facebook. Of course, when explaining SharePoint to new users, it's convenient to use the analogy because more people have used Facebook than SharePoint—so far.

Most users don't have rights to add sites—or even apps—on their corporate SharePoint server. This can severely limit your ability to share your files and information, and therefore may hinder your connection with other users. Personal sites can be the solution to this problem. Your personal site is where you can have increased control.

> **Note** Many of SharePoint's new social features, such as SkyDrivePro and Newsfeed, are not enabled out of the box. Organizations often like to analyze how these features will be used and train their staff prior to enabling them.

Naturally, you'll want to add some content to your personal site. As with any SharePoint site, you'll have the option to add apps to your personal site. Exactly which apps are available to you depends on the security setting on your server, as well as which apps have been added from the SharePoint store and your corporate catalog of apps.

Using Your Blog

One of the fundamental ingredients in the flavor of a personal site is a personal blog. On the right side of your Newsfeed page, you'll see that there is a link to your personal blog. When you click the blog link, you'll be taken to the main page for your very own blog (see Figure 7-1). On the right side of this page, you'll see a number of options for managing your blog.

FIGURE 7-1 The default blog page

From this page, you can access your posts, write new posts, manage your blog categories, manage comments, and even launch a local desktop client (such as Microsoft Word or Windows Live Writer) to write new blog content.

Viewing Your Newsfeed

At this point, you may be wondering what else was included with your personal site. At the top of most pages, you'll see a Newsfeed link.

The Newsfeed page will display your recent activity on the server (see Figure 7-2). For example, as you learned in Chapter 5, your tagging activities will be shown in your newsfeed. On the right side of the page, you'll see a summary of people, documents, sites, and tags that you're following. The main section of the page shows a running history of updates.

> **Note** Often, a user's profile is created only when that user logs in to SharePoint for the first time. So it's possible that you won't be able to add users who have not logged in to the system.

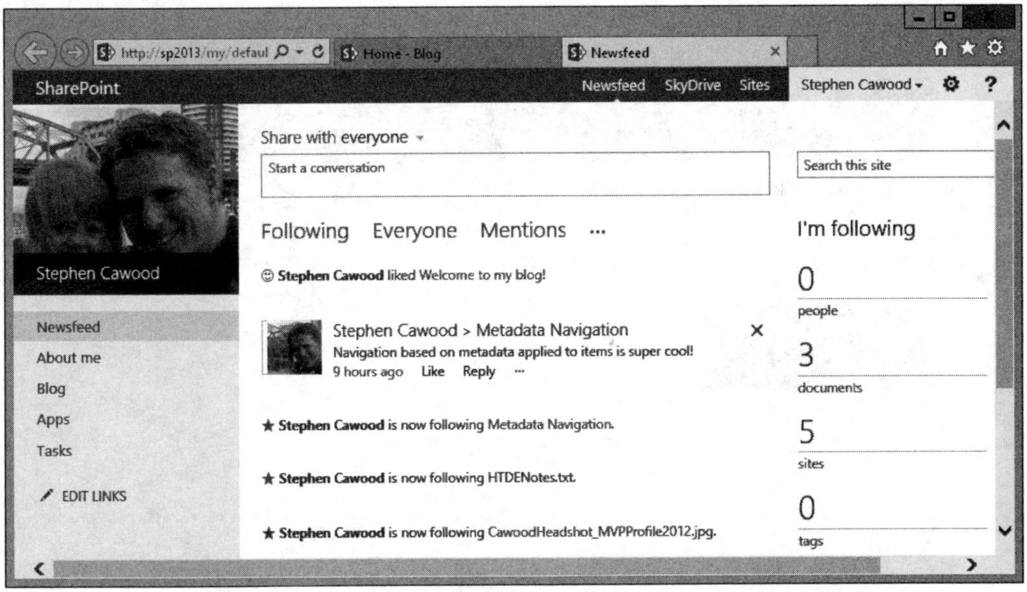

FIGURE 7-2   The Newsfeed page

Your SharePoint Profile

Your SharePoint profile allows you to provide useful information about yourself. To get to your profile page, expand the drop-down menu under your name and click the About Me link. From the About Me page, you can click the edit link near the top of the page to access your profile settings (see Figure 7-3). A profile includes sections for personal data, such as Basic Information, Contact Information, Details, Newsfeed Settings, and Language and Region.

Adding a Photo

You can make your presence more personal by adding a photo to your profile. To do so, in your profile, click the Choose Picture button under the Basic Information section. When you upload an image from your computer, it will be added to your SharePoint profile. After adding a picture, you'll see it shown in many places, but your profile page is one good example.

Microsoft clearly believes that this feature will be used by very large organizations, because the text under the Upload Picture option reads, "Upload a picture to help others easily recognize you at meetings and events."

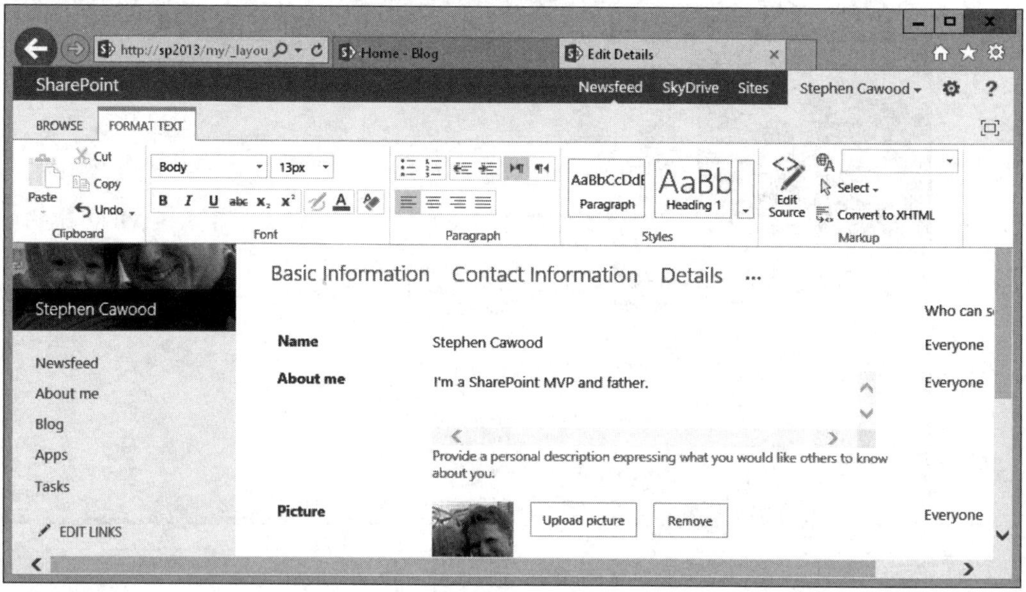

FIGURE 7-3 Editing a profile page

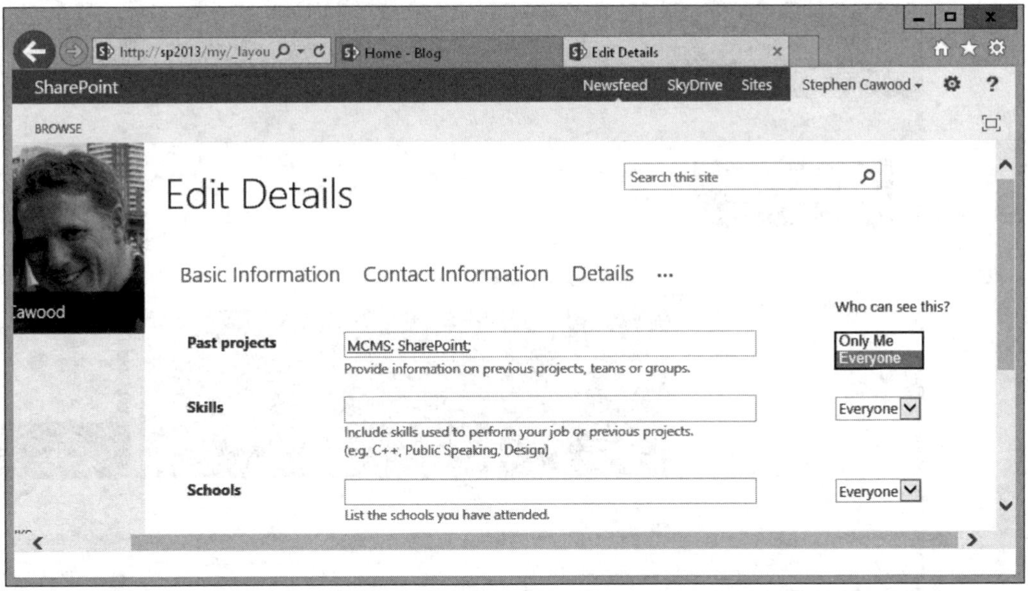

FIGURE 7-4   Setting the visible property for the Details section

Customizing Your Profile for Different Viewers

An interesting aspect of the profile page is that you can customize your profile page for different people. This feature is generally used for privacy reasons.

On the right side of the profile page, you can see who has permission to view the information. By default, everyone can see your basic information, but if you switch to the Details section, for example, you'll be able to change the setting for the information you add (see Figure 7-4).

Changing the Look of Pages

If the default blue page design and out-of-the-box fonts don't fulfill your aesthetic desires, you're in luck. Assuming you have rights to do so, many pages will allow you to alter the look of the page.

To customize the appearance of a page, click the gear icon in the top-right corner of the page and select the Change the look option (see Figure 7-5).

When you choose to change the look of a page, you'll be presented with a choice of templates. After you've selected the design, you'll be able to fine-tune it by altering elements such as the colors and fonts (see Figure 7-6).

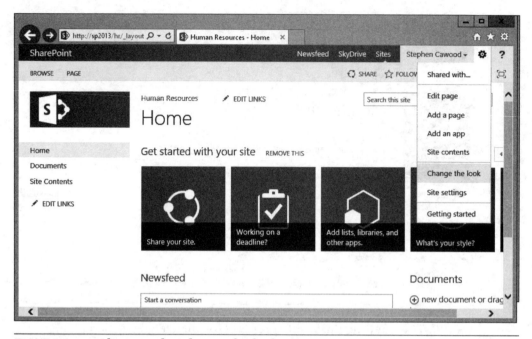

FIGURE 7-5 Choosing the Change the look option

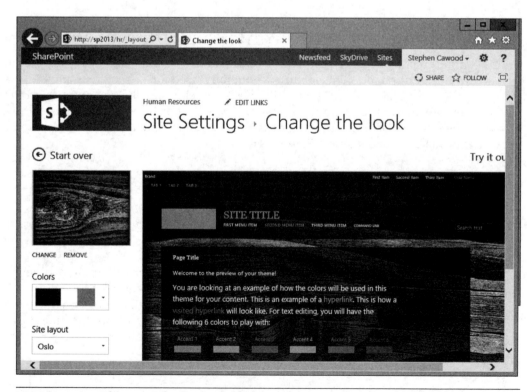

FIGURE 7-6 Changing the look of a page

Real-World Example: Blog Categories

I'm certainly not the most prolific blogger out there, but I do have more than 400 posts on my personal blog (www.geeklit.com). These posts are generally about software, video games, and writing, but there are plenty of random entries that give my blog a particularly eclectic feel. To help people who want to find posts on only one particular topic (including myself when I need to share a link) I use *blog categories*.

Categories are metadata tags associated with blog posts that allow the system to automatically generate an index of posts. This is a useful piece of functionality that is also available in SharePoint blogs. At one software company, I actually used this feature to track how many posts I had written on particular topics so I could show that I had met one of my formal performance goals (we all know managers love to see real measurable results).

To try out blog categories, you'll need to create some posts, but it's a good idea to plan your category taxonomy first. It is possible to go back and add or remove categories from posts, and you'll likely need to make some adjustments if you use this feature as much as I do, but you can make things easier on yourself by coming up with a starting list of categories.

First, navigate to your personal blog. The fastest way to do this is to click the Newsfeed link, and then click the blog link in the quick launch navigation (on the left side of the page). Once you're on your blog home page, click the Manage categories link on the right side. You'll be taken to a simple list interface that will allow you to add, edit, and remove blog categories (see Figure 7-7).

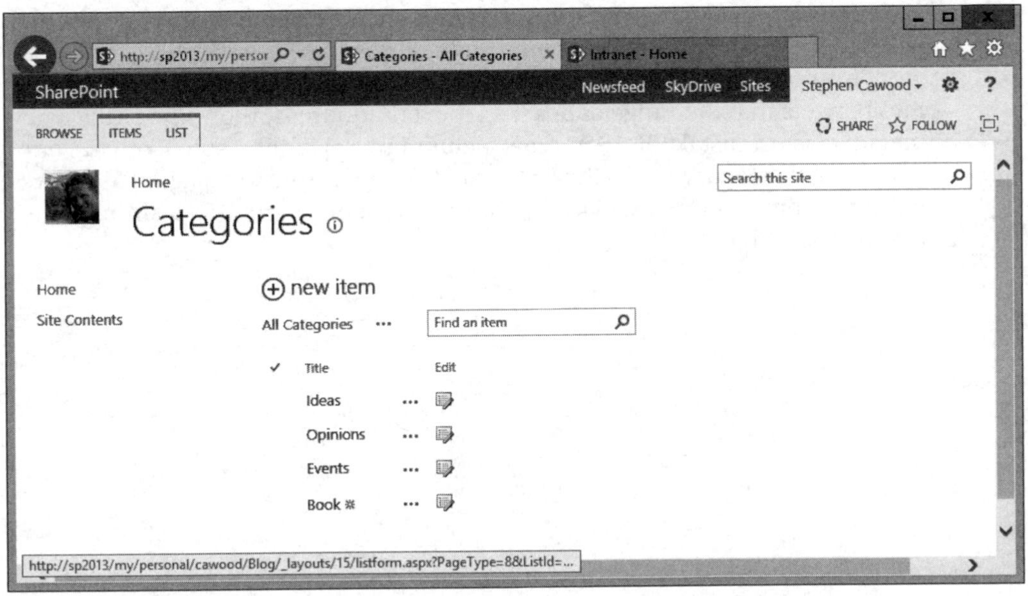

FIGURE 7-7 Managing blog categories

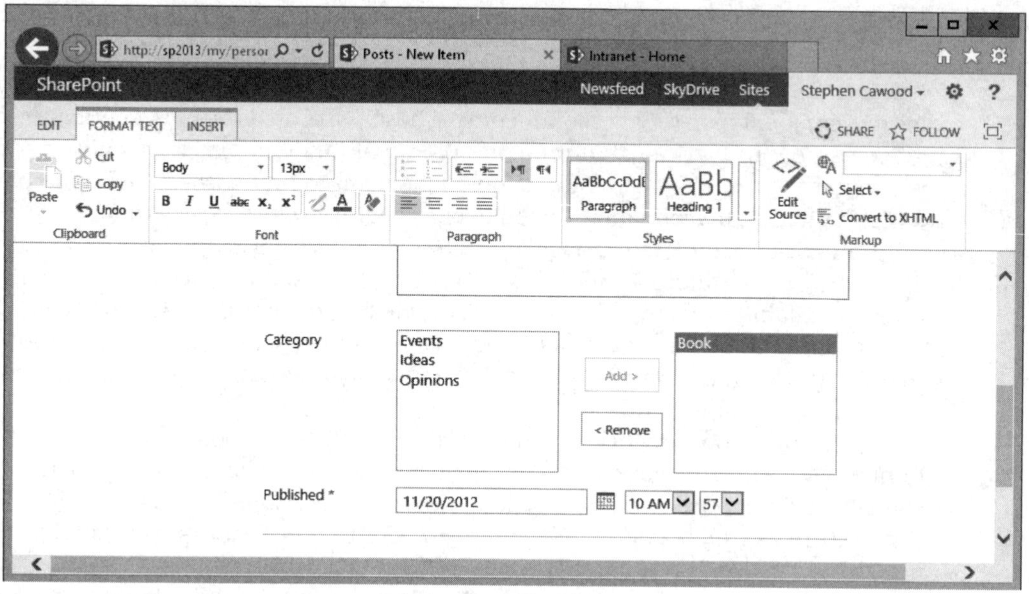

FIGURE 7-8 Adding the Book category to a blog post

Once you have added a few new categories, go back to the blog home page and choose create a post from the blog options on the right. Fill in the title and body, and then scroll down to find the Categories section. You can simply select categories and choose to add or remove them from the post (see Figure 7-8).

This may seem silly if you have only a handful of posts, but when that number gets into the range of dozens, or even hundreds, the value of the category metadata is unmistakable. Anyone (including you) will be able to go to your blog and see the category tags. Clicking a tag takes the user to a page that shows only posts that have been associated with that category, which is a simple and useful feature (see Figure 7-9).

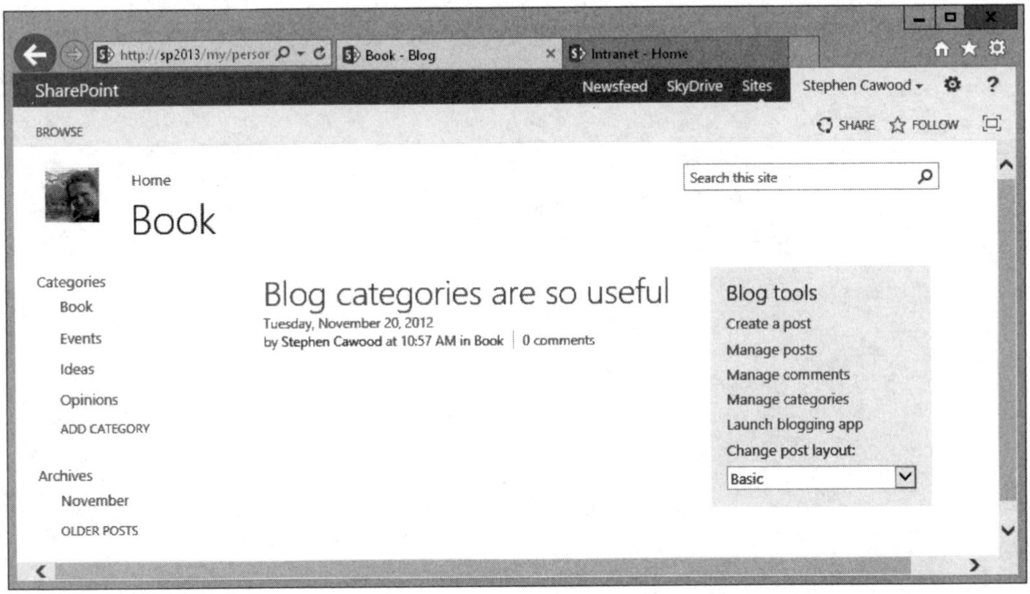

FIGURE 7-9   Filtering a blog by the Book category tag

Summary

With the mainstream popularity of social networking steadily growing, social features have become a hot topic in the SharePoint community. This chapter covered features of personal sites, such as blogs and newsfeeds. Hopefully, this introduction to some of the social-computing options in SharePoint will allow you to work with your colleagues more efficiently, and not result in rampant blogging and chatting about YouTube videos at your workplace.

8

Web Parts and App Parts

HOW TO...

- Add web and app parts to a page
- Customize web and app parts
- Use the out-of-the-box web and app parts

Web parts and app parts are flexible pieces of functionality that can be added to pages when they are needed. For example, if you want to show the contents of a list that's located in some other part of the site, you don't need to ask your users to click a link to see the data; instead, you can add a web part to your page that displays the data. Would you like to show your Microsoft Outlook calendar within SharePoint? You can use the Calendar app part to do just that.

The good news is that the Enterprise version of SharePoint Server comes with roughly 80 web parts and app parts. SharePoint Foundation and Office 365 provide a subset of these parts. The downside of that impressive number is that there aren't enough pages in this book to discuss all of these parts. This chapter covers the general process of adding parts and setting options to customize them, and then provides a quick reference to the app and web parts that come with SharePoint.

Adding App and Web Parts to a Page

If you want to experiment with app and web parts, the first thing you'll need is a web part page. I suggest trying this on a publishing or team site, since these have a built-in Pages library.

Creating a Web Part Page

To create a new page, click the Page tab on the ribbon, and then choose New (see Figure 8-1). In the Create dialog, give your page a name, and then click Create to have SharePoint create the new web part page.

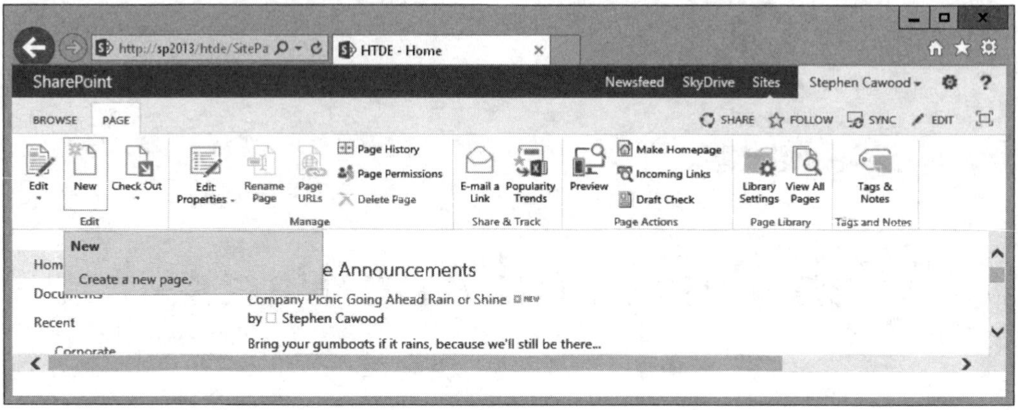

FIGURE 8-1 Choosing to create a new page

Tip You can also use the pages that are automatically generated when you create a site. Your site home page (that is, the default.aspx page) can also contain web parts.

In edit mode, you'll be able to see the zones defined by the page layout, but if you clicked Stop Editing, you would see that the new page is completely blank (see Figure 8-2).

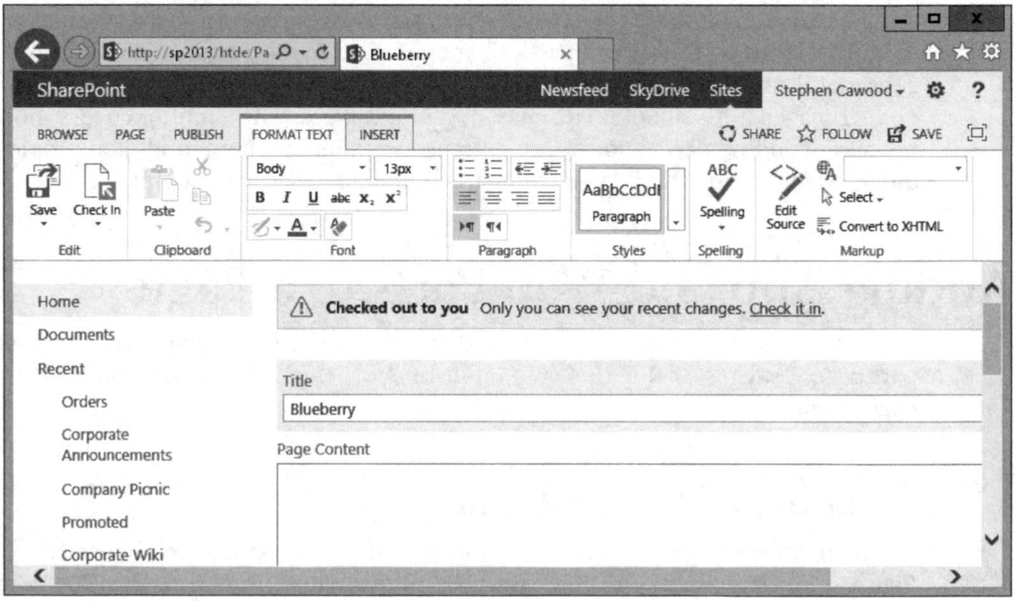

FIGURE 8-2 A new page

After you've created the page—and while you're still in edit mode—you can go to the Page tab on the ribbon and use the Page Layout drop-down menu to choose a different layout. The layouts will allow you to insert your parts in various columns.

The default option for an article page is body only, but you'll see that some site home pages have a header, a footer, and three columns. This essentially means that you'll have one wide zone, followed by three columns containing a zone each, and then another wide zone at the bottom. If you don't use a zone, it will collapse, and the screen real estate will be used by the other zones. This means that picking a layout with a lot of zones might be the best choice if you may need to make changes to the page in the future.

Adding Parts

To begin adding web parts, you'll need to be in edit mode. If you're not in edit mode already, click the Edit button in the Edit section of the ribbon or click the edit icon (the one that looks like a pencil) in the top-right area of the screen.

In edit mode, you can click any of the Add a Web Part links you see on the page, or use the insert option on the ribbon, to add an app or web part. You'll be able to choose the target web part zone after you make your selection. However, the link that you click will determine which zone is selected as the default for the add operation, so you may want to click the correct link rather than change the zone later.

 You might notice that some of the names of your apps appear in the web part gallery's app section. This is because some app parts are created specifically to show list content (for example, picture libraries). If you have those types of apps in your site, you'll be able to use them with these app parts without needing to do any configuration. Simply add the app part, and the data from your list will appear.

After clicking Add a Web Part, a list of the web parts available on your server will appear at the top of the page (see Figure 8-3). You'll still be able to see your page at the bottom of your screen. This allows you to choose the web parts you want and still have the context of the page you're editing.

For this exercise, choose the Table Of Contents web part from the Content Rollup category. If you are using SharePoint Foundation, this web part won't be available, so simply choose another web part.

Next, choose the target zone for the new web part. Since the layout defines the width of each web part zone, you'll want to add your web parts to zones that best fit their real estate needs on your page. For example, a web part that needs to be wide would fit best in the Header or Footer zone of the default page layout. If a narrower space is more suitable for your part, you can choose one of the three narrow columns.

Note Technically, the width of the zones in the page layout becomes a factor only when multiple web parts have been added to the page. If no web parts are in a zone, then that space can be used by web parts in other zones.

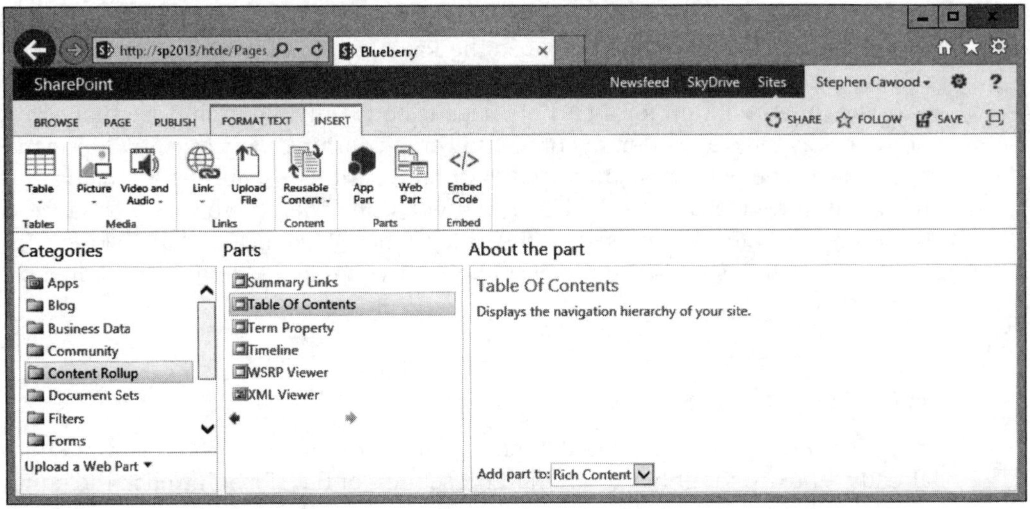

FIGURE 8-3 Adding a web part

Your new Table Of Contents web part will show links to the sites and lists under your site (see Figure 8-4).

Setting Options for Web and App Parts

After adding an app or web part, you can set various options that control how that part will behave. This allows you to customize the web part to suit your particular needs. Different web parts have different settings available.

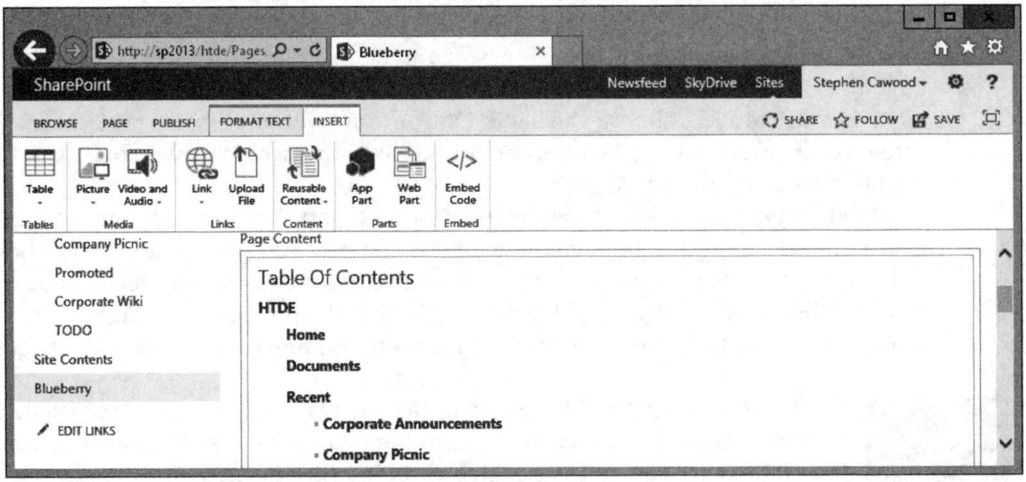

FIGURE 8-4 The Table Of Contents web part showing links

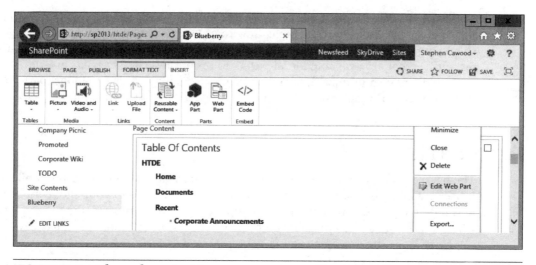

FIGURE 8-5   The web part actions menu open on the right side

To see the options for the Table Of Contents web part, make sure you have your page in edit mode, expand the drop-down menu next to the heading of the web part, and choose Edit Web Part (see Figure 8-5).

The web part options panel will open on the right. The options are neatly arranged in categories, so that you can find them with ease. For example, to change the width or height of the web part, expand the Appearance section (see Figure 8-6).

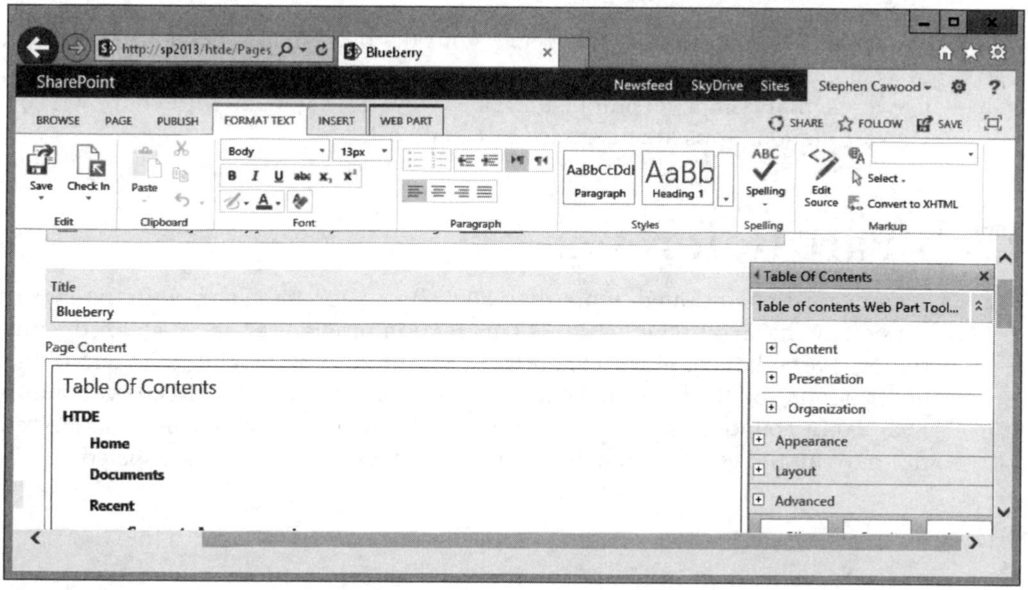

FIGURE 8-6   The web part settings

Other options for the Table Of Contents web part include specifying the level of your site hierarchy to start the table, how many levels to show, and whether pages should be included or hidden. The Layout and Advanced sections are generally used for settings that are available for all parts—for example, whether users are allowed to close the part, minimize it, or hide it. Some users may choose to hide a part if it is taking up room that they would rather see used by other elements on the page.

App Parts

The list of app parts you see when you choose to insert an app part is dynamic. This is because app parts can appear when you add certain apps to your site. For example, in Chapter 4, you saw that an app part appeared for the corporate announcements, which was because the announcements used the Announcements app part.

Here are some examples of app parts that you can use:

- **Announcements**   *Use this list to track upcoming events, status updates, or other team news.*
  This is probably one of the more commonly used web parts. Of all the content on a SharePoint server, announcements are likely the items that you'd least want to have lost in the shuffle of everything else. The Announcements web part keeps that from happening. Once you've added an announcements app to a site, you can add an Announcements web part to any page and you'll be able to ensure that the news is visible from different areas of the server. Announcement lists are discussed in Chapter 4.
- **Calendar**   *Use the Calendar list to keep informed of upcoming meetings, deadlines, and other important events.*

Add a Calendar web part and help your team keep on schedule. You'll find that this calendar offers a number of convenient features, such as the ability to attach files to events, maintain a version history, and view the calendar with your own custom views. Calendar apps are discussed in Chapter 4.

Web Part Reference

As previously mentioned, more than 80 web and app parts ship with the Enterprise version of SharePoint Server 2013. This section provides a reference for the out-of-the-box parts that come with SharePoint Server 2013, with a bit more detail than the descriptions you'll see in the SharePoint interface for adding parts. If you are using SharePoint Foundation 2013 or SharePoint Online in Office 365, or your server does not have all the features enabled, you will see a subset of the parts listed here.

Blog

The following parts are available for blogs:

- **Blog Archives**   *Provides quick links to older blog posts.*
- **Blog Notifications**   *Provides quick links to register for blog posts notifications using alerts or RSS feeds.*
- **Blog Tools**   *Provides blog owners and administrators with quick links to common settings pages and content lists for managing a blog site.*

Business Data

The web parts in this section help fulfill SharePoint's original mandate of being a portal to your company data. This category of web parts provides a vast array of tools for connecting to data sources and presenting the data in useful ways.

SharePoint may be used for many types of data storage today, but in the past, the same types of data would have been stored in an innumerable range of other systems. Rather than moving the data into SharePoint, your organization may have decided to leave that data where it is, and then use the business data web parts in SharePoint to show the information to the end user.

- **Business Data Actions**   *Displays a list of actions from Business Data Connectivity.*
- **Business Data Connectivity Filter**   *Filters the contents of web parts using a list of values from Business Data Connectivity.*
- **Business Data Item**   *Displays one item from a data source in Business Data Connectivity.*
- **Business Data Item Builder**   *Creates a business data item from parameters in the query string and provides it to other web parts.*
- **Business Data List**   *Displays a list of items from a data source in Business Data Connectivity.*
- **Business Data Related List**   *Displays a list of items related to one or more parent items from a data source in Business Data Connectivity.*

These web parts are added with the Enterprise edition:

- **Excel Web Access**   *Use the Excel Web Access web part to interact with an Excel workbook as a web page.*
- **Indicator Details**   *Displays the details of a single status indicator. Status indicators display important measures for an organization and may be obtained from other data sources, including SharePoint lists, Excel workbooks, and SQL Server Analysis Services KPIs.*
- **Status List**   *Shows a list of status indicators.*
- **Visio Web Access**   *Enables viewing and refreshing of Visio web drawings.*

Community

The following parts will work on community sites or any other site that has community features turned on.

- **About this community** *This web part displays the community description and other properties like established date. This web part will work on Community sites or any other site that has Community Features turned on.*
- **Join** *Provides the ability for non-members of a community site to join the community. The button hides itself if the user is already a member. This web part will work on Community sites or any other site that has Community Features turned on.*
- **My membership** *Displays reputation and membership information for the current visitor of a community site. This web part will work on Community sites or any other site that has Community Features turned on.*
- **Tools** *Provides community owners and administrators with quick links to common settings pages and content lists for managing a community site. This web part will work on Community sites or any other site that has Community Features turned on.*
- **What's happening** *Displays the number of members, topics and replies within a community site. This web part will work on Community sites or any other site that has Community Features turned on.*

Content Rollup

The Content Rollup category of web parts is highly popular because it allows you to reuse your content in different sections of your server. This allows you to maintain one authoritative store of the data, but at the same time, display the data in different pages.

- **Categories** *Displays categories from the site directory.*
- **Content Query** *Displays a dynamic view of content from your site. (Available if publishing is enabled.)*
  The Content Query web part is an easy way to display content from another part of the site. For example, you can configure the setting to show the contents of a particular list. After you choose a list and save your changes, the web part will dynamically update every time there is a change to the source list (see Figure 8-7).
- **Content Search** *Content Search Web Part will allow you to show items that are results of a search query you specify.*
  When you add the Content Search web part to a page, it will show recently modified items from the current site. You can change this setting to show items from another site or list by editing the web part and changing its search criteria. As new content is discovered by searches, this web part will display an updated list of items each time the page is viewed.
- **Project Summary** *Displays information about a project in an easy-to-read overview.*
- **Relevant Documents** *Displays documents that are relevant to the current user.*
- **RSS Viewer** *Displays an RSS feed.*
- **Site Aggregator** *Displays sites of your choice.*
- **Sites in Category** *Displays sites from the site directory within a specific category.*
- **Summary Links** *Allows authors to create links that can be grouped and styled. (Available when publishing is enabled).*

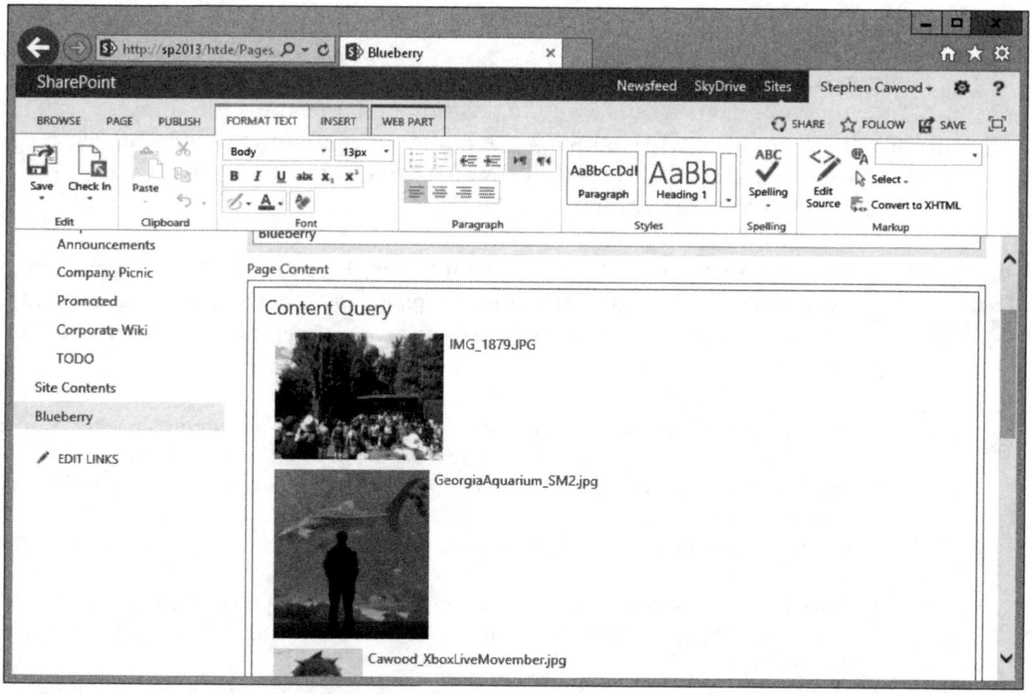

FIGURE 8-7   A Content Query web part showing the contents of a picture library

- **Table Of Contents**   *Displays the navigation hierarchy of your site.*
  The Table Of Contents web part, discussed earlier in this chapter, is available when
  publishing is enabled.
- **Term Property**   *Displays the specified property of a term.*
- **Timeline**   *Use this timeline to show a high-level view of data from another web part or
  tasks list.*
- **WSRP Viewer**   *Displays portlets from web sites using Web Services for Remote Portlets
  (WSRP) 1.1.*
  For more information about WSRP, read the article at http://en.wikipedia.org/wiki/
  Web_Services_for_Remote_Portlets.
- **XML Viewer**   Transforms XML data using XSL and shows the results.

Document Sets

Two document set parts are available:

- **Document Set Contents**   *Displays the contents of the Document Set.*
- **Document Set Properties**   *Displays the contents of the Document Set.*

Filters

Filter web parts are included with the Enterprise features. They give you the option of offering your users a quick way to customize the result set in another web part. For example, if you have a list showing the contents of an announcements list on your page, you can add the ability to filter which announcements are displayed based on the values in one of the columns in the list.

Note The filter web parts will not work with every type of web part, so you'll need to investigate whether your scenario is supported. The web parts that are supported will appear in the list of possible connections after you add a filter web part to the page.

- **Apply Filters Button** *Add this button to a page so users can decide when to apply their filter choices. Otherwise, each filter is applied when its value is changed.*
- **Choice Filter** *Filters the contents of web parts using a list of values entered by the page author.*
- **Current User Filter** *Filters the contents of web parts by using properties of the current user.*
- **Date Filter** *Filters the contents of web parts by allowing users to enter or pick a date.*
- **Page Field Filter** *Filters the contents of web parts using information about the current page.*
- **Query String (URL) Filter** *Filters the contents of web parts using values passed via the query string.*
- **SharePoint List Filter** *Filters the contents of web parts by using a list of values.*
- **SQL Server Analysis Services Filter** *Filters the contents of web parts using a list of values from SQL Server Analysis Services cubes.*
- **Text Filter** *Filters the contents of web parts by allowing users to enter a text value.*
  The Text Filter web part provides the option of filtering other web part data based on the text within a particular column, such as the Title column. Once you've added this web part to your page, you'll need to connect it to another web part on the same page. I personally found this to be a little tricky. To set the connection, first go to the right of the web part heading, find the web part actions drop-down menu, and choose Edit Web Part. Next, go back to the same menu, choose Connections, and then select Send Filter Values To. This will expand a menu of the web parts on the page that support the Text Filter web part (see Figure 8-8). After you choose the app you want to filter, a Configure Connection window will open and allow you to set the connection properties.

In the example in Figure 8-9, an announcements list is being filtered by the modified date value. Only the announcements with the specified filter value are being displayed. If you have thousands of items in your list, this type of filtering can save a substantial amount of time.

Caution The Text Filter web part filters by the entire string. For example, if you connected to an announcements list by the title and wanted to find an announcement called "Intranet is live," you would need to type the whole title.

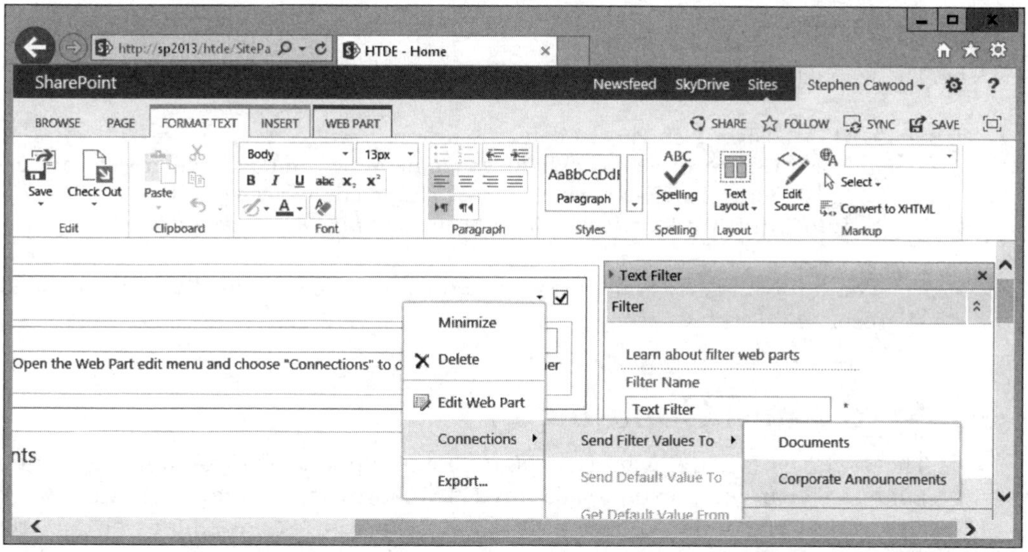

FIGURE 8-8   Connecting the Text Filter web part

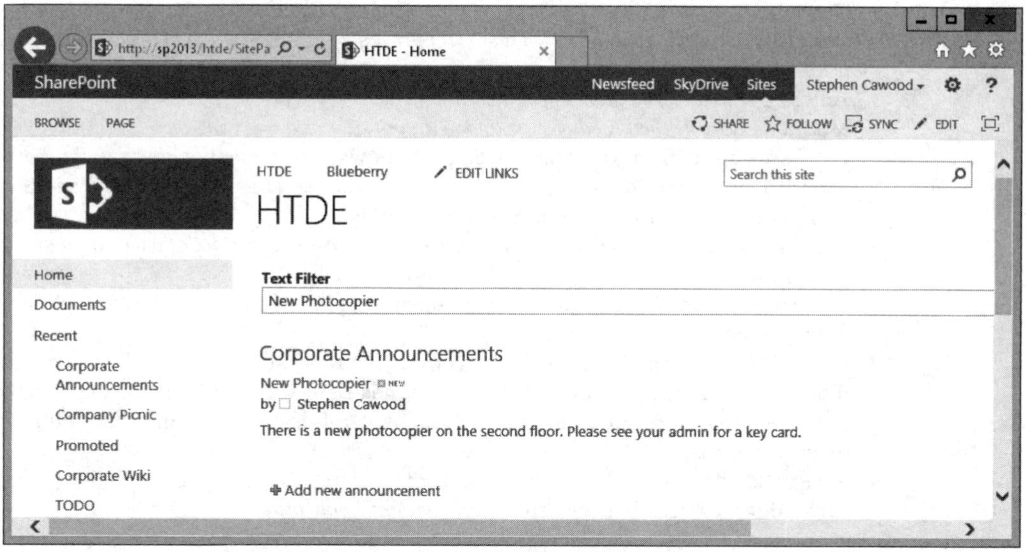

FIGURE 8-9   A text filter applied to an announcements list

Forms

The web parts in this category have highly specialized functions.

- **HTML Form Web Part** *Connects simple form controls to other web parts.*
  The HTML Form web part allows you to filter the contents of other web parts using HTML form elements, such as a check box or a drop-down box.
- **InfoPath Form Web Part** *Displays an InfoPath browser-enabled form.*

The InfoPath Form web part is used only to display forms that were created using Microsoft InfoPath.

Media and Content

These web parts add flexibility to your content options. For example, the Content Editor web part allows you to add any HTML-formatted content you want. Now that an Embed Code option is on the ribbon and there is a Script Editor web part, the Content Editor web part is used mainly for rich text, but you can use it to add your own custom HTML, including adding Adobe Flash content. Other web parts in this category make it easy to liven up your SharePoint pages with media such as images and video.

- **Content Editor** *Allows authors to enter rich text content.*
- **Get started with your site** *This web part displays a set of tiles with common SharePoint actions.*
- **Image Viewer** *Displays a specified image.*
- **Media** *Use to embed media clips (video and audio) in a web page.*
  As you would expect, the Media web part allows you to easily show media. You can choose a video from outside SharePoint; you don't need to store your videos in SharePoint. You can even insert videos into SharePoint wikis.
- **Page Viewer** *Displays another web page on this web page. The other web page is presented in an IFrame.*
- **Picture Library Slideshow** Used to display a slide show of images and photos from a picture library.
  In the 2007 version of SharePoint, this web part was called This Week in Pictures, but it didn't have anything to do with dates, so it has rightly been renamed. This web part has also been enhanced for SharePoint 2013. For example, you will find that you have more display options.
- **Script Editor** *Allows authors to insert HTML snippets or scripts.*
- **Silverlight** *A web part to display a Silverlight application.*

Search

Search is one of those features that requires no explanation. Sure, most of us don't need to index as many pages as Bing.com, but SharePoint is primarily targeted at large companies, and large companies have a lot of data. These web parts will help you make the most of the search feature.

- **Refinement**   *This web part helps the users to refine search results.*
- **Search Box**   *Displays a search box that allows users to search for information.* You can set multiple properties for the Search Box web part (see Figure 8-10).
- **Search Navigation**   *Helps users to navigate among search verticals.*

Note   Search Verticals are categories used to restrict search results. For example, people, content, conversations, videos or custom categories.

- **Search Results**   *Displays the search results and the properties associated with them.*
- **Taxonomy Refinement Panel**   *This web part helps the user to refine search results on term set data.*

To use this web part, you must also have a Search Data Provider web part on this page and use the Managed Navigation option. It's available when publishing is enabled.

Search-Driven Content

Many web parts are available for pages that show search-driven content. All of the parts in this category (except Catalog-item Reuse) will show items from the current

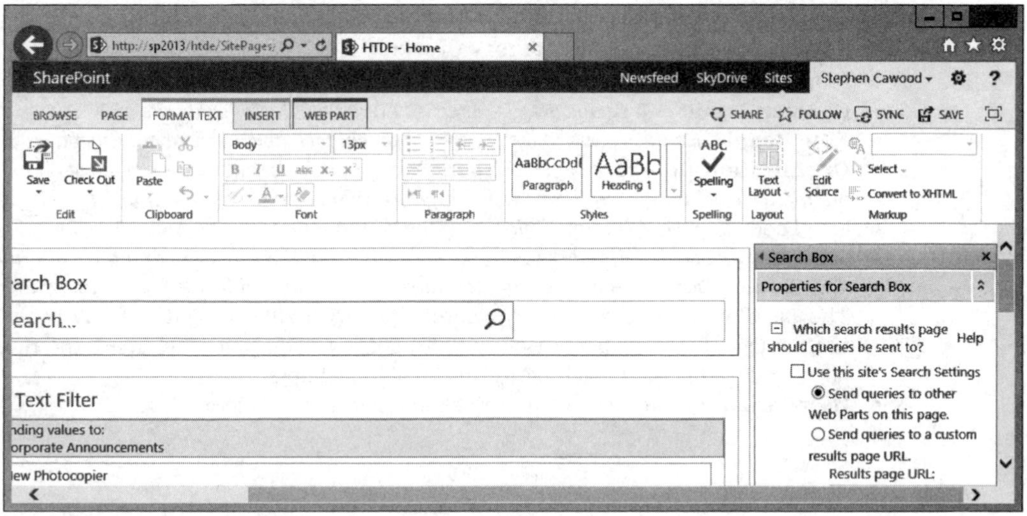

FIGURE 8-10   Setting the properties of a Search Box web part

site. You can change this setting to show items from another site or list by editing the web part and changing its search criteria. As new content is discovered by a search, the web part will display an updated list of items each time the page is viewed.

- **Catalog-item Reuse** *Use this web part to reuse or republish the content of an item from a catalog.*
- **Items Matching a Tag** *This web part will show items that are tagged with a term.* Along with being able to set this part to show items from another site or list, you can also specify whether you want the web part to display items associated with a different tag.
- **Pages** *This web part will show any items that are derived from the Pages content type.*
- **Pictures** *This web part will show any items that are derived from the Picture or Image content type.*
- **Popular Items** *This web part will show items that have been recently viewed by many users.*
- **Recently Changed Items** *This web part will show items that have been modified recently.* This part can help site users track the latest activity on a site or a library.
- **Recommended Items** *This web part will show content recommendations based on usage patterns for the current page.*
- **Videos** *This web part will show any items that are derived from the Video content type. It will sort items by number of views.*
- **Web Pages** *This web part will show any items that are derived from the Page content type.*
- **Wiki Pages** *This web part will show any items that are derived from the Wiki Page content type.*

Social Collaboration

I know what you're thinking: Isn't all collaboration social? Well, be that as it may, social collaboration is the next category of web parts.

- **Contact Details** *Displays details about a contact for this page or site.*
- **Note Board** *Enables users to leave short, publicly viewable notes about this page.*
- **Organization Browser** *This web part displays each person in the reporting chain in an interactive view optimized for browsing organization charts. It is commonly used on My Sites.*
- **Site Feed** *Site Feed contains microblogging conversations on a group site.*
- **Site Users** *Use the Site Users web part to see a list of the site users and their online status.*
- **Tag Cloud** *Displays the most popular subjects being tagged inside your organization.* The Tag Cloud web part is new in SharePoint Server 2013. It's a user-friendly way to see the tags that have been used in SharePoint and discover which are the most popular. The Tag Cloud web part is discussed in Chapter 5.
- **User Tasks** *Displays tasks that are assigned to the current user.*

Data View Web Part

The Data View web part allows you to choose how you want to display information from SharePoint. It is arguably the most versatile of web parts. However, to use it, you'll need to install the free Microsoft SharePoint Designer client.

Working with the Data View web part is more of a SharePoint designer or developer task than an end-user function, so it isn't discussed in this book. However, there are many resources online that will help you learn about this powerful tool. For example, the site www.endusersharepoint.com has published articles about the Data View web part.

Custom Web Parts

SharePoint developers can create custom web parts to fulfill an unlimited number of feature requirements. For example, at a SharePoint Saturday conference in New York, I used a population simulation web part called SharePoint Game of Life to demonstrate programming with the SharePoint taxonomy features (see Figure 8-11).

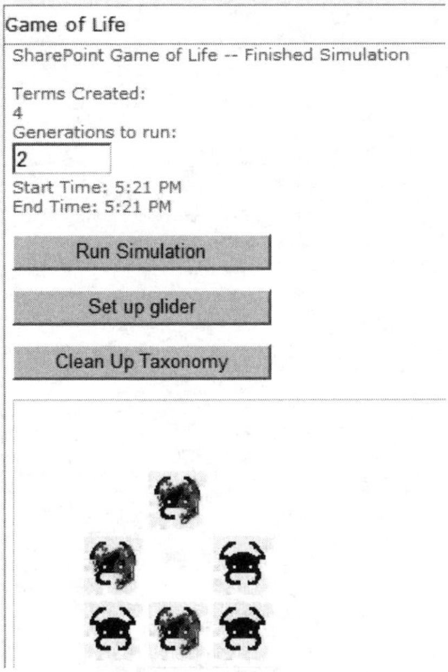

FIGURE 8-11   The SharePoint
Game of Life web part

If you're interested in creating your own web parts, you can find some useful tutorials online. For example, check out my blog post about developing SharePoint visual web parts, at http://geeklit.blogspot.com/2009/12/sharepoint-2010-visual-web-parts.html. Writing your own web parts is certainly an option. However, as you've learned in this chapter, roughly 80 app and web parts come with SharePoint Server. Be sure to investigate what's available before you or other developers in your company start writing anything new. Although it's true that the default web parts can't do everything you want, they are incredibly useful and flexible.

Summary

This chapter provided an overview of one of the most important elements of SharePoint: app parts and web parts. Now that SharePoint has an app model, obviously apps will be key to providing useful functionality to SharePoint users. However, it will likely take years before apps take over from web parts as the most widely used building blocks of end-user functionality.

9

Customization

HOW TO...

- Customize apps and lists
- Create custom app views
- Customize the look of SharePoint
- Customize navigation
- Create custom forms

SharePoint is a flexible system, and a large part of that flexibility is that you can implement considerable customization without needing to do any development. Without a doubt, there is no one-size-fits-all enterprise information management system that comes out of the box exactly the way that every organization would like. This chapter explores some of the many ways that you can tailor SharePoint to your needs.

SharePoint apps have been discussed in many parts of this book, but one aspect that hasn't been explored thoroughly is how to tweak and mold apps to suit your personal or business requirements. This is one of the most widely used customization options in SharePoint, so it seems fitting that the first topic on the customization list should be list customization.

Note In parts of this chapter, I use the terms *list* and *app* interchangeably. I have to admit that when I heard that SharePoint 2013 would refer to lists as apps, it didn't sound right to me. After all, I've been hearing the terms *SharePoint list* and *library* since 2001. However, I've come around and now see the value of associating SharePoint lists and libraries with the current popular understanding of the term *app*.

Custom Lists

Although SharePoint Foundation includes many app templates out of the box, and SharePoint Server includes even more, the solution to meeting SharePoint customers' needs is not to try to anticipate everything that they might require, but to provide flexible and user-friendly customization options.

Creating a Custom List with a New Column

Imagine that you're working in the marketing department of your company and one of your tasks is to organize your company presence at trade shows. To store the various data you need to track, you decide that you'll use a SharePoint app. The only problem is that there is no out-of-the-box template that includes a column for information such as the Twitter tag for each event or the sponsorship level for your company at each show. To store this specialized information, you can create your own list or customize an existing list type.

The options for creating apps are discussed in Chapter 2. The quickest choice is usually to choose Add an app from the gear icon menu. To begin this particular exercise, in the Create dialog, choose to create a custom list. When SharePoint has created the list, you'll see that it comes with one visible column: Title (see Figure 9-1). You need to add more columns to contain your data.

To begin, click the List tab on the ribbon, and then click the Create Column button (see Figure 9-2). This opens the Create Column dialog and allows you to specify exactly which type of column you would like to add.

For this example, you want to add a column to contain the Twitter hashtag for the conference, so choose a single line of text as the data type (see Figure 9-3). Twitter

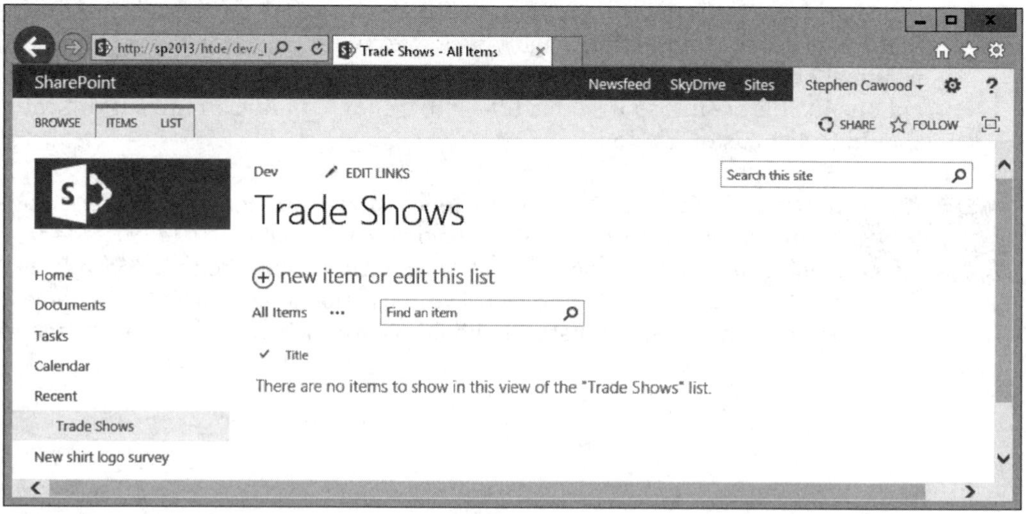

FIGURE 9-1 A new custom list

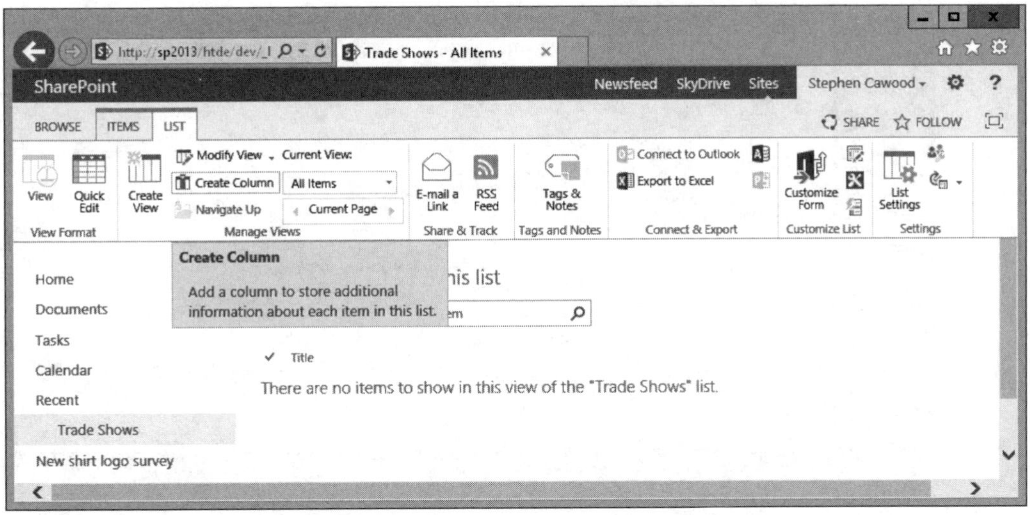

FIGURE 9-2 The Create Column option in the ribbon

hashtags allow Twitter users to search for tweets that are related to a particular subject. For example, people who are interested in one of the conferences can simply search for the hashtag to filter out all those noisy tweets about what people are having for lunch and the amazing tricks their pets have performed.

Scroll down the Create Column dialog to the Additional Column Settings section, and you'll see that there are also some other options, such as Add to Default View, which will make the new column visible within the default view. Since Twitter hashtags

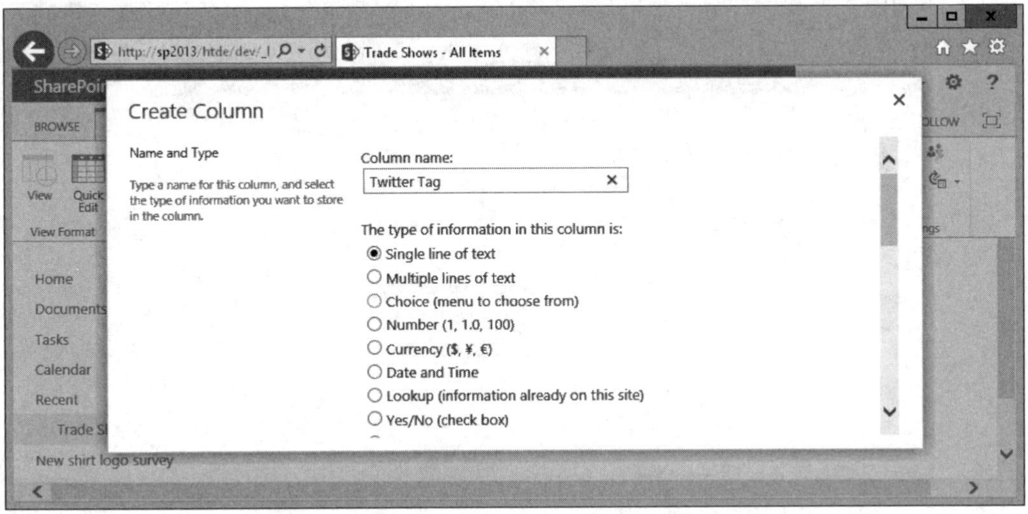

FIGURE 9-3 Specifying the data type for a new column

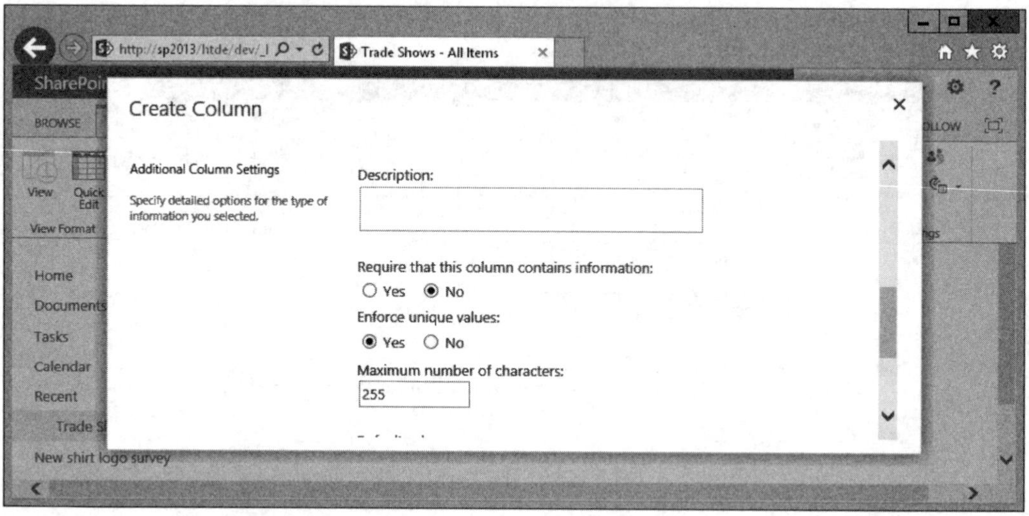

FIGURE 9-4 Setting properties for the new column

must be unique to be useful, select Yes for the Enforce Unique Values option (see Figure 9-4). When you choose this option, SharePoint asks you to index the column. Indexing is generally done as a means to make searching faster, but in this example, it also serves to provide a unique Twitter hashtag.

Now that you've added your new column, you can see it in action by clicking the Add New Item link in your custom list. Instead of just asking for a title, the New Item dialog will now also ask for a Twitter tag (see Figure 9-5). Because you

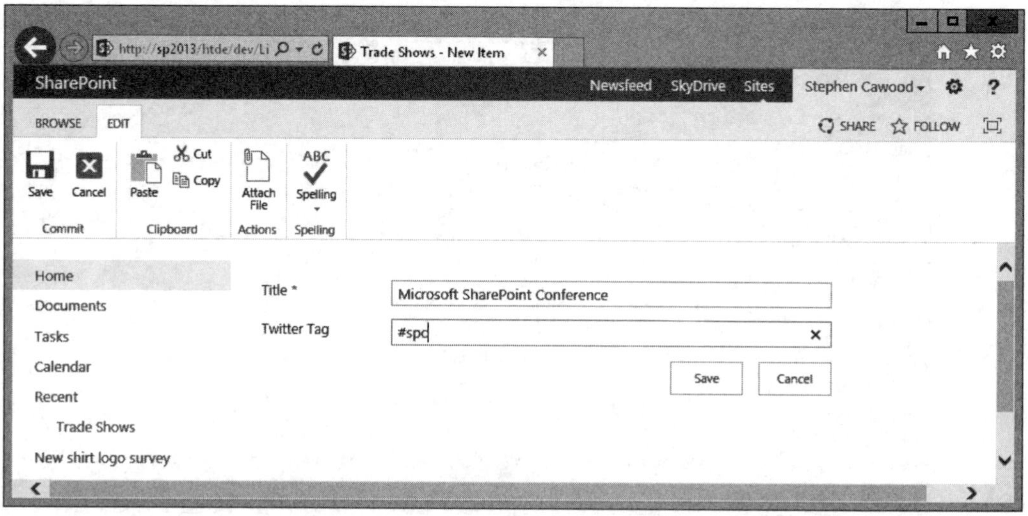

FIGURE 9-5 Adding a new item to the list

chose to provide one line of text, that's all your users will be able to enter. Twitter hashtags begin with the hash symbol, but since the default content for this field was set to #, your users will not need to type this symbol each time they make an entry. Furthermore, the list will enforce that each value in this column is unique.

Of course, using the Custom List type means that you'll need to add almost all the columns yourself. If there is an existing list that's similar to what you want, you might find that just augmenting that list is a faster way to go. However, you should keep in mind that some types of lists have other built-in functionality that you may or may not want to use. For example, calendar, task, contact, and discussion board lists are all able to connect to Microsoft Outlook.

Custom List Example: Mileage Tracker

In this exercise, you'll build on what you've already learned and create an entirely new list from scratch. The list that you'll build in this example enables a real-world scenario: a means of tracking mileage. In fact, this book's technical editors (including SharePoint MVP, Sean Wallbridge) use a list just like this at itgroove (www.itgroove.net).

The Mileage Tracker list will allow employees to easily track how many miles they have driven for work purposes and help them to produce mileage reports for use in their expense reports. The goal is to enable them to track the reason for each trip, the client account, the date of the trip, and the odometer readings at the beginning and end of the journey. The odometer readings will be used to calculate and store the total mileage for each entry.

The first step is to create a new custom list. Navigate to the site where you want the list to be created, and then choose to create a list.

From your new list, choose List Settings from the List section of the ribbon, scroll down to the list of columns, and click Title to edit the Title column's settings. Change the name of this column to **Reason for trip** and add the description **Please provide a brief description of your trip**. Once you have edited the column, save your changes.

Next, you need to add some columns. To ensure that employees are guided toward proper record keeping, in the Create Column dialog, set all of these columns to require data. This prevents employees from saving a new entry until they have provided all of this information. Create the following columns:

- **Company**   This column will track the name of the client and, therefore, should be a choice field. When you create the column, choose the type radio button Choice (Menu to Choose From) in the Create Column dialog. After selecting the type, scroll down to the Additional Column Settings section and enter a list of choices in the text box labeled Type Each Choice on a Separate Line. You might also prefer to use the Lookup (Information Already on This Site) data type and query against a list of companies in a separately created contact list.
- **Date**   This column will use the type Date and Time. To make the column more user-friendly, you can set the default value to be today's date.
- **Odometer Start**   This will be a number field with a minimum value of 0.
- **Odometer End**   This will be a number field with a minimum value of 1.

- **Total Mileage** The final column is used to calculate the total mileage. Not surprisingly, this will be a calculated column called Total Mileage. Create the new column using the type Calculated (Calculation Based on Other Columns). Since this field will track the difference between the two odometer readings, the formula to enter is **= [Odometer End]-[Odometer Start]**. You can create this formula quite easily by typing the equal sign into the Formula text box, double-clicking the first column in the Insert Column list, adding the minus sign, and then double-clicking the second column (see Figure 9-6).

Tip You can enable a wide range of functionality using calculated fields. For more information about calculated field formulas, refer to the online SharePoint documentation (such as examples of common formulas at http://office .microsoft.com/en-us/windows-sharepoint-services-help/examples-of-common-formulas-HA001160947.aspx and Keith Tuomi's post on the itgroove blog at http://yalla.itgroove.net/2012/09/sharepoint-calculated-column-formulas).

Once you have created your list, you can start to use it by entering a trip (see Figure 9-7). The required fields—in this case, all of them—will appear with an asterisk. This gives the end users a quick visual clue that they must fill in the field before they can save the new item.

When you add trips to this list, the Total Mileage column will automatically be calculated for you (see Figure 9-8). This can save time and reduce errors in your reporting.

This real-world example was intended to spark your imagination, and give you some ideas about creating useful custom lists of your own. Next, we'll take a look at customizing list views.

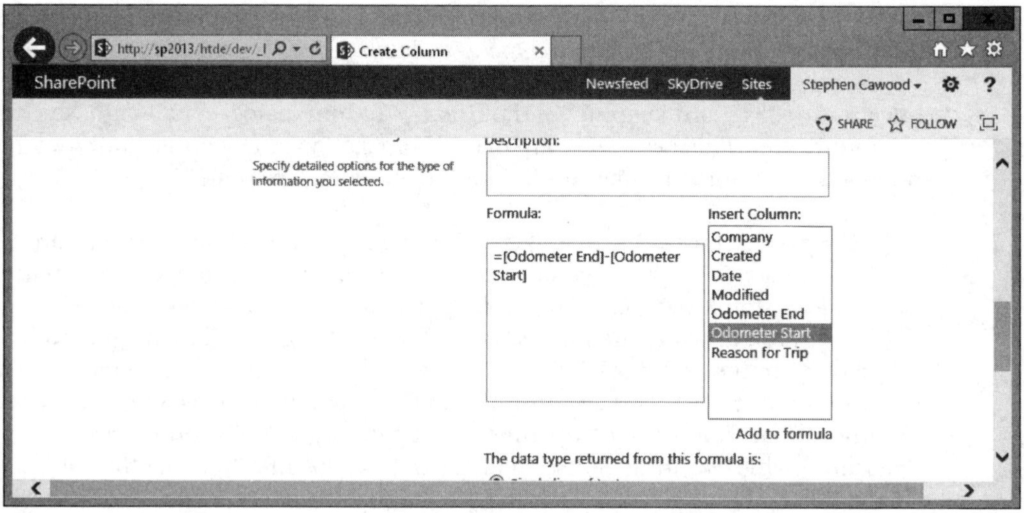

FIGURE 9-6 Adding a calculated field formula

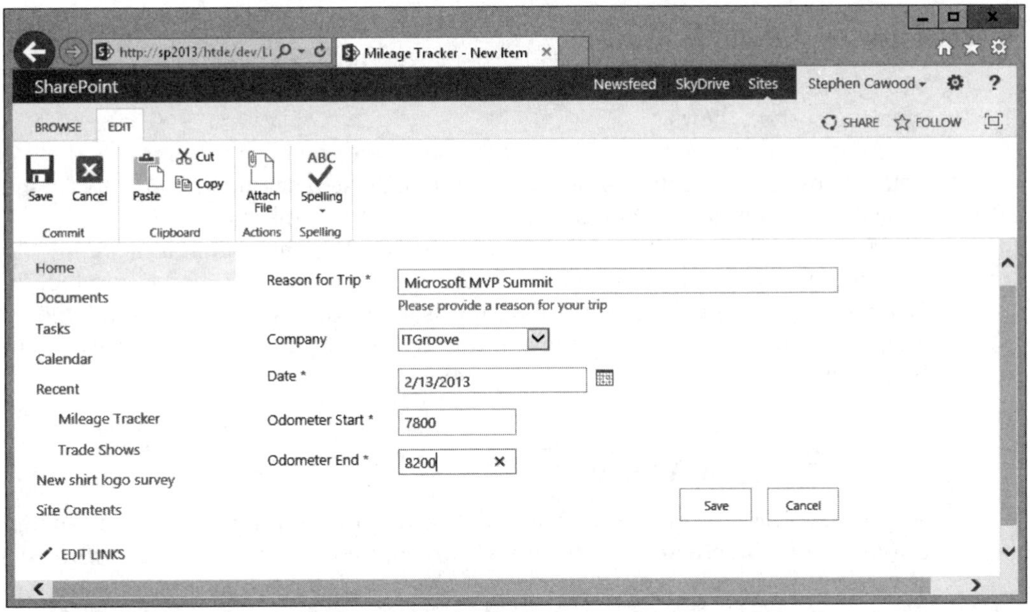

FIGURE 9-7   Adding a trip to the Mileage Tracker custom list

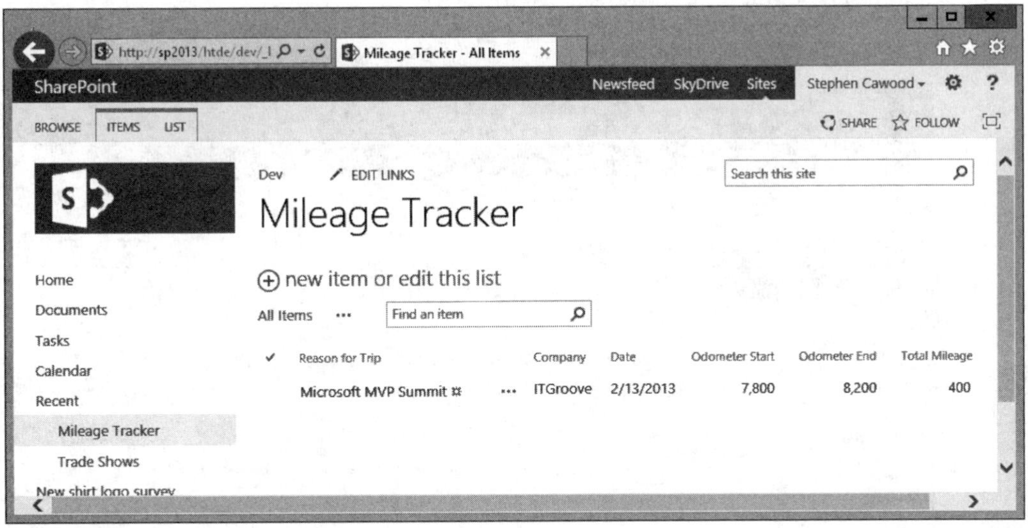

FIGURE 9-8   The Mileage Tracker custom list

Custom Views

Along with customizing lists, another useful dimension of list or app augmentation is creating custom views.

When you create a list, SharePoint also creates a view that presents the data to you. For example, a calendar list actually looks like a calendar, and a document library shows you a simple grid-based overview of your documents.

The view that is used to show a new list is called the *default view*. Some lists come with more than one view, providing additional choices. However, if you feel that there is a better way to present the data than it is displayed by the views available, you can create your own personalized view, either by modifying an existing view or creating a brand-new view.

Modifying a View

As you saw in the previous exercise, adding a new column to the default view is an option when you create the column. However, there are plenty of columns that aren't shown in the default view.

As an example, we will modify the default view for a document library to add a column. This will be the Checked Out To column, which will allow users to see at a glance who has each document checked out.

To begin this exercise, select Document Library in the Create dialog, and then upload some files. You'll see that the default view shows the columns Type, Name, Modified, and Modified By (see Figure 9-9).

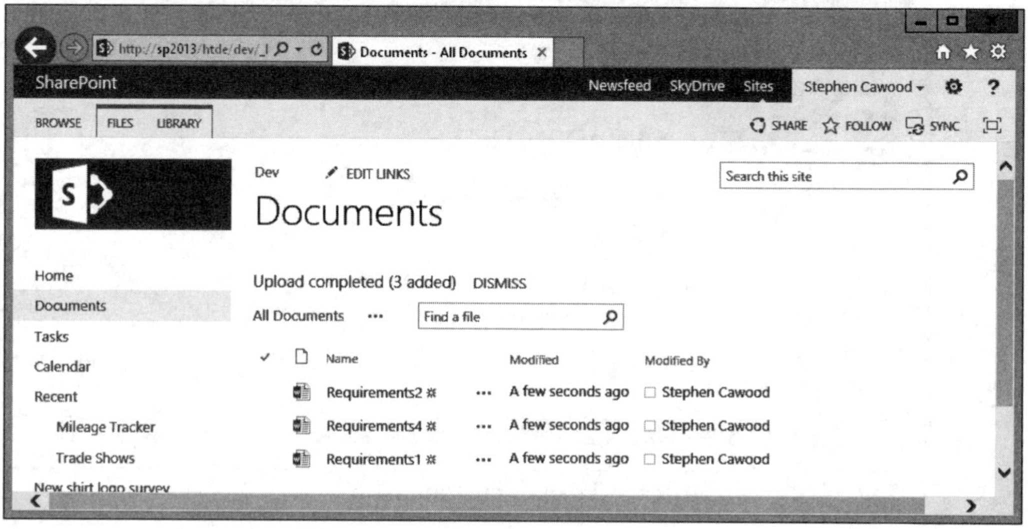

FIGURE 9-9 The default view for a document library

Click the Modify this View button in the Library section of the ribbon. This displays the Edit View dialog, which offers options to add columns and change the sort order (see Figure 9-10).

Simply check the box next to the Checked Out To column, and then click OK to save your changes. After you click OK, the default list view will show the Checked Out To column (see Figure 9-11).

Creating a New View

If modifying an existing view won't satisfy your needs, you can create a new view. For example, suppose that most of your users want to see the default view, but a few want an additional view. In this case, you can use the Create View button on the ribbon to create a brand-new view.

When you choose the Create View option, you're asked to pick from the available built-in view types:

- **Standard view**   *View data on a web page. You can choose from a list of display styles. Use this view type to show each instance of a recurring event.*
- **Datasheet view**   *View data in an editable spreadsheet format that is convenient for bulk editing and quick customization.*
- **Calendar view**   *View data as a daily, weekly, or monthly calendar.*

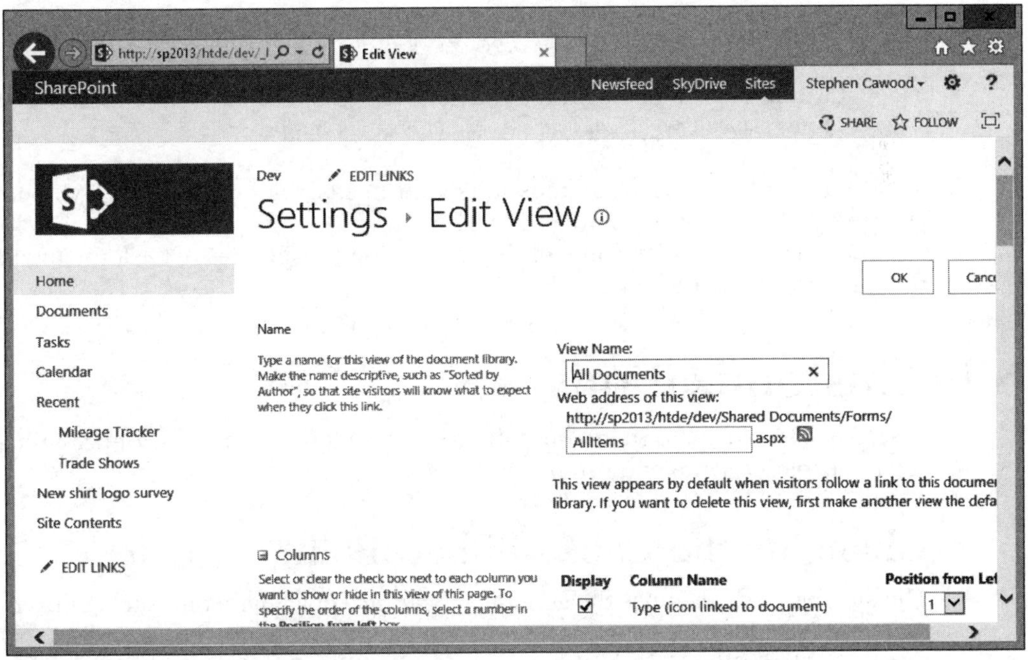

FIGURE 9-10   Customizing the default view

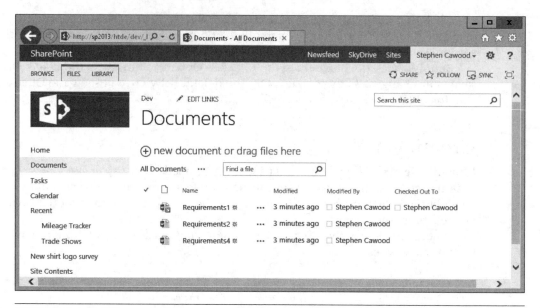

FIGURE 9-11 The new column appears after modifying the default list view.

- **Gantt view**   *View list items in a Gantt chart to see a graphical representation of how a team's tasks relate over time.*
- **Access view**   *Start Microsoft Office Access to create forms and reports that are based on this list.*
- **Custom view in SharePoint Designer**   *Start SharePoint Designer to create a new view for this list with capabilities such as conditional formatting.*

If none of the previous options suits your needs, then it is time to dive into creating custom views in SharePoint Designer.

Now that you've seen some of the interesting possibilities of customizing lists, it's time to move up to the site level.

Site Customizations

Just like lists and apps, SharePoint offers many options for site customization. This section explores some of those possibilities.

Changing the Look of SharePoint

The site theme determines the general appearance of a SharePoint site. For example, it defines the color scheme. In this way, it's similar to a Windows theme, or the Appearance setting in Microsoft Outlook Web Access. In SharePoint 2013, the term *theme* does not appear as much in the UI, but I'm going to use it here for simplicity.

To alter a SharePoint site theme, choose Site settings from the gear icon menu, and then choose Change the look from the Look and Feel section of the Site Settings page (see Figure 9-12). On site home pages with the default tiles showing, you can also click the tile that reads "What's your style?" to access these settings.

When the page opens, you can choose from the available templates, and then customize the site colors and fonts (see Figure 9-13).

You can also preview your customizations before applying the change. To preview the template, click the Try it out link on the right side of the page (see Figure 9-14). When you click the link, you'll be redirected to a page that shows what the site would look like if you applied the theme.

The preview isn't actually a working page—it's just meant to help you choose the theme that's best for your site (see Figure 9-15). If you click "No, not quite there," you'll go back to the Change the look page, and none of your changes will have been applied.

Note that changing the site theme template is not your only option for modifying your site's appearance. You can make more granular changes to the look of your site. On the left side of the template page, you'll find options to change the background image, customize the colors, switch the template layout, and change the fonts (see Figure 9-16). Changing these options can make a substantial difference in the look of your sites, so if you're not a fan of any of the default options, try out some of the customization features and see if you like the results.

One fun and potentially impactful change you can make to the site template is altering the background image. The options to change or remove the background

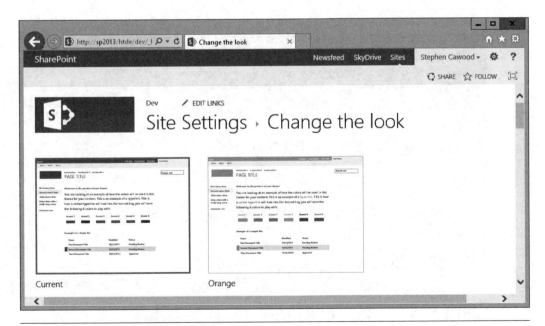

FIGURE 9-12   Site theme templates

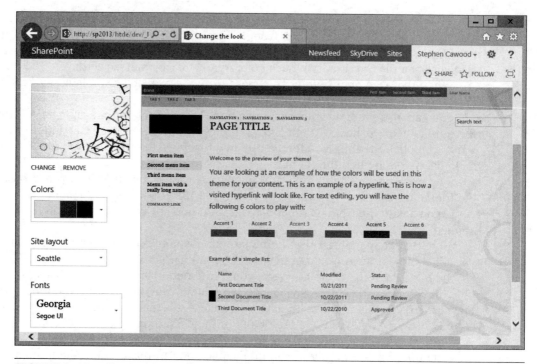

FIGURE 9-13 Customizing the template

FIGURE 9-14 Click the Try it out link for a theme preview.

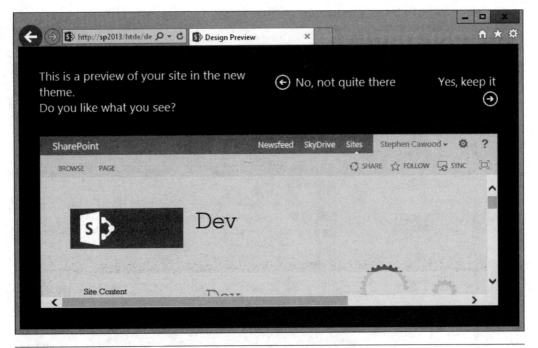

FIGURE 9-15 Previewing a site theme change

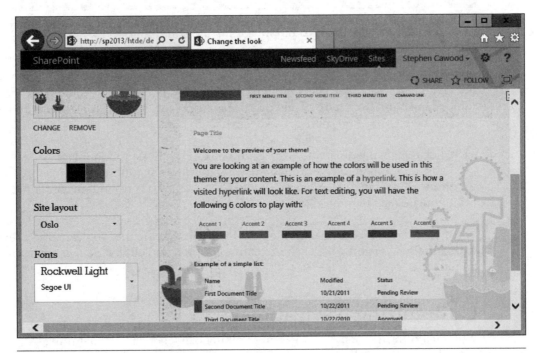

FIGURE 9-16 Site template style options

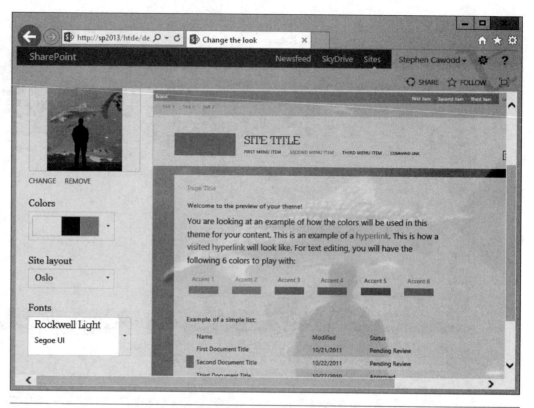

FIGURE 9-17 A new background image for the site theme

image are on the left side of the page. I chose the template you've seen in the past few figures precisely because I don't like the background image. I could click the remove link, and the image would disappear, but I would rather replace it with a more interesting picture. And there are two ways to do that:

- Click the change link below the thumbnail of the background image.
- Drag-and-drop an image from your computer onto the thumbnail. When you drop the new picture, SharePoint will set it as the background image for the site template (see Figure 9-17).

If you don't like the changes you made to your site theme, you can easily revert to the original version. Just click the Start over link, and all that you've done will be forgotten.

Customizing Navigation

When planning a website, navigation planning can be downright daunting. After all, what defines the usability of a website more than its navigation?

The Microsoft Office teams spend considerable time thinking about navigation. I know this because, during my time as a Program Manager at Microsoft, I helped design the navigation for Microsoft Office SharePoint Server 2007. Of course, more than just thinking is involved; the Office team also makes use of usability studies to help figure out the best possible navigation for SharePoint.

An essential part of providing user-friendly navigation is allowing SharePoint customers the opportunity to customize various navigation elements to suit their business requirements. You can take two approaches to revising your navigation. One approach is to go to the object in question (for example, a list of a site) and choose to show or hide it in the navigation. The alternative is to go to the navigation settings of the parent site and choose how the navigation will behave at the site level. The latter option is clearly more powerful because you can make decisions that apply to many apps, lists, libraries, pages, and subsites below the parent site.

To make changes at the site level, choose Site Settings. In the Look and Feel section, the following navigation settings are available:

- **Current Navigation**   Current Navigation is the new name for the quick launch menu that appears down the left side of the page. It is used on most SharePoint pages. You can choose to edit the Current Navigation settings using the Structural Navigation section of the settings. For example, you can add or remove items and change the sort order (see Figure 9-18). If you don't like the heading, you can add your own by clicking New Heading.

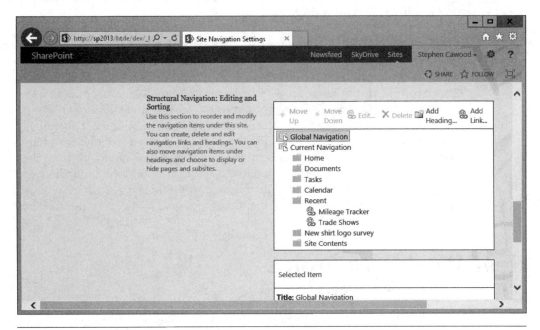

FIGURE 9-18   Editing the quick launch navigation

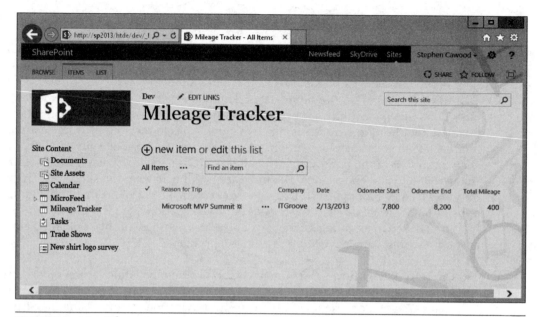

FIGURE 9-19 The tree view navigation

If something does not appear in the quick launch navigation (for example, a page or a list), check the settings of that object. It may have been hidden in the Current Navigation settings.

- **Global Navigation** As you'd expect, the top link bar appears at the top of the page. One option in this section is "Display the same navigation items as the parent site." If you select this option, the current links will be hidden, and the top link bar links from the parent site will replace them. Some users prefer to have the top link bar the same on every page and subsite, and the Global Navigation option can be used to implement that type of navigation and consistency.

- **Tree view** The tree view is usually disabled, but if you'd like to have a handy hierarchical view of the site content, then click the Tree View link from the Site Settings page. You can choose to enable the tree view and the quick launch. The only option for this control is to turn it on or off. When it is enabled, you can click the arrow image to expand the hierarchy—just like you would in Windows Explorer (see Figure 9-19).

Real-World Example: Custom InfoPath Forms

Microsoft InfoPath electronic forms can be huge time-savers. Instead of producing paper forms that might eventually end up being scanned for archiving anyway, why not just cut out the middle steps and go directly to digital?

In this example, you're going to add a new electronic form to SharePoint that will collect the information for a product order. Once you are finished, you'll be able to navigate to the form library in SharePoint, add a new item, and be presented with the custom form to fill out. Each time you fill out a form, it will be saved in the form library as a new order.

 This example will work completely only in SharePoint Server Enterprise Edition because InfoPath Forms Services is not available in other versions. For example, SharePoint Foundation does not offer this functionality.

To start the process, you need to create the form template in Microsoft InfoPath Designer 2013. If you have InfoPath installed, you can try this example.

First, open InfoPath Designer, select the SharePoint Form Library template, and then click Design Form (see Figure 9-20).

Caution You might be tempted to start by creating the form library in SharePoint. However, when you create a form library in SharePoint, it won't have an associated form template, and therefore won't be usable. In this case, it's actually easier to create the form library as part of the publishing process.

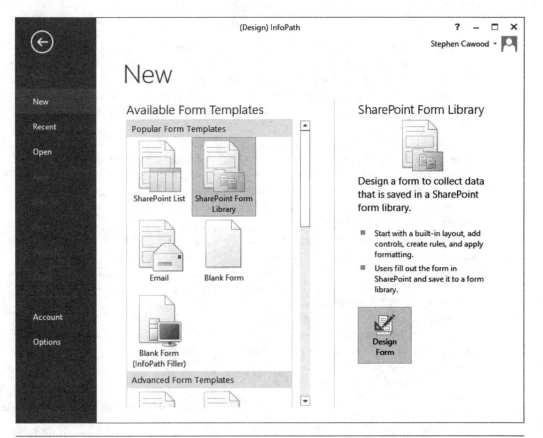

FIGURE 9-20   Selecting the SharePoint form template in InfoPath

FIGURE 9-21 The new form in edit mode

After you make your choice, InfoPath will open the template for editing. In this case, you're creating an order form, so change the title to **Order Form** and change the first heading to **Personal Information**. To make these changes, simply click the text and start typing. To allow users to enter information into the form, you'll need to add fields. This example is meant to be straightforward, so we will just add a Name field (see Figure 9-21).

To add the Name field, click in the Add Control cell next to Add Label and type **Name**. On the right side of the page, expand the drop-down list under myFields and choose Add. The Add Field or Group dialog opens, and you can enter the name and data type for your field (see Figure 9-22). In this case, enter **Name** in the Name field, use the data type Text (string), and then click OK. Next, drag the new field onto the form next to the label for name.

At this point, you may want to save your form locally so that you have a backup copy. To do this, just click the Save button on the ribbon and choose a folder.

Next, you'll be publishing the form template to a SharePoint form library. Fortunately, InfoPath makes this whole process pain-free. You can do everything from within the client.

To publish your new custom form template, switch to the InfoPath File menu, and then select the Publish tab on the left side of the application (see Figure 9-23).

FIGURE 9-22 Adding a new field to the form

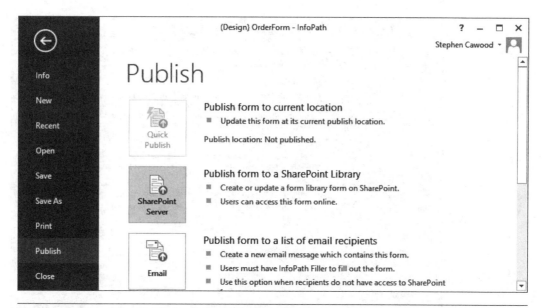

FIGURE 9-23   The Publish tab in InfoPath 2013

The first thing you'll be asked is which SharePoint site you would like to use to host the form template. Enter the URL of the site that will contain the form. For example, the URL of the site used in this example is http://sp2013/htde.

After you enter the URL, the Publishing Wizard will start and give you a few choices. The first is whether you want the form to be used from a browser. You should check the box to enable this option. You also need to choose what you would like to create or modify. For this example, choose Form Library (see Figure 9-24).

Caution This rest of this example will work only with SharePoint Server Enterprise Edition. You can, however, continue with the example by clearing the Enable This Form to Be Filled Out by Using a Browser check box. This means that using your form will require the InfoPath client instead.

After selecting the options in the first dialog, click Next to continue to the next one. The next step allows you to either create a new form library in SharePoint or upload your custom form template to an existing library. Creating the form library from the publishing step—the approach we'll take here—is a handy option because InfoPath manages the whole process for you, so you don't need to complete the manual steps of creating a library and assigning the InfoPath template. Click Next, and you'll be asked to supply a name for your new library (see Figure 9-25).

After adding the name, and optionally a description, click Next again. At this point, you'll decide which form fields will be available as columns within SharePoint. In this example, you want the Name field to be added because that will allow users to sort and filter the orders by the name. Click the Add button in the column section of the dialog. This opens the Select a Field or Group dialog and allows you to choose the Name field from your custom form (see Figure 9-26). Click OK, and the field will appear in the column section of the available fields.

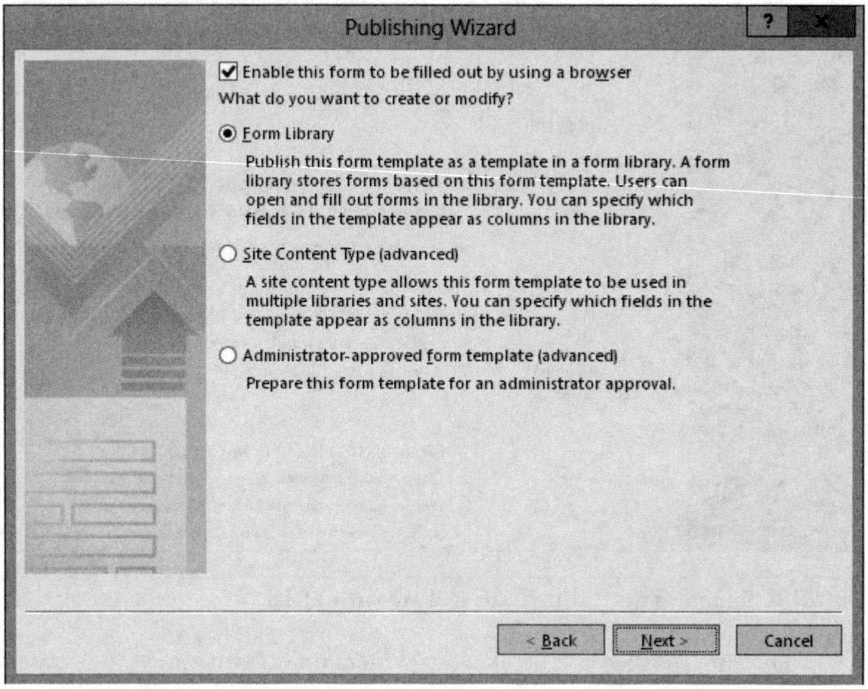

FIGURE 9-24 Choosing the first of the form publishing options

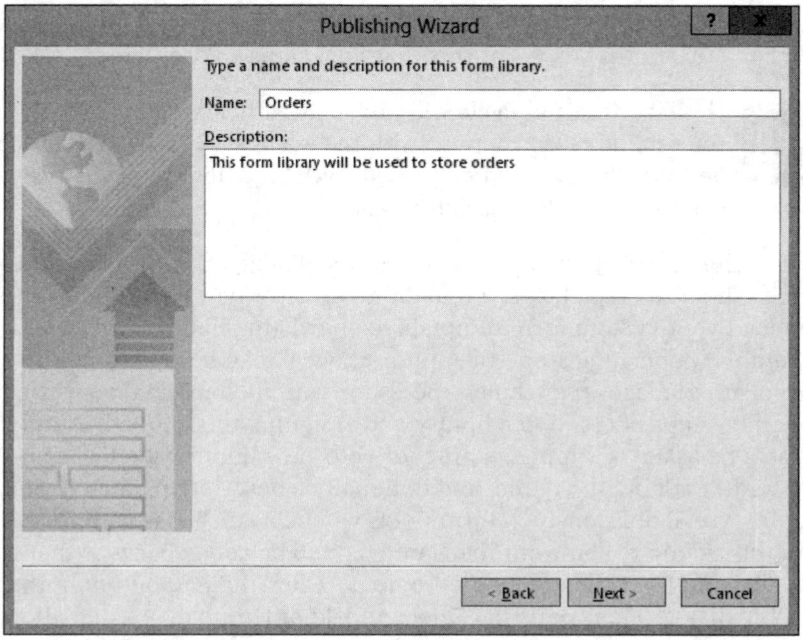

FIGURE 9-25 Choosing where to upload the form

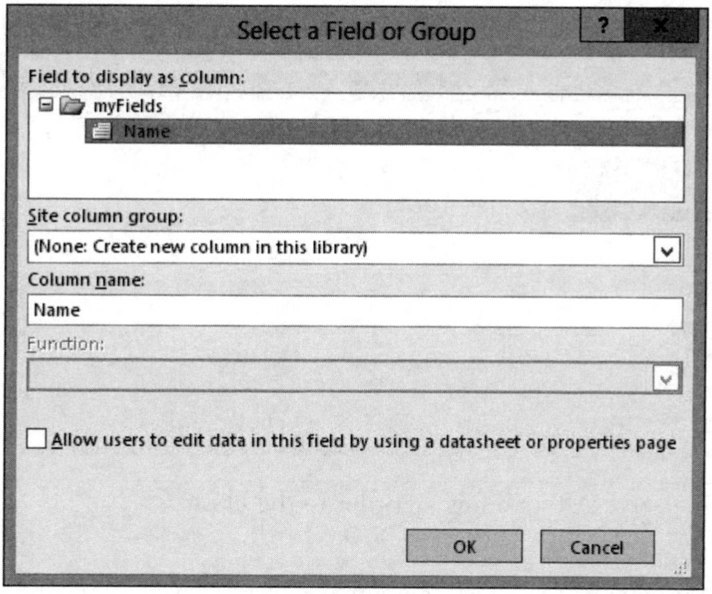

FIGURE 9-26 Adding the Name field as a column in SharePoint

When you click Next, you will be presented with a summary of some of your choices, and you can either go back and make changes or click the Publish button to proceed. After publishing your form template, you will receive a success message. Choose the Open This Form Library option so that you can try out your new form template.

When you choose to continue, InfoPath will open the new form library. Of course, it will be empty, so you'll want to choose Add Document to create an order. Since you chose to allow web editing, this will open the form directly in Internet Explorer and allow you to enter the name into the Name field (see Figure 9-27).

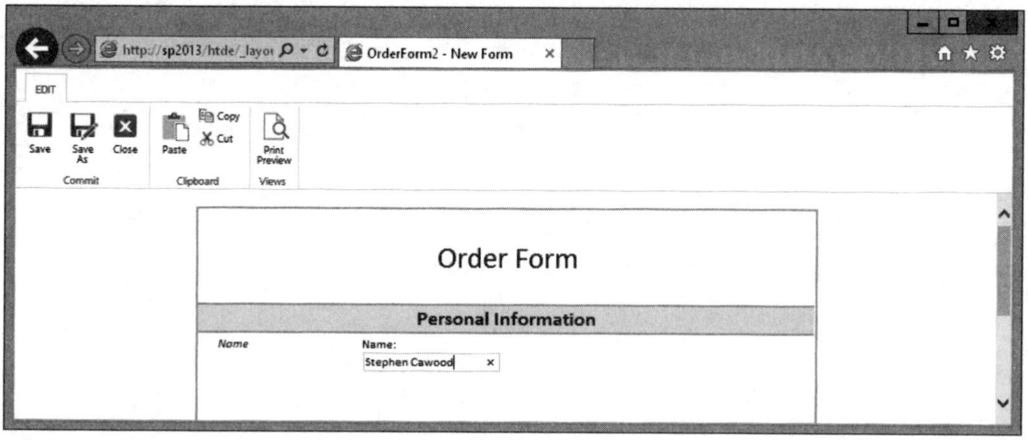

FIGURE 9-27 Filling out the new form template

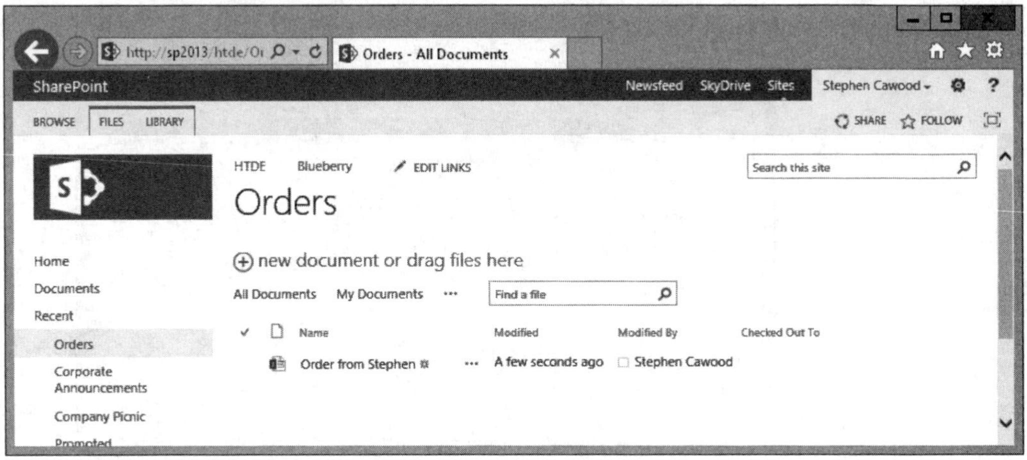

FIGURE 9-28 After adding an order to the library

Once you have entered the name, click the Save button, and then close the order. SharePoint will return you to the form library, where you can see that the order has been created and the name you entered is visible in the Name column of the documents list (see Figure 9-28). Congratulations, you've created your own customized SharePoint form using InfoPath!

Summary

The customization options within SharePoint are numerous and varied. This chapter gave you a taste of that variety. If you're interested in learning more about specific aspects of customizing SharePoint, search online for videos and blog tutorials related to your topic of interest. Just bear in mind that SharePoint customization and development is a massive topic. It's best to have specific objectives in mind and start with small projects. Have fun!

10

Using SharePoint with Client Applications

HOW TO...

- Use Microsoft Office Backstage
- Use the Connect to Office option
- Work with SharePoint through Microsoft Outlook
- Create forms with Microsoft InfoPath
- Customize SharePoint with SharePoint Designer
- Use third-party clients with SharePoint

The goal of this chapter is to introduce you to some of the rich clients that you can use with SharePoint. People choose to use these applications for various reasons, such as because the software makes certain tasks easier, or because it enables use cases that simply aren't available through the SharePoint web-based user interface.

Microsoft Office Backstage

The Microsoft Office Backstage view replaced the traditional File menu in early versions of Office. After you have already opened a document from SharePoint with Word, you will find that SharePoint appears as one of the targets for saving files.

Saving Office Files to SharePoint

To try out saving an Office file to SharePoint, open Microsoft Word 2013 and create a new document. Once you have your document ready to save into SharePoint, click the File tab to open the Backstage view, choose Save As, and then click SharePoint (see Figure 10-1). You'll be able to browse SharePoint for the right place to save the file.

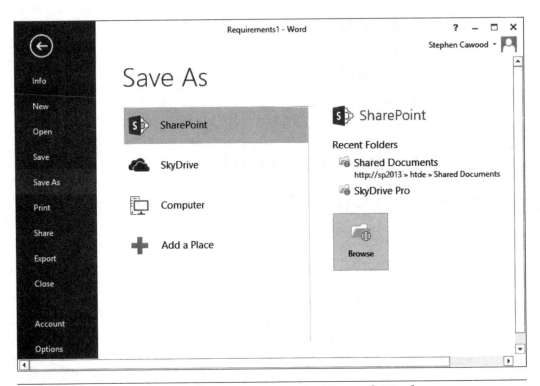

FIGURE 10-1 The Office Backstage view open in Microsoft Word

> **Note** If you've already saved a document to SharePoint, you will be shown the last location in the Recent Locations area. However, if it is the first time you've used this feature, you need to use the Save As button.

Click Save As, and you'll be asked where you would like to save the document (see Figure 10-2). You can enter the URL of your SharePoint server in the address box at the top of the dialog (click the little folder icon, and then paste in the URL address of your SharePoint site). The dialog will show the available SharePoint document libraries, and you'll be able to choose where you want to save the file.

Connecting to Office

If you want to continue to use Office applications to save files in SharePoint, you can quickly add lists to the Favorites section of the Backstage browse dialog. Just click the Connect to Office button in the SharePoint ribbon (see Figure 10-3). To add the current list to the Favorites list in the Backstage dialog, open a list, and then click the button.

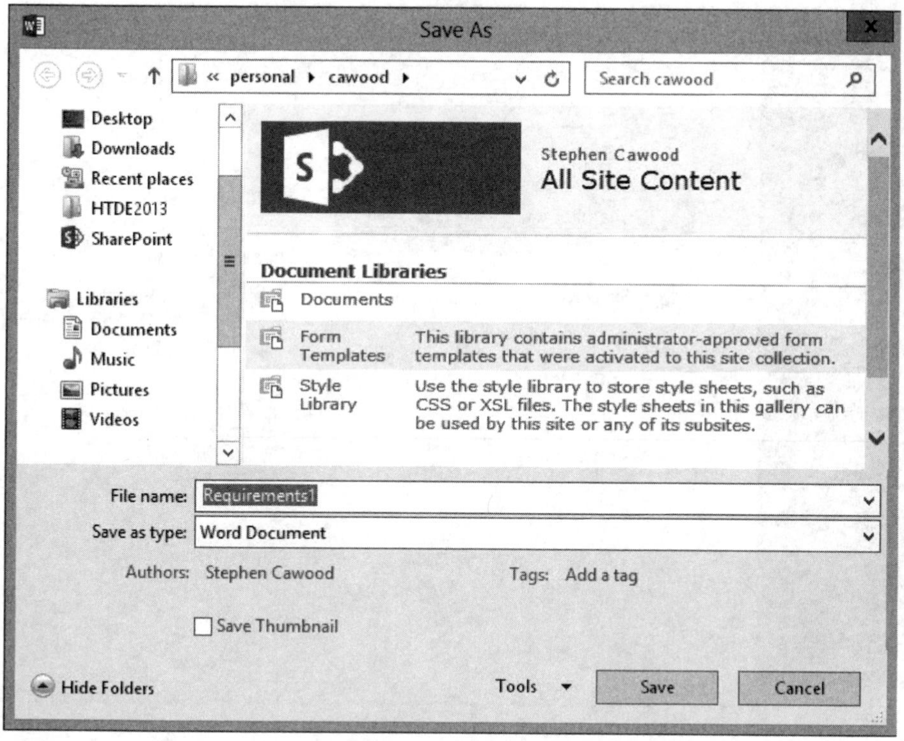

FIGURE 10-2   Saving to a SharePoint document library

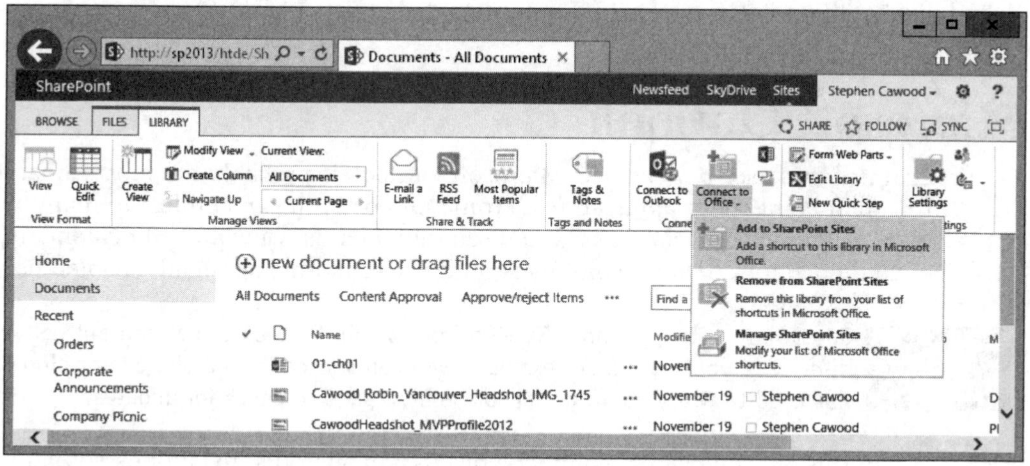

FIGURE 10-3   The Connect to Office button in the ribbon

FIGURE 10-4 The list of connected SharePoint libraries

After you have selected to connect the document library to Office, it appears in the list of SharePoint sites in the Save As dialog (see Figure 10-4).

Microsoft Outlook

From an end-user perspective, Microsoft Outlook is probably the most integrated of the SharePoint client applications. From Outlook, you can connect to many types of lists, including contacts, tasks, and discussion boards; view and edit calendars; and even upload files to SharePoint by sending attachments to e-mail–enabled lists.

 Subscribe to a SharePoint RSS feed from within Outlook to get content delivered directly to your Inbox. For example, you can subscribe to a SharePoint blog and not need to worry about going to the blog page to check for updates.

In this example, you'll connect a discussion board list to Outlook so that you can read and contribute from within Outlook. To begin, navigate to the list, and then click the Connect to Outlook button on the ribbon (see Figure 10-5).

After you confirm that you want to connect the list to Outlook, SharePoint will open Outlook for you (see Figure 10-6).

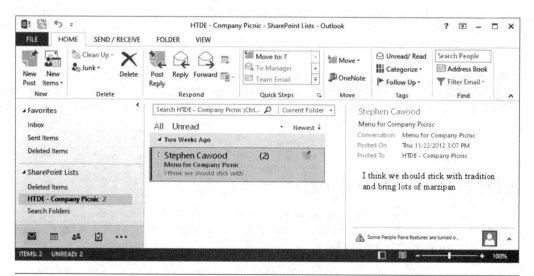

FIGURE 10-5   Connecting to a discussion board list in SharePoint

Many people find that they spend most of their time in their e-mail client—probably more than they should. If you're one of them, you may appreciate the ability to reply directly to a SharePoint discussion thread from within the application that you already have open (see Figure 10-7).

 You can right-click any SharePoint list from within Outlook and choose Open in Web Browser. Also, you can "share" the list with others by right-clicking and sending colleagues direct links via e-mail to wire their Outlook client to the list.

FIGURE 10-6   The discussion list open in Outlook

FILE | DISCUSSION | INSERT | OPTIONS | FORMAT TEXT | REVIEW

Menu for Company Picnic - Discussion

Post To HTDE - Company Picnic
Menu for Company Picnic

Conversation

Great idea! I'm on board...

From: Stephen Cawood
Posted At: Thursday, November 22, 2012 3:07 PM
Posted To: HTDE - Company Picnic
Conversation: Menu for Company Picnic
Subject: Menu for Company Picnic

I think we should stick with tradition and bring lots of marzipan

Some People Pane features are turned off because Windows Desktop Search isn't available.

FIGURE 10-7 Replying to a SharePoint thread from Outlook

To see your SharePoint calendar from within Outlook, connect a calendar list
to the client. Back in SharePoint 2003, calendars were read-only in Outlook, but in
recent versions, you can make changes to calendars. This is very useful, particularly
if you use the Outlook overlay mode.

 Calendars are another type of list that can be e-mail enabled. After you have
connected the calendar, you can choose to share the calendar with other people by
sending them an e-mail. This allows you to quickly create a shared office calendar
system.

Microsoft InfoPath

Microsoft InfoPath can be used to create custom electronic forms for use in
SharePoint. InfoPath provides many powerful features for building new forms
or converting existing forms.

You can use the client to create a form template, and then use that template in a SharePoint form library. An example of using InfoPath to create a custom form is provided in Chapter 9.

SharePoint Designer

Microsoft SharePoint Designer is a free client application that provides added customization options for SharePoint. If you want to do a lot of SharePoint development, Microsoft Visual Studio could be the tool of choice. However, if you need to create custom master pages, add custom lists, create powerful new views, or add custom formatting, then SharePoint Designer might be the right choice.

You can also use SharePoint Designer to create new lists, add or remove columns, edit the properties of lists, and even create new master pages.

Colligo Briefcase and Email Manager

Of course, not all SharePoint client applications are created by Microsoft. Dozens of independent software vendors (ISVs) create software for SharePoint. One such company is Colligo (www.colligo.com), which provides solutions for mobile SharePoint collaboration and content management, including the Colligo Briefcase, Email Manager, and Administrator apps.

Colligo Briefcase

Award-winning mobile app, Colligo Briefcase (see Figure 10-8), solves the SharePoint mobility challenge by providing secure access to SharePoint on Windows, Mac OS X, Apple iOS, and Android mobile devices. Full offline support, advanced metadata support, and industry-leading sync and security capabilities enable organizations to embrace "bring your own device" (BYOD) concept, while maintaining control of their corporate data.

Compatibility with all major Mobile Device Management (MDM) solutions, coupled with Colligo's customization and deployment services, ensures a secure and manageable mobile solution.

Colligo Email Manager

Colligo also provides seamless integration between SharePoint and Microsoft Outlook, for managing e-mail, connected or offline, on both Windows and Mac

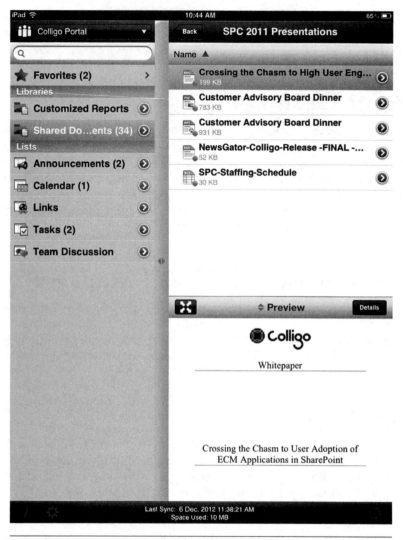

FIGURE 10-8 Colligo Briefcase

systems (see Figure 10-9). Advanced metadata support that is not available with out-of-the-box SharePoint 2013, reduces corporate risk by ensuring content is accurately tagged and readily accessible.

Colligo Administrator

Colligo's client apps can all be centrally configured and managed, ensuring a consistent user experience, on every platform and device. The suite of powerful tools for SharePoint administrators reduces IT overhead and supports corporate governance, while providing easy, consistent access for end users.

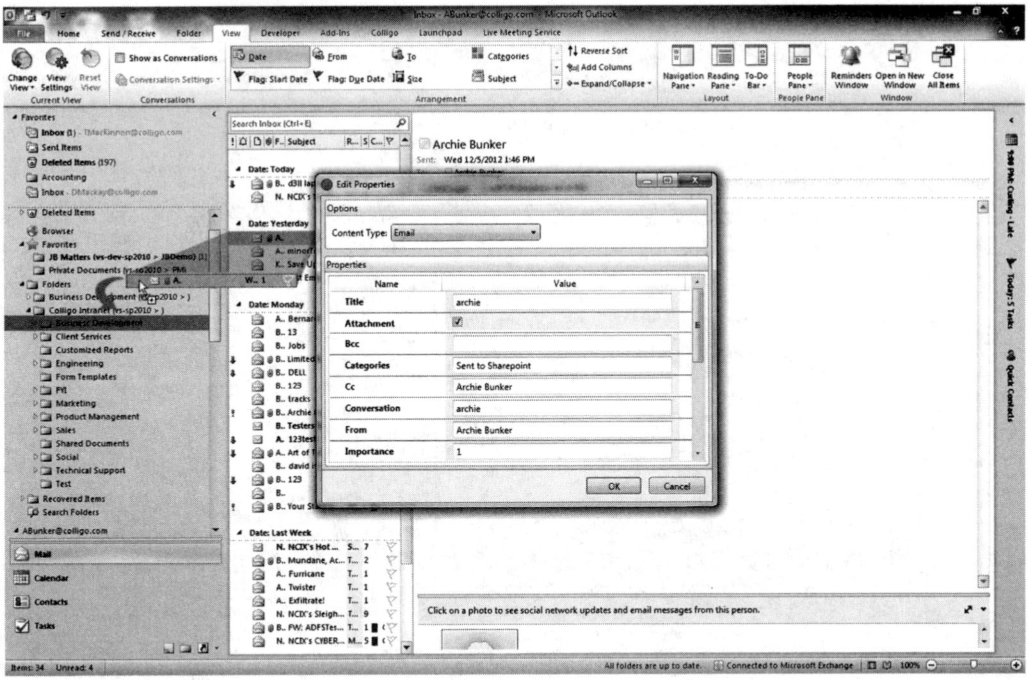

FIGURE 10-9   Colligo Email Manager

Metalogix Content Matrix

Another prominent SharePoint ISV is Metalogix Software Corporation (which also happens to be where I used to have my day job). Metalogix (www.metalogix.com) offers a number of Microsoft SharePoint and Microsoft Exchange administration solutions, but it is best known for SharePoint migration, archiving, and storage management.

The Metalogix migration applications include SharePoint upgrade features and support for numerous source systems. Whether you're looking to move content to SharePoint from file shares, other web systems, or earlier versions of SharePoint, Metalogix has a product that will help.

However, the products are not just for migration. Metalogix Content Matrix offers a number of management features that make it a useful SharePoint client application (see Figure 10-10). For example, Metalogix Content Matrix can do the following:

- Move assets such as lists or sites to different servers or different locations
- Split list contents or merge lists together
- Migrate SharePoint sites, lists, and libraries between servers
- Upgrade from SharePoint 2007 and SharePoint 2010 to SharePoint 2013
- Reorganize or use different templates for your SharePoint content
- Migrate to hosted SharePoint environments such as Microsoft Office 365

Visit www.metalogix.com to download a free trial.

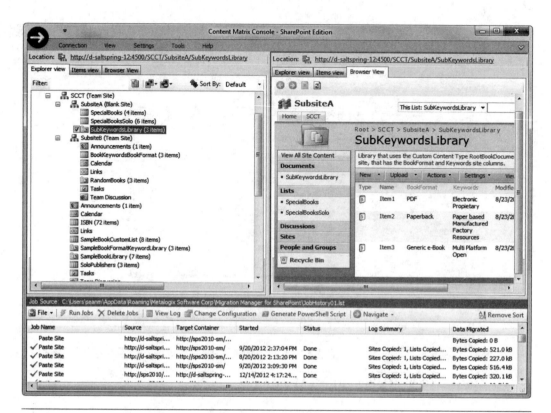

FIGURE 10-10 Metalogix Content Matrix

Summary

As you've seen throughout this chapter, many SharePoint client options are available. Whether you're just a fan of rich clients or you need the power of a product such as SharePoint Designer, you may find that you prefer to interact with SharePoint through an interface other than a web browser.

Colligo and Metalogix are not the only third-party vendors creating management software for SharePoint. If you're looking for SharePoint client applications, take some time to surf the Web and check out what's available. Many companies offer free trial downloads so that you can see their applications in action before you buy. You can also read reviews on sites such as SharePoint Reviews, at www.sharepointreviews.com.

11

Introduction to SharePoint Administration

HOW TO...

- Install SharePoint
- Use SharePoint Central Administration
- Change the document maximum size upload setting
- Administer managed metadata (SharePoint taxonomy)
- Activate SharePoint features
- Use PowerShell to administer SharePoint

You can think of this chapter (and the next chapter, which is an introduction to SharePoint development) as additional reading if you want to go beyond what the typical SharePoint user needs to know. Many SharePoint users may not have an interest in SharePoint administration, but plenty of readers out there will be curious about various aspects of administering a SharePoint server. If you fit into the curious category, then this chapter is meant for you.

Installing SharePoint

If you want to install SharePoint, I strongly suggest that you sign up for a free account with the Critical Path Training program and use its SharePoint setup guide. In this section, we'll walk through a short installation for people who want a relatively simple setup on a Windows 8 client machine (that is, not running Windows Server 2012 as the host operating system).

Note At the time of writing, the SharePoint 2013 version of the setup guide had not been posted yet. However, it should be available from the Critical Path website: www.criticalpathtraining.com/Members/ContinualLearning.

201

For me, one of the biggest enhancements in Windows 8 is the ability to run Hyper-V in the client operating system (O/S). This means I don't need a server O/S running on my laptop (or desktop for that matter). I can simply run virtual machines (VMs) with whatever I need—for example, the shiny new RTM build of SharePoint Server 2013.

Note Microsoft Hyper-V is a virtualization platform that allows users to run virtual machines within their computer. This is commonly done to allow different operating systems to run (often simultaneously) on the same computer.

You don't need to install SharePoint in a virtual environment, but if your goal is to have your own SharePoint environment for development or to learn more about SharePoint, I strongly suggest that you go with a VM setup. Installing SharePoint in a VM allows you to easily create a backup version and move the image from one machine to another. Of course, if you're setting up a production SharePoint server, then you should read the Microsoft TechNet SharePoint installation guide (http:// technet.microsoft.com/en-US/library/cc303424(v = office.15).aspx), and stick to the best practices for production environments.

Caution Hyper-V will work only if your BIOS, hardware, and CPU support Hyper-V. It's a really good idea to check first before you try to use it and get frustrated. Whenever I order new hardware, I explicitly ask if it supports virtualization and Hyper-V. That way, when I get something (such as a CPU) that doesn't work—and that happens—it's easier for me to return it for something that will work.

This setup is "relatively simple" because I chose a particular setup and I repeat it often. I run SharePoint in a Hyper-V VM in a single-server farm. I install Microsoft SQL Server and the domain controller role on the same VM. This means I can export the VM and import into a different Hyper-V instance, and it all just works. Because the whole setup is self-contained and doesn't require Internet access, it's great for demos, webinars, conference sessions, and other presentations. However, this is not the best practice for a production SharePoint installation. For example, you should not install a SharePoint production server on a domain controller.

Here are the steps for my basic SharePoint setup on a Windows 8 client machine:

1. Install Windows 8 and add the Hyper-V feature.
   Once you have Windows 8 running, scroll to the top or bottom corner on the right side to open the fly-out menu, and then choose Settings | Control Panel | Programs and Features | Turn Windows features on or off. Then check the box next to Hyper-V and install it (see Figure 11-1). This will require a reboot.
2. Create a new virtual hard disk (VHD) in Hyper-V.
   I'm choosing Windows Server 2012, so I've downloaded that ISO file from MSDN and selected it as the OS when I created the new VM in the Hyper-V Manager (see Figure 11-2). I'm going with a 50GB VM with 8GB of RAM (but I can always increase these numbers later). If you don't need Office and/or Visual Studio, you may not need 50GB of space.

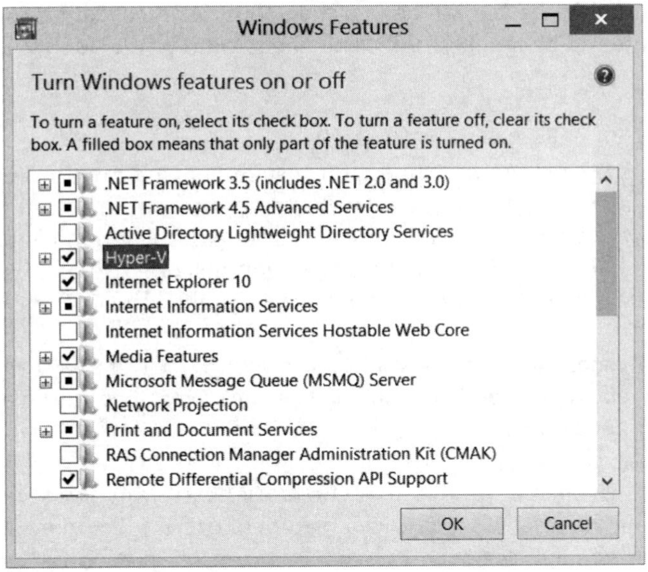

FIGURE 11-1   Installing the Hyper-V feature

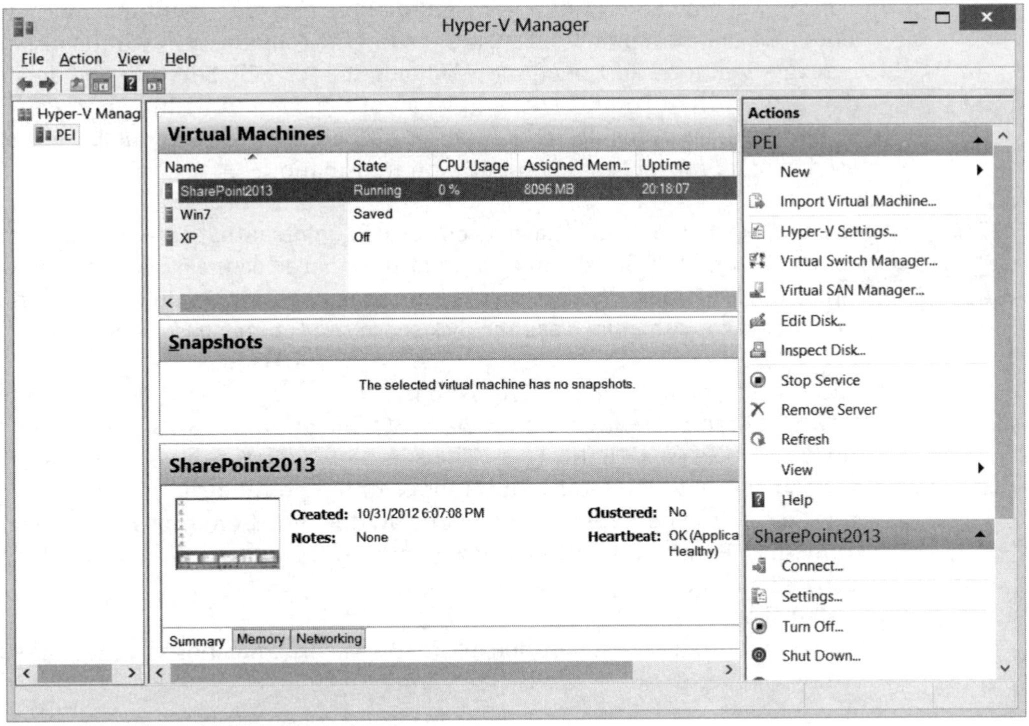

FIGURE 11-2   The Hyper-V Manager

The initial image file will be less than 10GB. After installing SharePoint Server, the VHD file will be roughly 19GB, and about 20GB of the 50GB will be free.

3. Install Windows Server 2012 and name your VM.
   Changing the machine name after installing SharePoint has historically been tricky, so pick a name you want to use right from the start. I'm installing Windows Server 2012 Datacenter Edition with the graphical user interface (GUI). Remember to activate Windows after you install it. No one likes a VM with an OS that hasn't been activated. After you've installed the O/S, run Windows Update.

 If you choose Windows Server 2008 as your OS, it will take a while to update, and many reboots will be required. The last time I installed it, there were 123 Windows Server 2008 updates.

4. Add the web server and Active Directory (AD) Domain Services roles.
   I add the Wireless LAN Services feature because I like to be able to use my VMs on my laptop, which I obviously use a lot on wireless connections. Once you've installed AD, you'll have the option of promoting the server to a domain controller. After that is finished, create the domain accounts you'll need. I always add one for myself and another to use as the SharePoint administrator account.
5. Install Microsoft SQL Server.
   I install Microsoft SQL Server as a stand-alone server (default instance). It's a simple installation process. I install the engine (obviously) with the client and management tools. If I need more, I'll add it later. SQL Server is the database that powers SharePoint. For example, all of the content within SharePoint is stored, by default, inside SQL Server. A different SQL Server database is also used to store most of the configuration information.

 I often export the VM and save a copy at this point so that I have a base image of the OS with SQL Server. Since both of them have been released recently, that's what I did this time. You can also create a snapshot, but I would rather just export a reusable copy than increase the disk space needs of my base image.

6. Run the SharePoint 2013 prerequisite installer.
   Download the SharePoint Server 2013 ISO image from MSDN and launch the default.hta file (see Figure 11-3). The setup file will run the product installation, so don't run that first. You want to first run the prerequisite installer. If you don't have access to SharePoint Server, you can download the free version available from SharePoint Foundation at www.microsoft.com/en-us/download/details .aspx?id=35488.
7. Install SharePoint 2013.
   The actual product installer doesn't really ask any questions—that's saved for the two configuration wizards (see Figure 11-4).

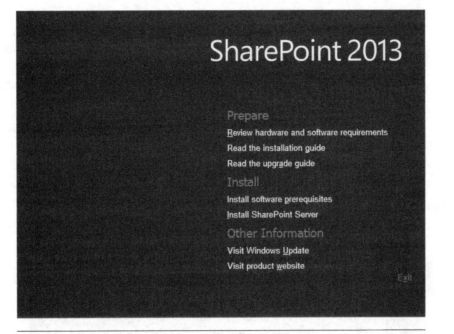

FIGURE 11-3   The SharePoint install splash screen

FIGURE 11-4   Choosing to run the SharePoint
Configuration Wizard

8. Run the SharePoint 2013 Configuration Wizard.
   This wizard asks a lot of questions, and you can find plenty of posts on that topic. One key point is that you likely do want to run the Configuration Wizard at the end of the installation (see Figure 11-5). There are few times that you wouldn't want this selected, such as if you are planning to manually set up SharePoint by using PowerShell.
9. Run the Farm Configuration Wizard.
   After running the SharePoint Configuration Wizard, you'll be asked to run the Farm Configuration Wizard. This step includes creating a root site collection and choosing which services will run on the server (see Figure 11-6).

That's it—you're finished! Now you have a SharePoint 2013 image on Windows 8, and that's so handy.

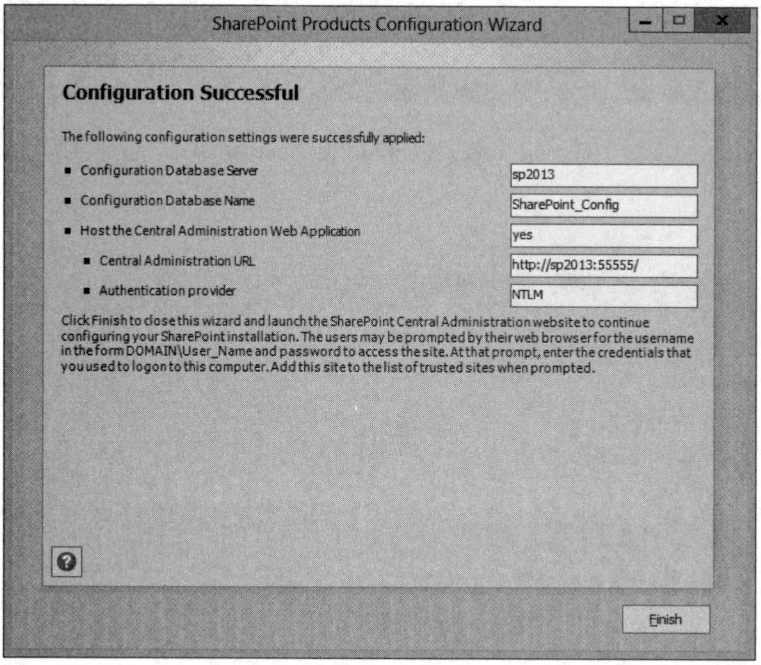

FIGURE 11-5 The confirmation screen in the SharePoint Configuration Wizard

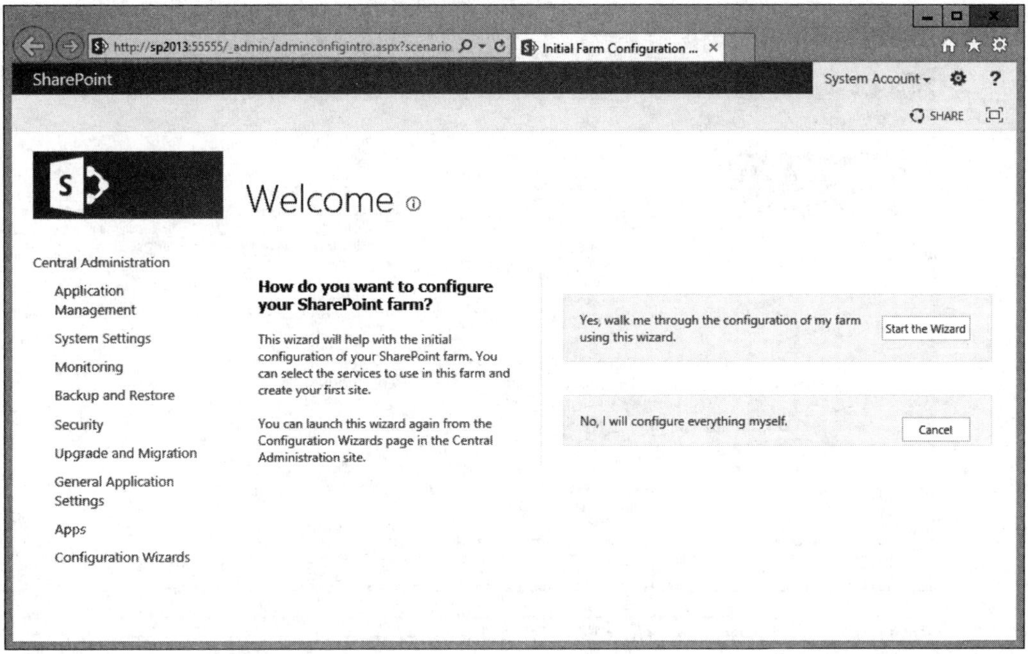

FIGURE 11-6   The SharePoint Farm Configuration Wizard

Using SharePoint Central Administration

As with the rest of SharePoint, the main interface for SharePoint administration is web-based. This means that you can bookmark the URL on other machines and access it remotely, if the security settings allow remote connections.

To open SharePoint Central Administration (commonly referred to as "central admin") on your SharePoint server, go to the app search bar (or the Start menu on older versions of Windows) and type in **SharePoint**. One of the results will be SharePoint 2013 Central Administration. When you choose to launch it, central admin will open in your favorite browser (see Figure 11-7).

From the administration interface, you can configure many settings. Everything from SharePoint security settings, web application settings, and various SharePoint services can be managed from within central admin. Along with the technical changes

FIGURE 11-7 SharePoint Central Administration opens in your browser.

you can make to your SharePoint environment, you can also configure options to quickly improve the experience for your end users. One such example is changing the maximum upload size for documents. Here, to give you an idea of how central admin works, we'll walk through making that change. If you're interested in diving into the depths of SharePoint administration, pick up a good reference and start reading. For example, *Professional SharePoint 2013 Administration* by Shane Young, Steve Caravajal, and Todd Klindt.

Real-World Example: Changing the Document Size Upload Setting

The document size upload setting is meant as a precaution against unrestrained disk bloat on SharePoint servers. However, it can be frustrating to users who routinely work with files that exceed the default limit of 250MB.

To find the upload setting, open Central Administration, and then choose Application Management from the main screen. Click Manage Web Applications under the Application Management section.

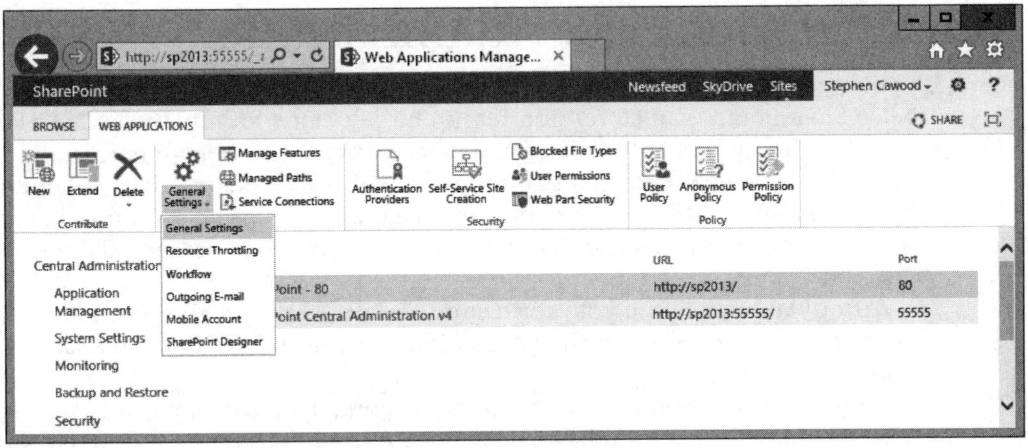

FIGURE 11-8   The ribbon options for Web Application settings

Next, click the site collection you wish to modify, and open the drop-down menu under the General Settings link in the ribbon. From the drop-down menu, choose General Settings (see Figure 11-8) and then scroll down the long page until you find the Maximum Upload Size setting (see Figure 11-9). You can change this setting to match the requirements of your end users. By most standards, 250MB is a large file, but it might be the case that you have larger files that you would like to store in SharePoint.

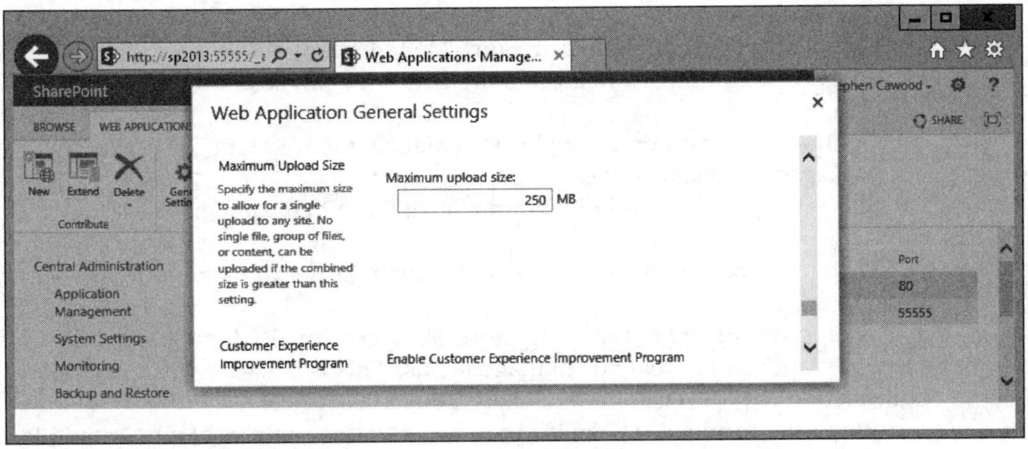

FIGURE 11-9   Changing the Maximum Upload Size setting

Managed Metadata Administration

If you need to administer SharePoint taxonomy, the first step is to learn how to use SharePoint term stores and research the details for creating a SharePoint taxonomy hierarchy. You'll also want to read Microsoft's best practices and make use of the managed metadata planning data sheets. To ensure that you end up with the best possible taxonomy for your organization, you'll likely want to collaborate with some business users so that you can determine the best possible terms, term sets, and groups.

After you have set up your term store and decided how your taxonomy will be organized, you'll need to set the permissions on your term store and enable various contents for tagging.

Remember that there are two types of tagging: managed keywords and managed metadata. Managed keywords are used for informal "folksonomy" style tagging, and managed terms are used for centrally controlled and delegated hierarchical term structures.

Enabling Managed Metadata on Your Server

In the SharePoint Enterprise Managed Metadata (EMM) features, all taxonomy data is stored within a SQL Server database called the *term store*. Creating a managed service application creates a term store that you can use to build your taxonomy hierarchy.

Here are the steps to enable managed term tagging on a SharePoint list or library:

1. Add an administrator to your term store.
2. Create some terms.
3. Add a column of type Managed Metadata to the list or library.

SharePoint provides the Term Store Management Tool for working with managed metadata. To open the Term Store Management Tool, select either of these options:

- Central Administration | Application Management | Manage Service Applications | Managed Metadata Service
- Site Settings | Site Administration | Term Store Management

Both of these options open the same Term Store Management Tool interface (see Figure 11-10).

When you first go to the Term Store Management Tool, you'll find that you don't have any options to create or manage terms. This is because you must be in the administrators group for the managed metadata service.

When the term store page is open, you can use the SharePoint People Picker to add administrators in the Term Store Administrators section (see Figure 11-11). Here's where you can add yourself to the administrators group for the managed metadata service.

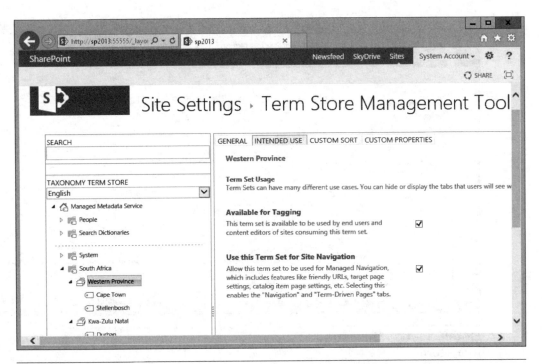

FIGURE 11-10   Opening the Term Store Management Tool in Site Settings

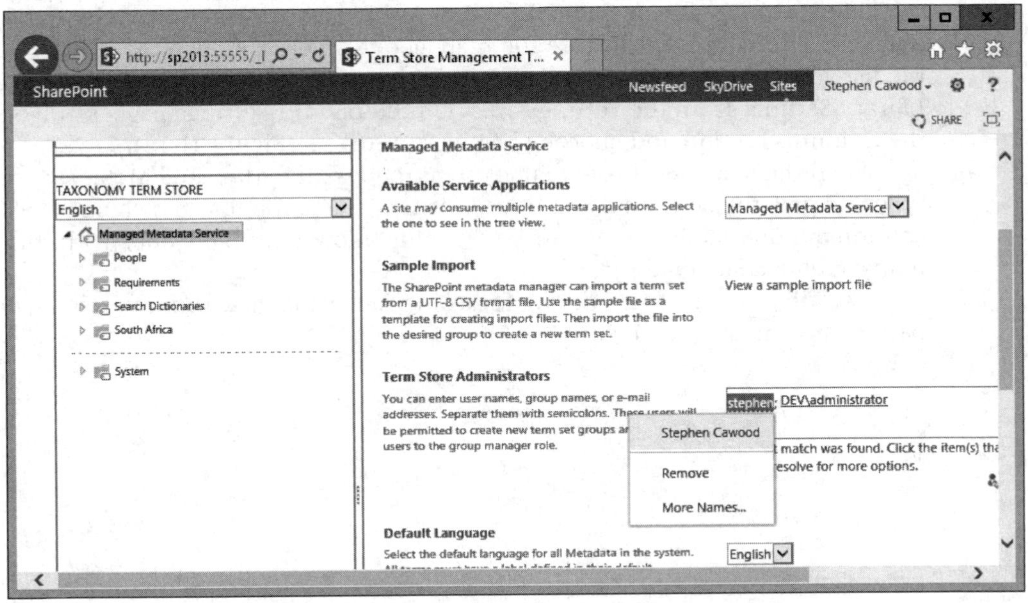

FIGURE 11-11   Adding an administrator to the term store

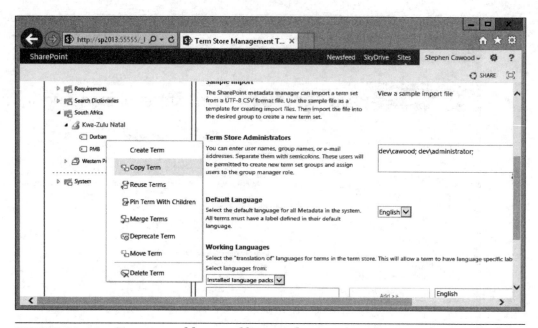

FIGURE 11-12 Once you add yourself as an administrator, you can start to use the term store.

After you add yourself and save the changes, you'll be able to create groups, term sets, and terms (see Figure 11-12).

To use managed terms, you'll need to add a new column to your lists and libraries. This column will store the managed term data. To add the column, go to the list you want to enable, choose the Library tab from the ribbon, and then choose Library Settings from the Settings area. On the Library Settings page, scroll down to the Columns section and choose Create Column (see Figure 11-13).

When the Create Column dialog opens, choose the Managed Metadata column type and give the column a name (see Figure 11-14). You'll also be able to set column options, such as whether you want to allow multiple values with this managed metadata column.

You will also have the option of filtering the available taxonomy tree down to a particular term set (see Figure 11-15).

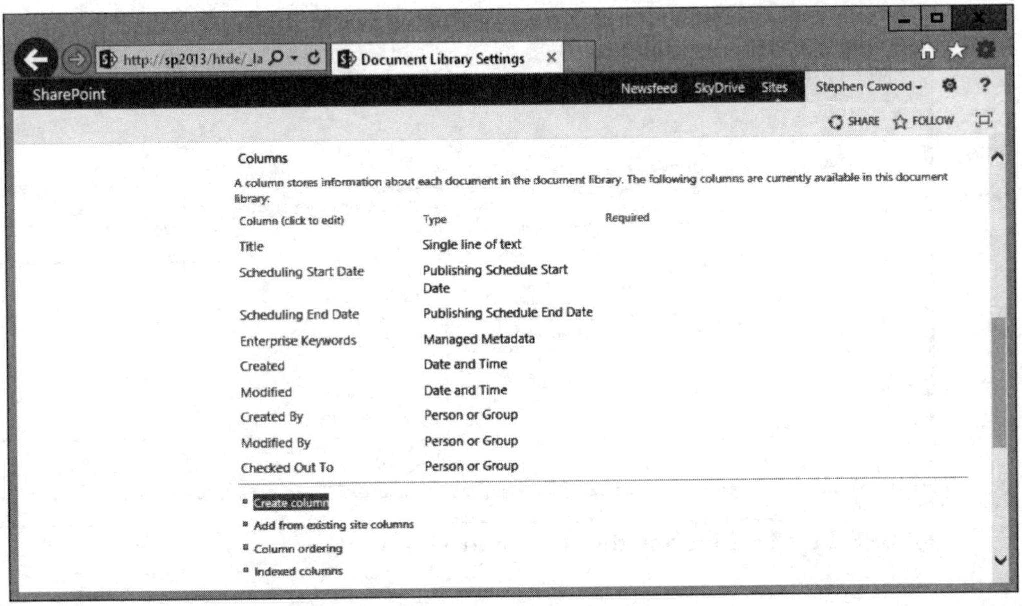

FIGURE 11-13 Create Column is available in the Columns section.

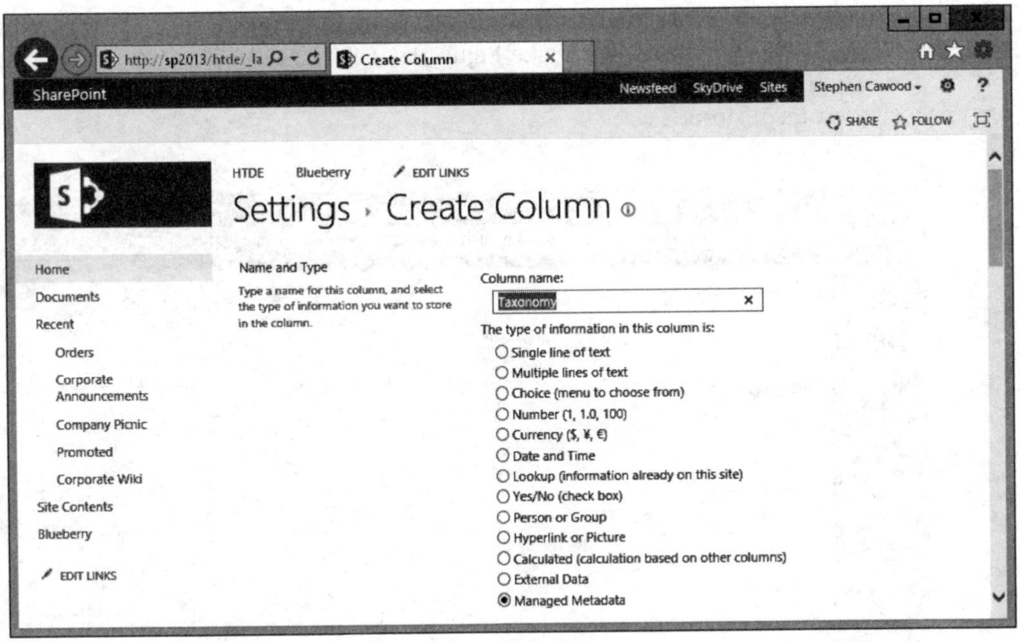

FIGURE 11-14 Use the Managed Metadata column type for managed terms.

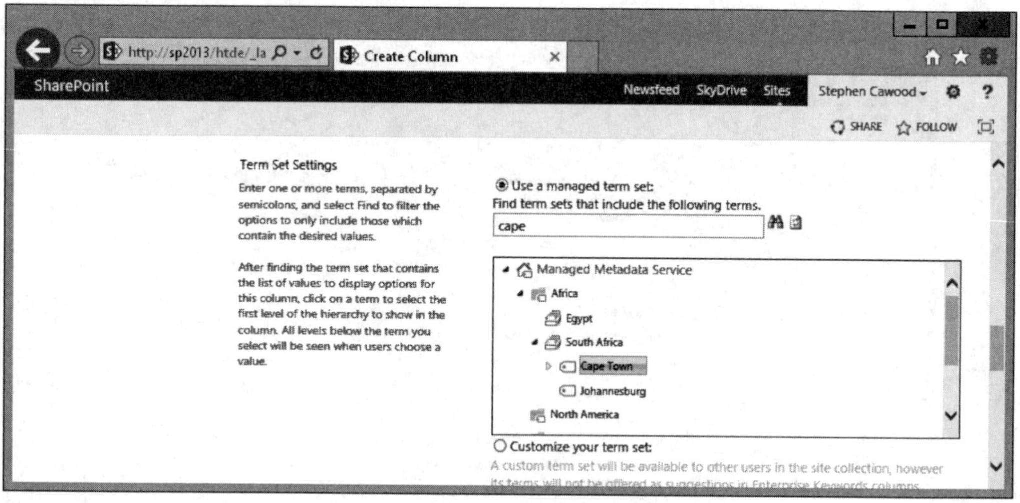

FIGURE 11-15 Filtering the column to a term set

After adding this column, when you edit the properties of a document in the document library, you will see a new option to choose managed terms to put into the new managed metadata field. You have two options for adding terms:

- Start typing in the field, which prompts SharePoint to suggest tags that match the characters you have typed (see Figure 11-16).
- Click the little tags icon on the right of the field, which enables you to browse your term store.

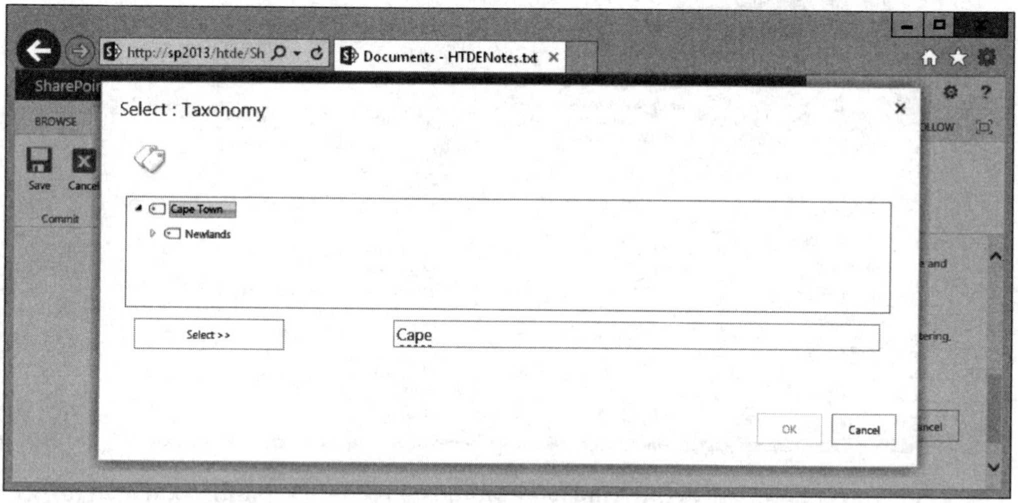

FIGURE 11-16 After adding the managed metadata column, you can add terms.

Understanding the SharePoint Taxonomy Hierarchy

If you're wondering how to organize your SharePoint EMM, you should start by reading the TechNet article "Plan terms and term sets in SharePoint Server 2013" (http://technet.microsoft.com/en-us/library/ee519604(v = office.15).aspx). This section highlights some of the key points of that article and also adds a few points from other sources.

While the TechNet article reminds you that you could simply allow your users to add keywords, and then use their input to create your taxonomy—promoting keywords to managed terms as necessary—it seems likely that most organizations will want to start with an organized metadata hierarchy.

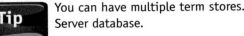 Unlike managed terms, managed keywords are not stored in a hierarchical fashion.

SharePoint EMM managed terms are organized into a hierarchy. The objects within this hierarchy are term stores, groups, term sets, and terms. These are the rules for the taxonomy hierarchy:

- When a managed metadata service is created, a term store will be created. Once you have a term store, you can create a group. A group is a security boundary.
- Once you have a group, you can create a term set. A term set must be the child of a single parent group.
- Under a term set, terms can be created.
- A term can be added as a child of another term.
- Terms can be nested to seven levels.

Note The previously referenced TechNet article "Plan terms and term sets in SharePoint Server 2013" clearly states that "You can nest terms to a maximum of seven levels deep." However, SharePoint Server does not enforce this constraint. The best advice is to stick to seven levels, even though it's possible to have more.

One of the key points of the TechNet article about planning your terms and term sets is that a group is a security boundary. A group contributor can manage the term sets in the groups and create new term sets. All users who have access to a term set under a group can see all of the other term sets—even if they don't have rights to manage the other term sets. Therefore, you should organize your term sets into groups based on the groups of users who will manage them. For this reason, your taxonomy may correlate to your organizational structure. Take a look at the example shown in Figure 11-17, which has the following hierarchy:

- **Term store**   The term store is simply titled Taxonomy.

Tip You can have multiple term stores. Each term store is stored in a separate SQL Server database.

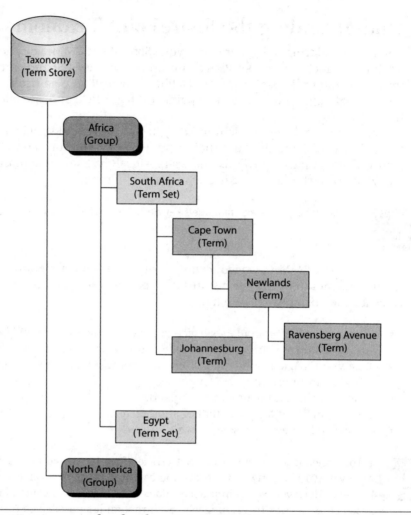

FIGURE 11-17   An example of a SharePoint EMM hierarchy

- **Groups**   Under the term store are two groups: Africa and North America. The idea is that these could be significant geographical locations to this particular fictional organization. Remember that the groups are a security boundary, so the users assigned to the Africa group don't have to have any access to the North America group. However, if users are given rights to a term set under one of the groups, they will be able to see the names of all the term sets under that group.
- **Term sets**   Inside the Africa group, there are two term sets: South Africa and Egypt.
- **Terms**   At the top level, the South Africa term set contains the terms Cape Town and Johannesburg. In this case, the Cape Town term contains the child term Newlands (a neighborhood in Cape Town), and that term contains the child term Ravensberg Avenue.

When you're creating your managed terms, you're free to identify synonyms, and you can also specify which is the preferred term. For example, you can set up a term so that when a user types in "Joburg," she will be asked to assign the term "Johannesburg."

> **Tip** You can specify a custom sort order for terms, so it isn't necessary to show them in alphabetical order.

Term sets can be open or closed. Open sets allow all users to add terms. Terms can be added to closed sets only by users who are contributors to the group.

As you've seen, in addition to terms, SharePoint EMM contains keywords. Keywords aren't restricted, and that's why they can be used informally to create folksonomy.

If you've been tasked with creating the taxonomy for your EMM hierarchy, the points outlined in this section are important, but I strongly recommend that you also take advantage of the articles and the planning worksheets available on TechNet. Setting up a taxonomy is a potentially complex task, and a lack of proper planning or a poorly designed taxonomy could be worse than not having one at all.

Promoting a Managed Keyword to a Managed Term

One philosophy for building out a taxonomy hierarchy is to let the users decide which terms are important. In SharePoint, there are two ways to achieve this:

- You can allow "fill-in" keywords in your term sets.
- You can allow users to tag with managed keywords, and then you can choose to promote some (or all) of them to managed terms.

To change a managed keyword to a managed term, you simply open the Term Store Management Tool (from Central Administration or Site Settings) and use the Move option to move the keyword into the term hierarchy. To access the Move action, right-click the term that you would like to move (see Figure 11-18).

> **Note** It is not possible to move a managed term to the keyword store. In other words, you can promote a managed keyword to a managed term, but you can't demote a managed term to a keyword.

Creating Your Own Term Store

If you want to create your own term store, you'll need to follow the steps provided in this section to create a new managed metadata service. Generally, this won't be necessary, because one term store will be enough for most organizations.

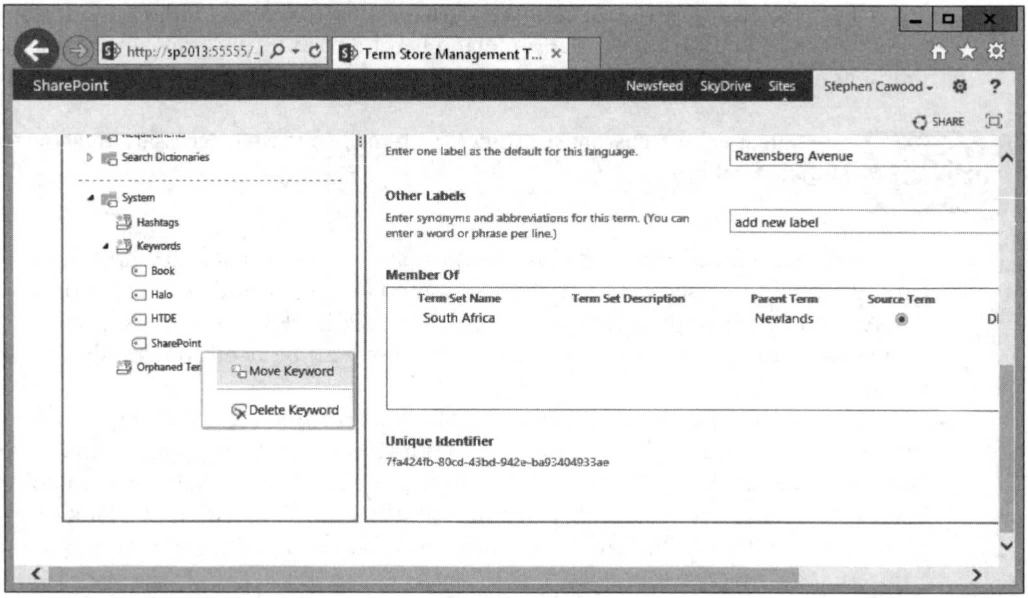

FIGURE 11-18 Moving a keyword to the term store will convert it to a managed term.

First, open SharePoint Central Administration and select Manage Service Applications from the Application Management section. At this point, the Service Applications tab should be selected at the top of the page. Next, click the drop-down arrow under New, and then click Managed Metadata Service (see Figure 11-19). This opens the Create New Managed Metadata Service dialog.

The dialog contains the following fields:

- **Name**   The name of your new managed metadata service.
- **Database Server**   The name of your database server.
- **Database Name**   The name of the database you want to use on the selected server. If the database does not exist, it will be created.
- **Database authentication**   The recommended option is Windows authentication, but SQL authentication is also available.
- **Failover Database Server**   If you're using a failover database server, you can enter its name here.
- **Application Pool**   You can either create a new pool or choose an existing one from the drop-down menu.

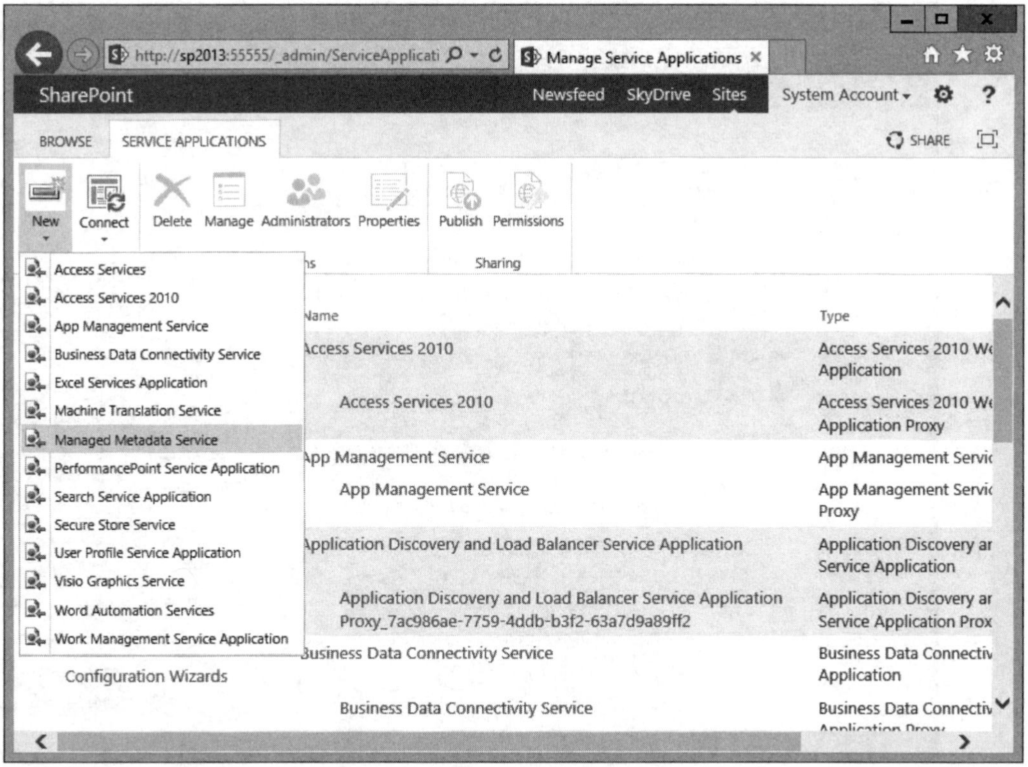

FIGURE 11-19   Creating a new managed metadata service

Note   Ensure that the selected application pool is actually running before you try to use your term store.

- **Content Type Hub**   From Microsoft: *If you want the managed metadata service to provide access to a content type library as well as to a term store, type the URL of the site collection that contains the content type library in the Content Type hub box. The service will share the content type library at the root of the site collection.*

From the same area of Central Administration, you have options to perform numerous other operations on your term store. For example, you can delete a term store, modify the term store permissions, add term store administrators, and more (see Figure 11-20).

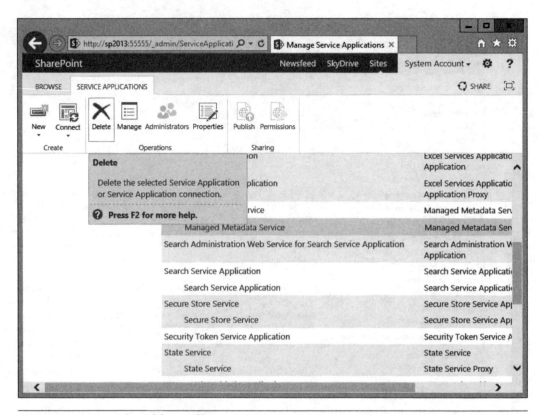

FIGURE 11-20 The ribbon offers more term store management options.

Activating SharePoint Features

SharePoint ships with a number of useful site features. These include the Content Organizer, which allows you to define an automated process for filing your content; the Getting Started feature, which enables the introductory tiles you see by default on the home page of a new team site; and the SharePoint Server Publishing feature, which allows you to create sites with all of the publishing functionality available in SharePoint.

These are just a few examples of the features that come out of the box with SharePoint. However, they are not all activated on every site template by default—that simply wouldn't make sense. If you find that you want to use functionality provided by a feature that has not been activated, you can go into the Site Settings page and activate it yourself.

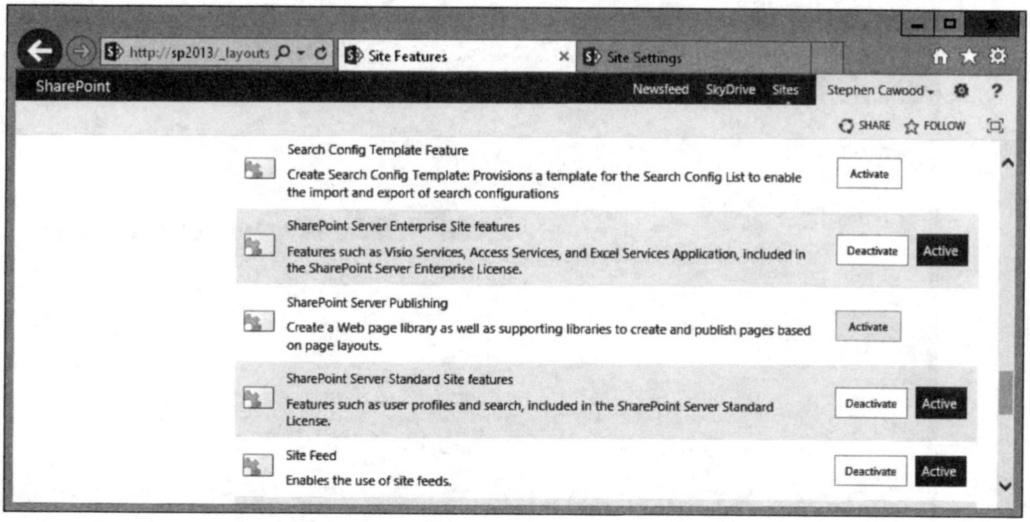

FIGURE 11-21 Enabling SharePoint Server Publishing

In this example, you'll learn how to activate the publishing feature. The interesting thing about publishing is that it must first be enabled at the site-collection level before it is possible to activate it at the site level. This isn't true for all features, but it's important to know that some features require a two-step activation.

The first thing you'll need to do is activate the feature at the site-collection level. To do this, go to the Site Settings page for your site and then choose the Go to the top level site settings link from the Site Collection Administration category at the bottom of the page (this appears if you're not at the root of the site collection). Once there, choose the Manage site collection features option from the Site Collection Administration category. To enable the feature, scroll down to the SharePoint Server Publishing Infrastructure feature and simply click the Activate button (see Figure 11-21).

Once you have successfully enabled publishing at the site-collection level, you can return to the Site Settings page for your site in that site collection and choose to enable SharePoint Server Publishing for the site. You'll also find it under the Manage site features option from the Site Actions category. After activating this feature, the publishing site templates will appear in the list of available templates for your site (see Figure 11-22).

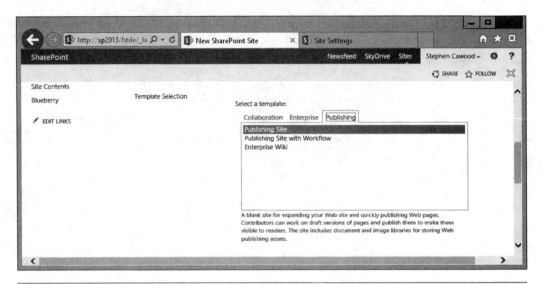

FIGURE 11-22 The publishing site templates

Introduction to PowerShell

PowerShell is a relatively new command-line interface in Windows. PowerShell has become incredibly popular with administrators, as it allows them to perform many tasks quickly and in a repeatable—scriptable—fashion. Anyone interested in SharePoint administration as a career will need to learn the ins and outs of PowerShell. To the average user, however, PowerShell is not a requirement to get the most out of SharePoint.

The usefulness of PowerShell for SharePoint administration is described in the Microsoft TechNet article "Use Windows PowerShell to administer SharePoint 2013" (http://technet.microsoft.com/en-us/library/ee806878.aspx#section2), as follows:

> After you install SharePoint 2013, applicable Windows PowerShell cmdlets are available in the SharePoint 2013 Management Shell. You can manage most aspects of SharePoint 2013 in the SharePoint Management Shell. You can create new site collections, web applications, user accounts, service applications, proxies, and more. Commands that you type in the SharePoint Management Shell return SharePoint objects that are based on the Microsoft .NET Framework. You can apply these objects as input to subsequent commands or store the objects in local variables for later use.

To open the SharePoint PowerShell management console, navigate to the Start menu, or if you're using Windows Server 2012, open the app search box and type **SharePoint**. Once you have the list open, click the SharePoint Management Shell (see Figure 11-23).

Unless you're actually logged in as Administrator, it's likely that you'll need to run the management console under the administrator account. To do this, pin the console to the task menu, close it, and then open it again using the Run as Administrator option. Alternatively, you can right-click the icon in the Start menu, and it will present you with the same Run as Administrator option.

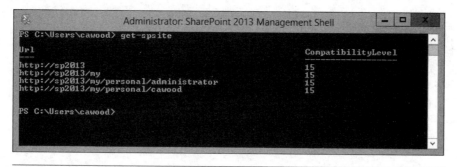

FIGURE 11-23   Launching the SharePoint PowerShell management console

Once you have the SharePoint PowerShell management console running with sufficient privileges, you can try some commands. The simplest (read: safest) example is a read-only operation. For example, the command get-spsite will return a list of all the site collections on the server (see Figure 11-24). Another read-only command you can try is get-spwebtemplate, which returns all of the globally installed site templates.

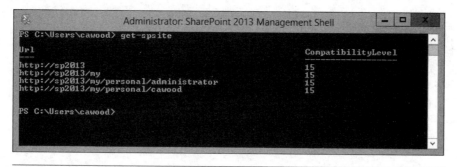

FIGURE 11-24   Running get-spsite in PowerShell

You might find it odd that `get-spsite` returns the list of site collections instead of a list of sites. This is because SharePoint site collections were originally called "sites," and subsites were originally known as "webs." This naming has continued in both the SharePoint administration and SharePoint development context. So if you hear SharePoint administrators referring to how many top-level "sites" there are in a SharePoint farm, it's possible that they are referring to site collections.

If you would like to learn more about using PowerShell to administer SharePoint, take a look at the Windows PowerShell Command Builder. It's a handy web application that allows you to build PowerShell commands (see Figure 11-25). To get going, you can download the *Windows PowerShell Command Builder Getting Started Guide*, available from http://www.microsoft.com/en-ca/download/details.aspx?id=27588.

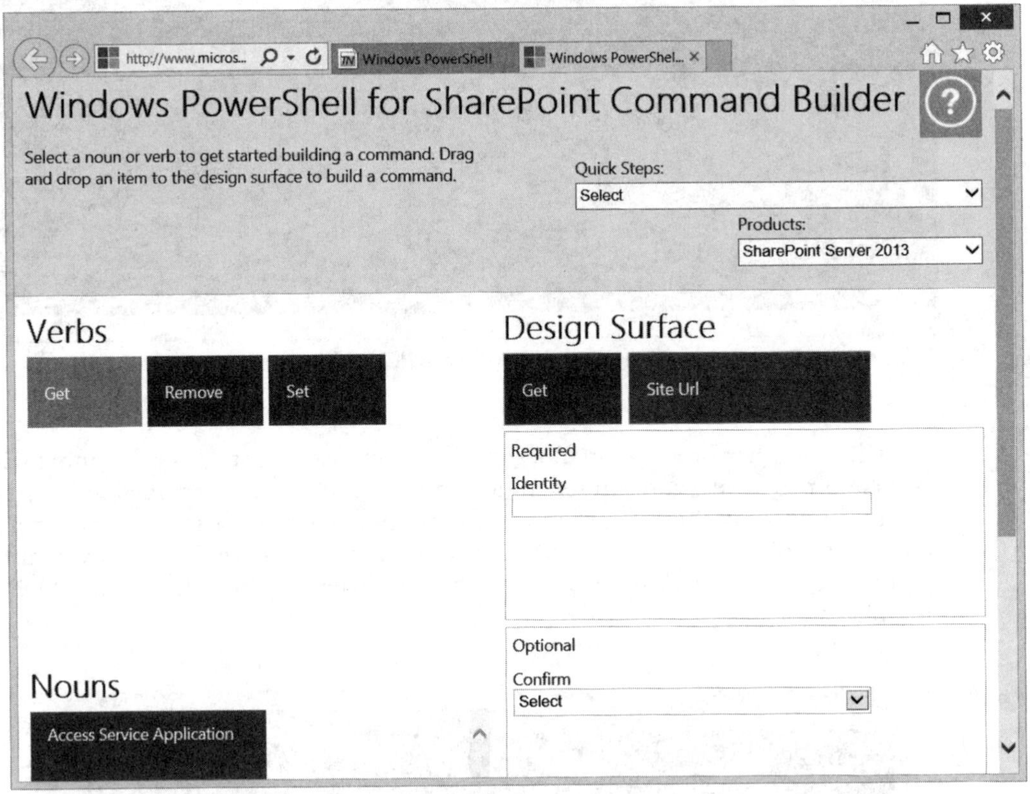

FIGURE 11-25 Windows PowerShell for SharePoint Command Builder

Summary

The topics in this chapter were chosen to give you a broad overview of SharePoint administration tasks. As with SharePoint development, SharePoint administration is a giant topic.

You may never need to install SharePoint, use SharePoint Central Administration, or use PowerShell to administer SharePoint, but at least now you have some understanding of what those tasks entail.

12

Introduction to SharePoint Development

HOW TO...

- Set up a SharePoint development environment
- Develop visual web parts
- Develop SharePoint apps

Like SharePoint administration, SharePoint development is a huge topic in itself. This chapter will give you a taste of the various SharePoint development options. If you are not familiar with Visual Studio or .NET programming, you might want to try a few introductory .NET lessons before working through this chapter. A good place to start is http://msdn.microsoft.com. For example, for Visual Studio basics, you could read *Getting Started with Visual Studio* (http://msdn.microsoft.com/library/vstudio/ms165079.aspx).

The first thing to learn about SharePoint development is that there are a number of different programming interfaces for SharePoint. One reason for this is that Microsoft wants to give SharePoint developers as much flexibility as possible. Another reason is simply that SharePoint has been around long enough to see some coding options come and go. For example, when SharePoint was first released, native web services were in their infancy. More than ten years later, that interface has been deprecated in SharePoint 2013. In other words, this interface will work in SharePoint 2013, but support could be removed in the future, so it's best to avoid using it.

SharePoint Programming Interfaces

In SharePoint 2013, the main programming interfaces are the server-side API, the Client-Side Object Model, and the brand-new SharePoint App model.

Note As you saw in Chapter 11, it's also possible to code against SharePoint with PowerShell. However, PowerShell is generally used by administrators rather than by SharePoint developers.

The SharePoint Server-Side API

The server-side API is certainly the most powerful option for SharePoint developers. In terms of functionality, it's clearly the programming interface that provides the best breadth of coverage.

The clear disadvantage of the server-side API is that this type of code must actually run on the SharePoint server—there is no remote option. In practice, this limits when the server-side API can be used. For example, it cannot be used with Office 365, since SharePoint developers do not have the ability to run their own code on Office 365 servers.

The SharePoint Client-Side Object Model

The SharePoint Client-Side Object Model (CSOM) is a relatively new addition to the SharePoint platform. In early versions of SharePoint, the only remote interface for SharePoint developers was the native web services. The CSOM is a more modern version of that interface, and thanks to the CSOM, the native web services are no longer recommended.

SharePoint App Model

The new SharePoint App model is not so much a method of programming against SharePoint as it is a method of deploying code to SharePoint.

The SharePoint App model uses the CSOM under the hood, so it's limited to what is provided in the CSOM interface. However, it's important to include the App model in this conversation, because it does use a specific framework, which needs to be considered during the planning stage of a development project. In other words, you can save yourself a lot of time if you consider whether you're going to use the SharePoint App model when you are deciding which programming interface to use.

For more information about the different methods for programming in SharePoint, refer to the MSDN article, "Choose the right API set in SharePoint 2013" (http://msdn .microsoft.com/en-us/library/jj164060.aspx).

Setting Up a SharePoint Development Environment

The good news about setting up a SharePoint development environment is that you'll be able to find free (or trial) versions of all the software you need. However, it will take some time to get up and running. Don't expect the following examples and setup to be quick.

Note If you've never done any development, it will take some time, and you'll likely have some questions along the way. Just remember that you can get help from the community 24/7 via the MSDN forums (http://social.msdn.microsoft.com/Forums).

The first step is to install Visual Studio with the SharePoint development tools (see Figure 12-1). Run Windows Update to see if there are any updates for Visual Studio. You can go to Tools | Extensions and Updates to check for updates to the add-ins for Visual Studio.

Note At the time of writing, the Office Developer Tools were in Preview 2 (available from www.microsoft.com/web/handlers/WebPI.ashx?command=GetInstallerRedirect&app id=OfficeToolsForVS2012GA).

For more information about getting your machine ready for SharePoint development, refer to the MSDN article, "Set up the development environment for SharePoint 2013" (http://msdn.microsoft.com/en-us/library/ee554869.aspx).

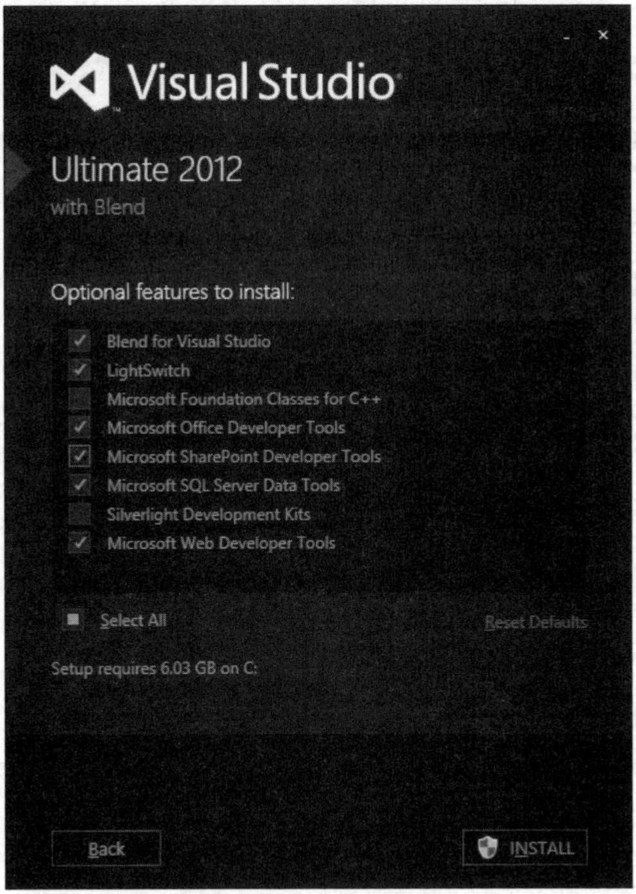

FIGURE 12-1   Installing Visual Studio 2012

Creating Visual Web Parts

One of the SharePoint 2010 features that I was most excited about is the ease with which developers can create web parts, which were introduced in Chapter 8. To distinguish the old from the shiny new, SharePoint now provides the Visual Web Part project type. In this section, I'll quickly cover the basics of getting a new web part working in debug mode.

Setting Up a Visual Studio Project

Obviously, you'll need a working SharePoint 2013 development machine. Once you have everything set up, the first step is to create a new project in Visual Studio 2012 (see Figure 12-2). To create a new SharePoint 2013 Visual Web Part project, launch Visual Studio 2012 as Administrator, and then choose the File | New Project option from the main menu.

The New Project dialog gives you the ability to choose a myriad of project types. For this example, choose Visual C# | SharePoint 2013 | Visual Web Part. As usual, you also have the option of choosing a project name, the path for the project files, and a solution name.

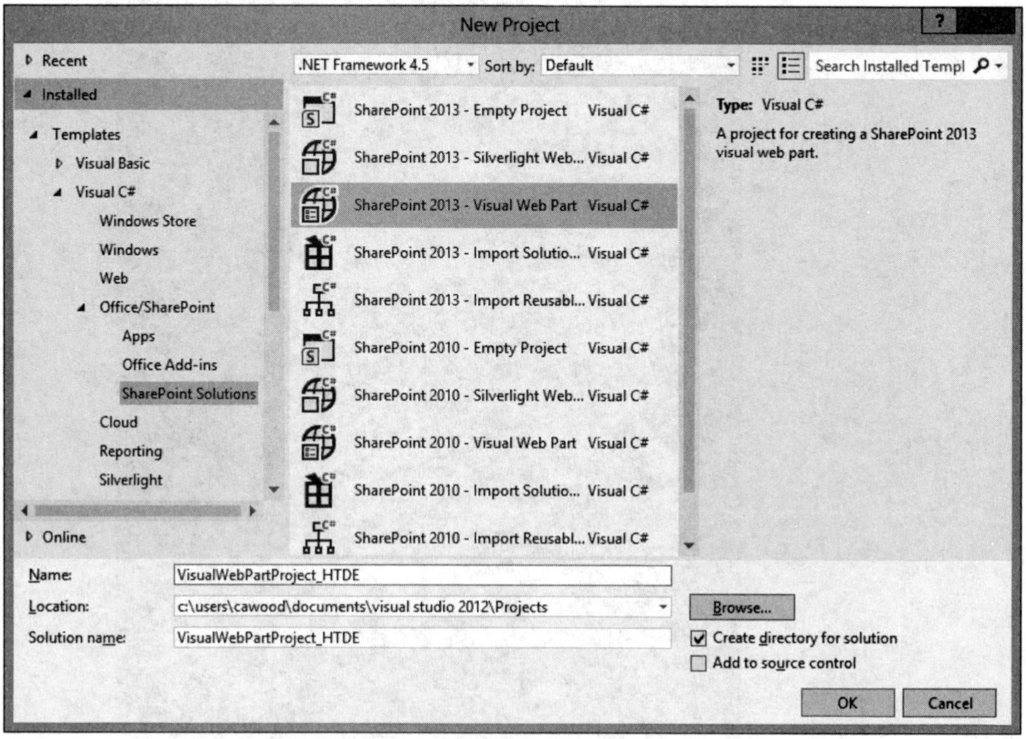

FIGURE 12-2 Creating a new SharePoint 2013 Visual Web Part project

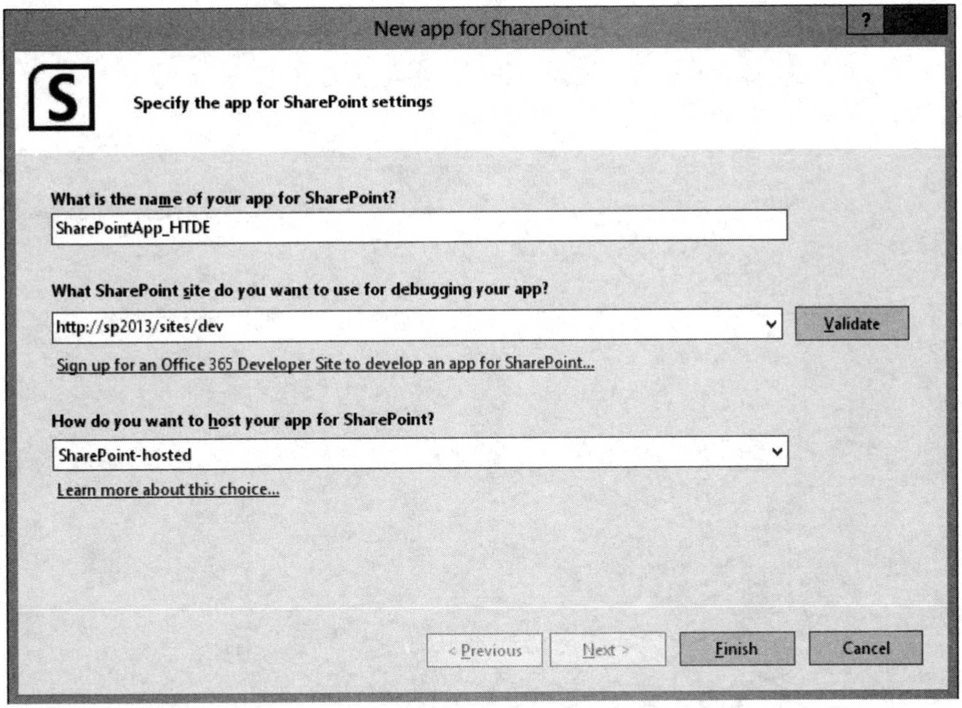

FIGURE 12-3   Choosing the debugging and trust level settings

Visual Studio will also ask which SharePoint site you would like to use to debug your web part (see Figure 12-3) and which type of solution you want to create. The two choices for the trust level are Farm Solution and Sandboxed Solution. Farm Solutions are the most powerful since they provide the complete power of the server-side API. Sandboxed solutions are more secure because they are restricted to a lower level of trust.

> **Note**   SharePoint sandboxed solutions are deprecated in SharePoint 2013. This means that they may not be supported at all in the next major release. For this reason, I recommend developing a SharePoint app rather than using sandboxed solutions.

When the project is created, you will see that the plumbing of your new web part is provided in the project template (see Figure 12-4).

Running the Visual Web Part

Rather than dive into the code, we're just going to get this blank web part running. Add a simple `<H1>Hello World</H1>` line below the content on the web part page, and then run the project in debug mode. To start the debugger, press F5 or click the green start arrow on the main menu.

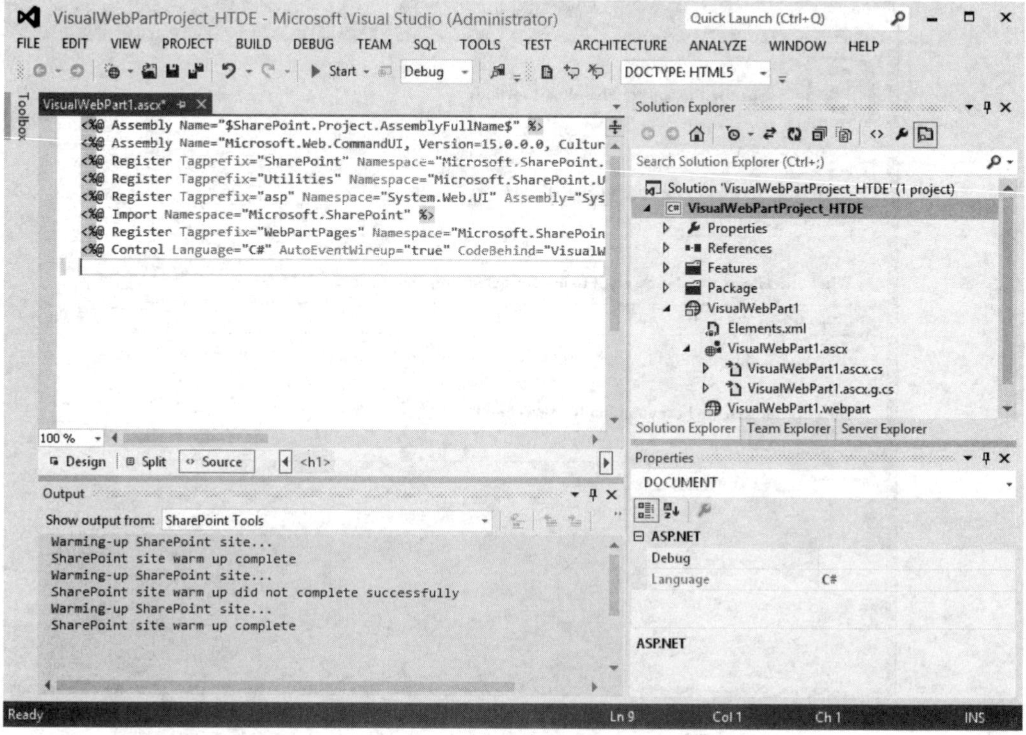

FIGURE 12-4 Your blank template for web part creations

The first time you try to debug the project, you'll be told that the web.config file is not set to allow debugging. When you see that message, choose the option to enable debugging. After you enable debugging, the home page for the site you chose will open. If you close this browser window, you'll be returned to Visual Studio.

To add your custom web part to another page, you can choose Insert | Web Part from the ribbon. Your new web part will appear in the Custom category. After you choose to add it, you'll see the name appear on your web part page (see Figure 12-5).

And that's it—your new custom web part will be visible on the page (see Figure 12-6). You now have a blank web part project that you can use to build what you want. Sure, it doesn't actually do anything, but just enjoy how simple it is to get a working web part running in debug mode on your SharePoint server. Now you can drag-and-drop controls from the Toolbox, just as with any other ASP.NET page, and start your creation.

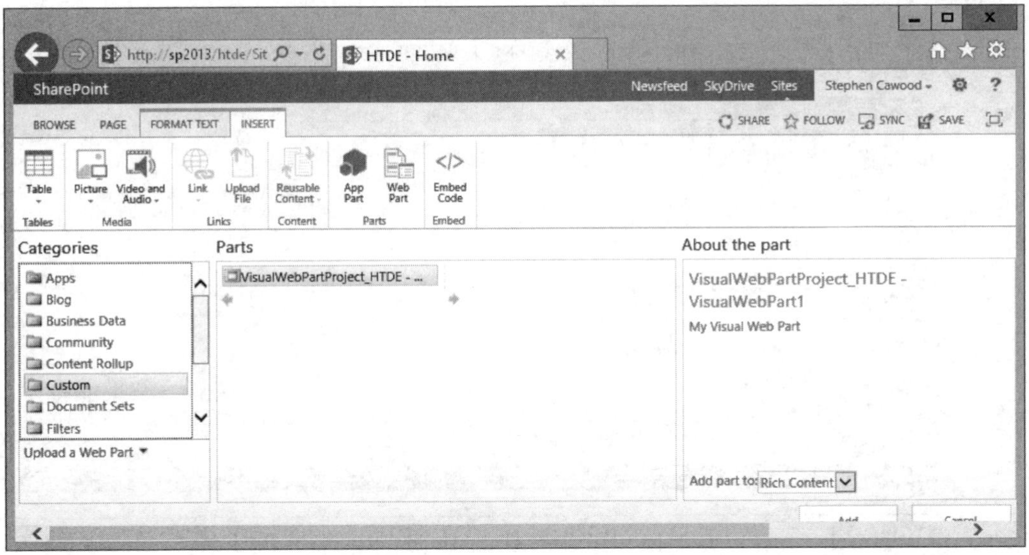

FIGURE 12-5   Choosing the new custom web part from the available web parts

Debugging and Adding Breakpoints

One of the great advances in web part coding is ease of debugging. To see how easy it is to debug and step through your code, simply insert a breakpoint in your visual web part (see Figure 12-7). In this example, a breakpoint has been added to the .ascx.cs page.

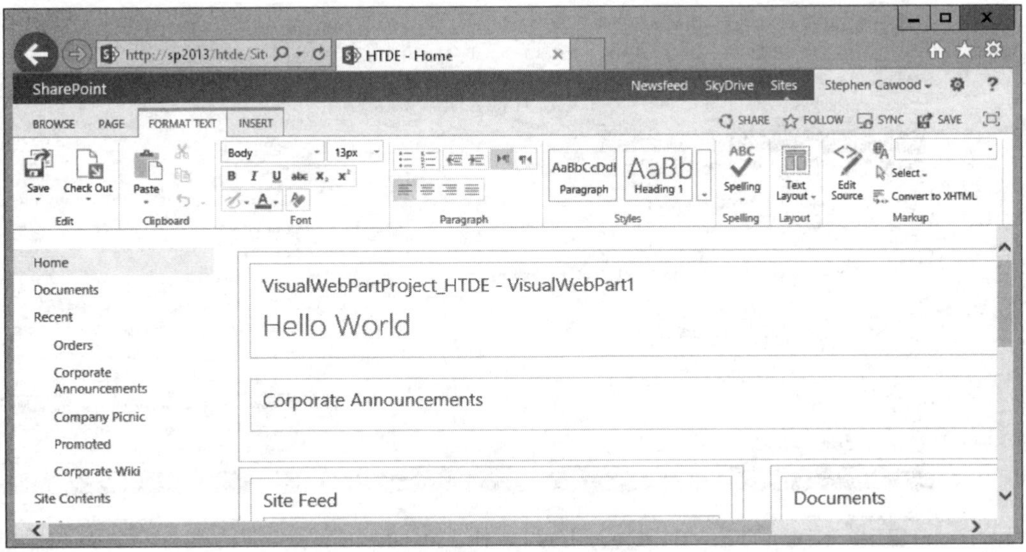

FIGURE 12-6   The new web part has been deployed

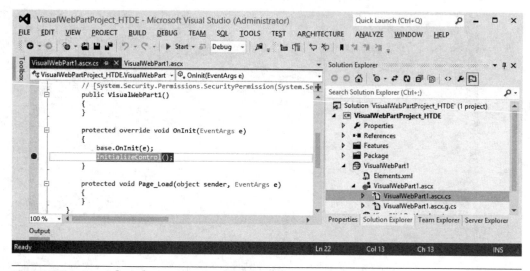

FIGURE 12-7   A breakpoint set in the SharePoint web part

When you now run the debugger, code execution will stop at your breakpoint and let you step into or over, or do whatever you desire in debug mode (see Figure 12-8).

Visual web parts make it fairly easy to build and deploy custom functionality to SharePoint. Now the trick is to figure out what you want to do, but isn't that better than worrying about the plumbing?

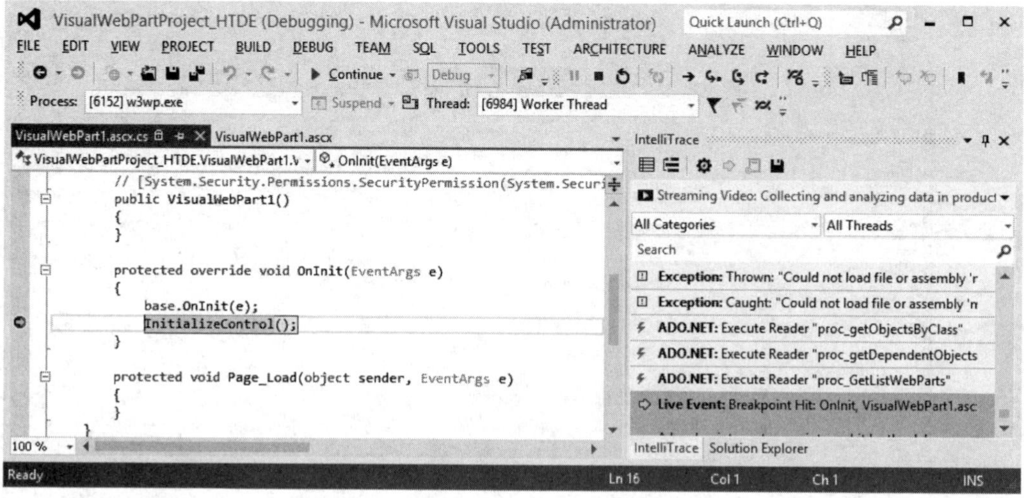

FIGURE 12-8   The debugger has hit the breakpoint.

Developing a SharePoint App

The new SharePoint App model is an exciting option for SharePoint developers. While it's true that the server-side object model offers more power, SharePoint apps can be developed both publicly and privately. SharePoint apps can be sold in the SharePoint App Store, in much the same way as apps for cell phones and Windows apps are sold.

Creating a Developer Site

If you would like to try developing a SharePoint app, you should first create a new site collection using the Developer Site template. Note that you must create this site collection from SharePoint Central Administration (discussed in Chapter 11). You will not find the Developer Site template in the regular site templates list.

Once you have your Developer Site collection created, the next step is to create a new SharePoint App project in Visual Studio 2012. To create the new project, choose File | New Project | C# | Office/SharePoint | Apps | App for SharePoint 2013 (see Figure 12-9).

Choose the name and the site to use for debugging your app. For this example, choose the SharePoint-hosted option (see Figure 12-10). Three options are available:

- SharePoint-hosted means that your app will run on the SharePoint machine.
- The Autohosted option will deploy the app to the Windows Azure cloud development platform, which is run by Microsoft.

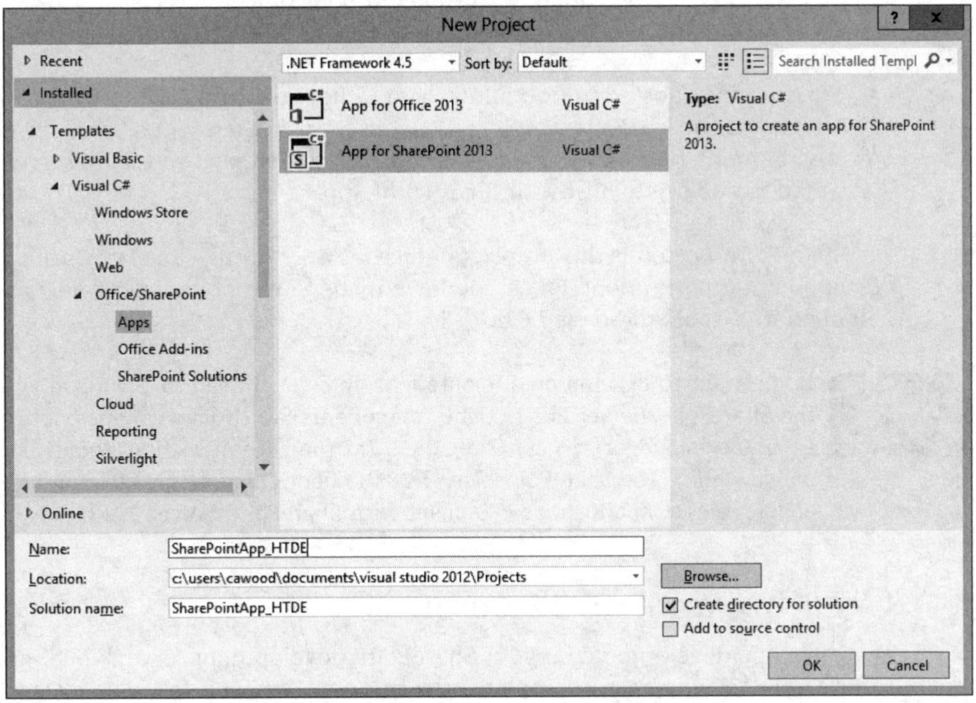

FIGURE 12-9   Creating a new SharePoint app project

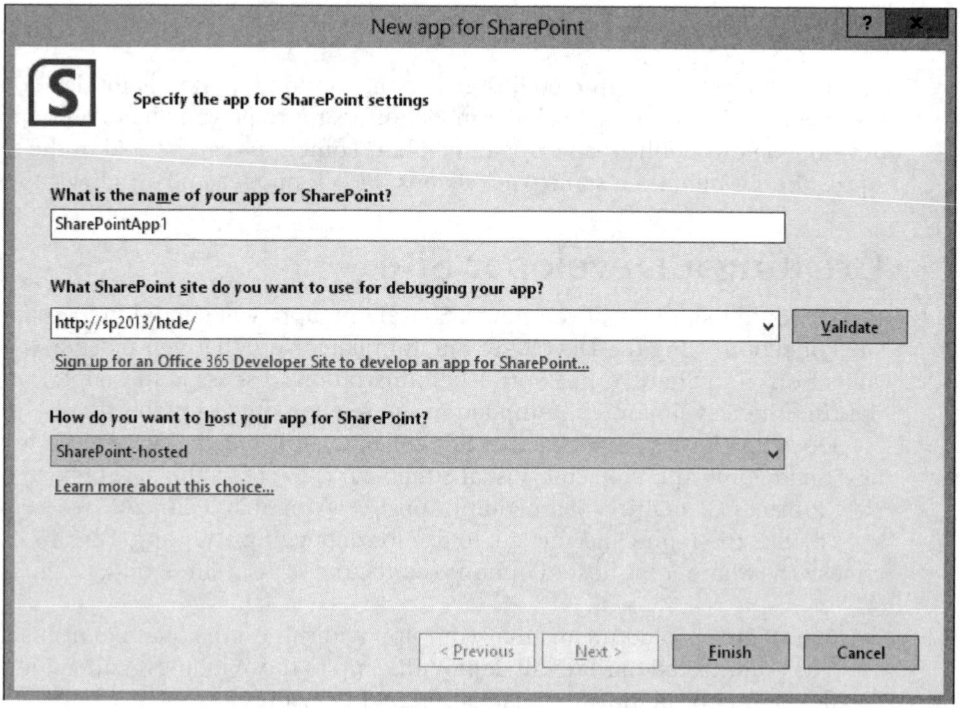

FIGURE 12-10 Choosing the settings for your new app

- The Provider-hosted option allows you to host the app on any web-accessible server you choose. For example, you might want to use a cloud-based development environment, but not Windows Azure, or you might have your own server that you would like to use to host your SharePoint app.

SharePoint-hosted is the simplest choice, as everything can stay within your local development environment. Once you have made your choices, your new app project will open in Visual Studio (see Figure 12-11).

> **Note** If you want to develop on a remote machine, you'll need to download and install the SharePoint Server 2013 Client Components SDK from www.microsoft.com/en-us/download/details.aspx?id=30355 (at the time of writing, this is still the preview link). The SharePoint Server 2013 Client Components SDK can be used to enable remote and local development with SharePoint Server 2013.

Creating an App Domain

To enable app development on your SharePoint development server, you'll need to do some setup. You've already completed the first step, which is to create a Developer Site to test your apps. The next step is to create an isolated app domain for your apps to use.

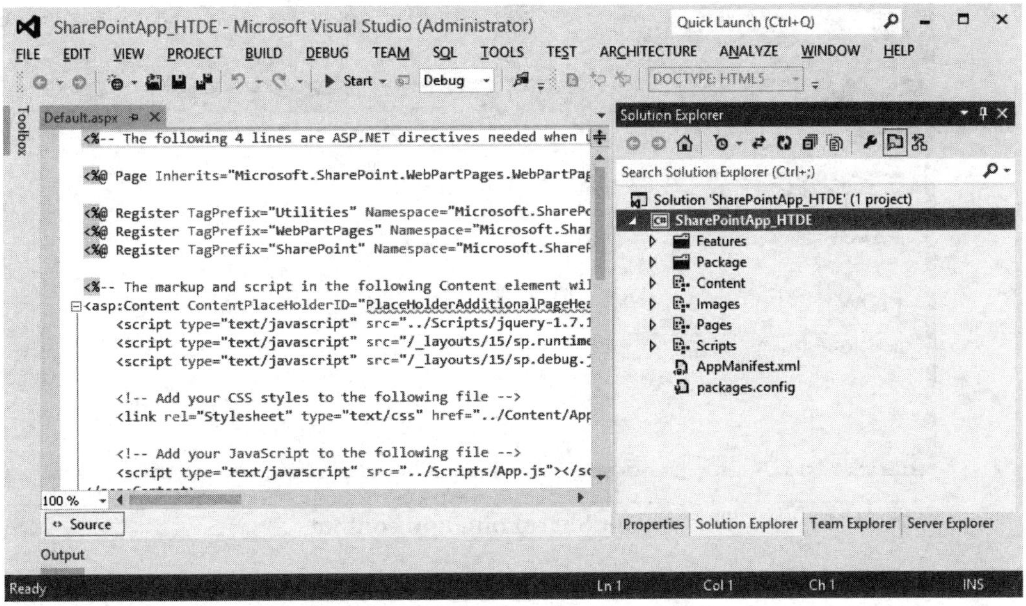

FIGURE 12-11   A new app project in Visual Studio

Creating this domain is a required step, but the good news is that you can get a PowerShell script to make this task a lot easier. (It is possible to create the domain without this particular script, but I suggest you use the script.) First, download the PowerShell script to create an isolated app domain from http://tomvangaever.be/blogv2/2012/08/prepare-sharepoint-2013-server-for-app-development-create-an-isolated-app-domain/. (See Chapter 11 for details about running a PowerShell script for SharePoint.)

First, the script asks for your app domain name. If you're using dev.com as your domain name, then your app domain name will be contosoapps.com, and your app prefix will be added—for example, apps.contosoapps.com.

The next step is to create a managed account. You'll first need to create a new account using the AD Users and Computers interface. Then you'll need to set this new user as a SharePoint managed account. To do this, open a new PowerShell window as Administrator and run the command `New-SPManagedAccount`. You'll be asked to supply the username and password that you want to use for this account.

Next, return to your original PowerShell window and enter the login name of the new managed account you created. At this point, the PowerShell script will run through six steps, providing feedback when each has been completed.

Once you choose to debug your app, the system will create a feature for the app, and your new app will launch (see Figure 12-12).

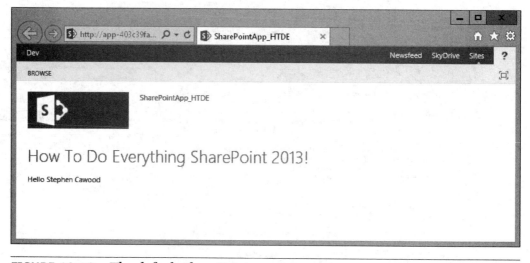

FIGURE 12-12 The default SharePoint app content

Note that under the hood, SharePoint will create an entry in your development machine's hosts file (C:\Windows\System32\Drivers\etc). It will look something like this:

```
127.0.0.1 app-403c39fa0bd661.contosoapps.com # 84526754-a966-4be6-
a7a7-a1258cc76114;http://sp2013/sites/dev/
::1 app-403c39fa0bd661.contosoapps.com # 84526754-a966-4be6-a7a7-
a1258cc76114;http://sp2013/sites/dev/
```

The hosts file entry allows your dev machine to find the app at the domain you specified when you ran the PowerShell script. When you stop debugging, the entry is removed.

To read more about developing apps for SharePoint, refer to *Apps for Office and SharePoint* (http://msdn.microsoft.com/en-us/library/fp161507.aspx) on MSDN.

Summary

This chapter is meant to give you a small taste of SharePoint development. There are many topics within the umbrella of "SharePoint dev," and most SharePoint developers don't even have to deal with all the topics. If you're taking on your first SharePoint development project, I highly recommend that you scope out a small project at first and only move on to tackling something complicated after you have your first project working.

If you would like to learn more about SharePoint 2013 development, I strongly suggest you start with the training videos available on MSDN. An example is "SharePoint 2013 training for developers" (http://msdn.microsoft.com/en-US/sharepoint/fp123633).

13

Template Reference
for Apps, Pages, and Sites

HOW TO...

- Choose the right app
- Differentiate between types of SharePoint pages
- Learn about SharePoint site templates

As you've learned in this book, the end-user functionality within SharePoint is largely determined by the apps, site templates, app parts, and web parts that are provided out of the box. This chapter is a reference for the apps, pages, and sites that are available in SharePoint Server 2013.

Remember that some of the types of apps or sites listed here may not be available on your server. Your options will depend on the version of SharePoint you are using, the features that are installed, the site template for the current site, and your permissions within the system. For example, if you're using SharePoint Server 2013 with the enterprise features enabled, you will see most, if not all, of the items listed in this chapter. If you're using SharePoint Online within Office 365 or SharePoint Foundation, you may not see all of the apps and sites listed in this chapter.

Many of the templates that fit into this chapter have already been discussed in other parts of this book; in those cases, you can follow the reference to the relevant chapter. Conversely, some of the important templates that didn't fit nicely into the other chapter topics will be covered here. For your convenience, the description of each template is included from the SharePoint UI.

Note While it's true that you can get the descriptions from the UI, to do that takes some time. Hopefully, by providing that information in a more accessible format, this chapter will save you some time and effort.

239

Apps

If you polled SharePoint end users, many would identify apps as the fundamental pieces of a SharePoint server. Apps add functionality, and they are the containers for items—what type of item is determined by the app template.

In SharePoint 2013, lists and libraries have been renamed to "apps." Why did Microsoft change the terminology? The answer seems to be that they are simply using language that people foreign to SharePoint will understand. In this way, SharePoint is more accessible to an end user. Thanks to the growing popularity of smartphones and tablets, the average person on the street has heard of apps, and many have a good understanding of how apps are used to add functionality.

> **Note** At the back end of every SharePoint server is a set of databases, and among those databases, the most heavily used is the content database. App items are rows in that database, and their associated metadata is stored in the columns.

Libraries are actually lists—lists with attachments. Whether you need to manage documents, images, or forms, SharePoint can help make the task easier. Libraries combine the benefits of SharePoint lists with features specific to the type of content being stored.

Access App

Access Web App

This app allows you to use Access 2013 web apps in SharePoint. Some configuration is required to get this type of app to work. To read more about Access web apps, refer to the Access blog (http://blogs.office.com/b/microsoft-access/archive/2012/07/20/introducing-access-2013-.aspx).

Announcements

A list of news items, statuses and other short bits of information.

Announcements help you get out news and updates within your organization. Announcement lists were covered in Chapter 4. Announcement lists are among the handful of list types that can be e-mail–enabled. In other words, you can send an e-mail to the announcement list and have it appear in announcement form. The subject line will become the title, and the body will become the announcement text.

Asset Library

A place to share, browse and manage rich media assets, like image, audio and video files.

If you're looking for a central place to store image, audio, and video files, an asset library might be the right choice for you. One advantage of using an asset library is

FIGURE 13-1   Asset library item options

the various metadata that's made available as part of the list template. For example, you can specify whether the file is an image file, an audio file, or a video (see Figure 13-1). If you were working on a presentation that required various types of media, this library would allow you to store them in one location, and then filter by the metadata, such as the media type.

The asset library in SharePoint 2013 features a new video control that allows you to easily share video within SharePoint. Upload a WMV video file, and you can play it directly from SharePoint.

Calendar

A calendar of upcoming meetings, deadlines, or other events. Calendar information can be synchronized with Microsoft Outlook or other compatible programs.

Calendar lists provide the functionality that you would expect from a calendar—and probably a little bit more. Calendars are discussed in Chapter 4.

Note   Calendars can be connected to Microsoft Outlook so that you can share and overlay SharePoint calendars with your own. As well, calendars are another list type that can be e-mail–enabled, which means that you can "invite" a SharePoint calendar to your meetings.

Contacts

A list of people your team works with, like customers or partners. Contacts lists can synchronize with Microsoft Outlook or other compatible programs.

If you need to store a list of contacts in a location that is accessible through a web browser, the SharePoint contacts list can address your needs. When you add a new contact, you'll be asked for all sorts of information, such as names, address, e-mail address, and more (see Figure 13-2).

Note Contacts lists can be linked to Microsoft Outlook, and then shared among your team as a global or team contacts list.

Custom List

A blank list to which you can add your own columns and views. Use this if none of the built-in list types are similar to the list you want to make.

With so many different sites, pages, and lists, people may be led to believe that SharePoint is an application that comes with the functionality they want right out of

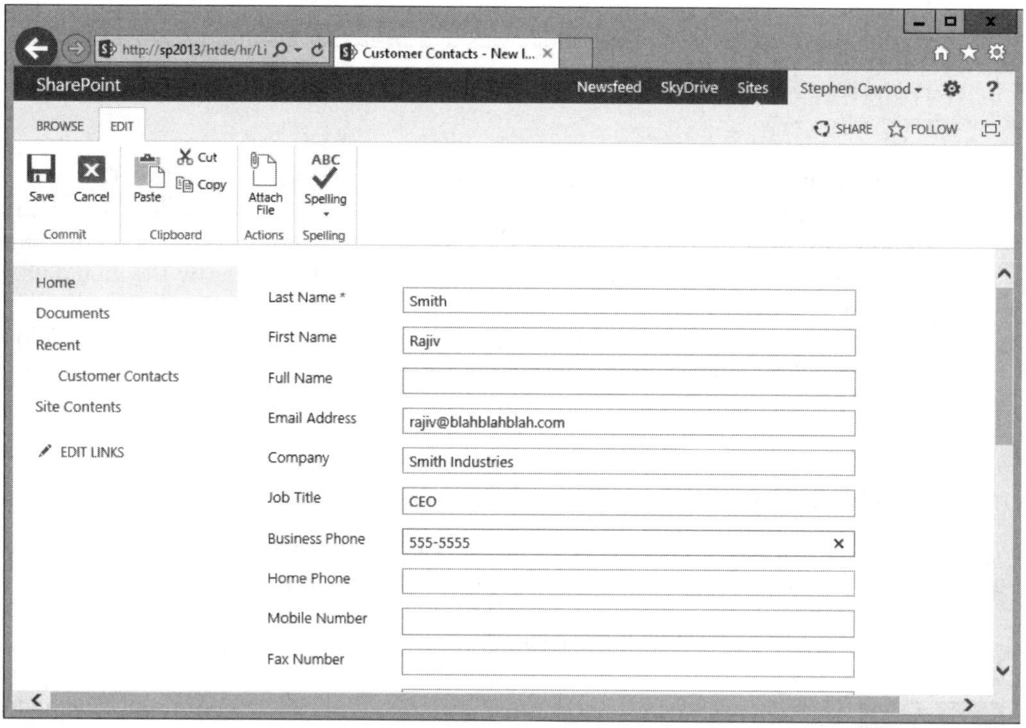

FIGURE 13-2 The new contact dialog

the box. However, as any large enterprise is already aware, it's simply not possible to develop a one-size-fits-all information management system. Microsoft is keenly aware of this fact, and thus has developed SharePoint as a platform; if there is something you need, you can add it. This is where custom lists fit into the picture. If you need to build your own list from scratch, you can still use the functionality that comes with a list, but you can define your own custom type.

A custom list allows you to start creating your own list with the standard item view as the default. When you create a new custom list, only one column is visible: Title (see Figure 13-3). It is up to you to add the rest of the functionality you need.

Custom List in Datasheet View

A blank list which is displayed as a spreadsheet in order to allow easy data entry. You can add your own columns and views. This list type requires a compatible list datasheet ActiveX control, such as the one provided in Microsoft Office.

This type of list also allows you to start with just a Title column, but the default view is a datasheet (see Figure 13-4). As the description states, the datasheet view requires additional software, but it does have its benefits. The datasheet view allows users to quickly make edits to the list data—simply click in a field and start editing.

Data Connection Library

A place where you can easily share files that contain information about external data connections.

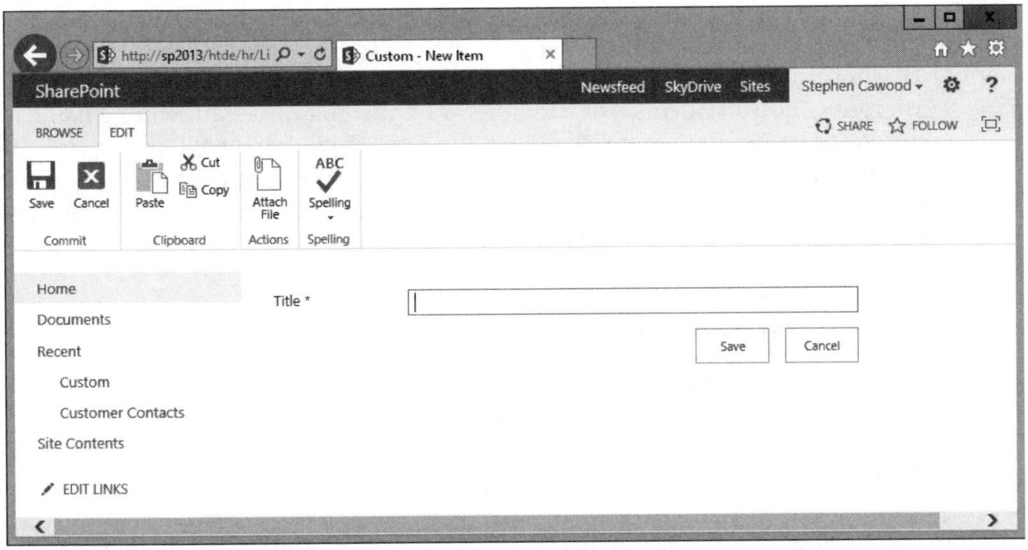

FIGURE 13-3   The custom list add new item dialog

FIGURE 13-4 A custom list in datasheet view

Data connection libraries are used to store files that define data connections. This includes Office Data Connection (ODC) files and Universal Data Connection (UDC) files. These files can define connections to databases, web services, or even SharePoint libraries and lists.

By storing these connection files in SharePoint, you can use them when creating Microsoft InfoPath forms. For example, if I know that my team will be using a web service to gather data that will be used in our InfoPath forms, I can create a data connection file in InfoPath and store that file in a data connection library, thereby making it easier for anyone who wants to use that connection in their InfoPath forms to do so.

Discussion Board

A place to have newsgroup-style discussions. Discussion boards make it easy to manage discussion threads and can be configured to require approval for all posts.

Discussion boards enable a back-and-forth conversation among people in different locations. This type of list is discussed in Chapter 4.

Note Discussion boards can be connected to Microsoft Outlook so that you can carry on a SharePoint conversation using Outlook as your conversation tool.

Document Library

A place for storing documents or other files that you want to share. Document libraries allow folders, versioning, and check out.

Document libraries are the backbone of document management in SharePoint. They are covered extensively in Chapter 2.

 Document libraries and certain types of lists can be e-mail–enabled to allow you to simply e-mail a document to the library or list instead of uploading the files through the SharePoint web UI.

External List

Create an external list to view the data in an External Content Type.

This list will show data from an external content type, but you will need to first have an external type created by a SharePoint administrator. These lists are used by SharePoint's Business Connectivity Services (BCS). You can define a connection in BCS (often in SharePoint Designer) to an external Microsoft SQL Server database, a Microsoft Access database, or some other type of data source. SharePoint will then present the data as though it were a list in SharePoint.

Form Library

A place to manage business forms like status reports or purchase orders. Form libraries require a compatible XML editor, such as Microsoft InfoPath.

Form libraries can be used with Microsoft InfoPath to create custom electronic forms for your organization. Creating forms is covered in Chapter 9.

Import Spreadsheet

Create a list which duplicates the columns and data of an existing spreadsheet. Importing a spreadsheet requires Microsoft Excel or another compatible program.

If you have Microsoft Excel, you'll have the option of importing data quickly from one of your spreadsheets. The import spreadsheet list allows you to import data from a spreadsheet as part of the list-creation process. When you choose to create the list, you'll be asked to specify which spreadsheet file contains the data you would like to import. When you click the Import button, the file will open in Excel, and you can choose which cells to import (see Figure 13-5).

After you import the spreadsheet, your data will be imported into the list (see Figure 13-6). Once the import has been completed, there is no connection between the original spreadsheet file and the import spreadsheet list.

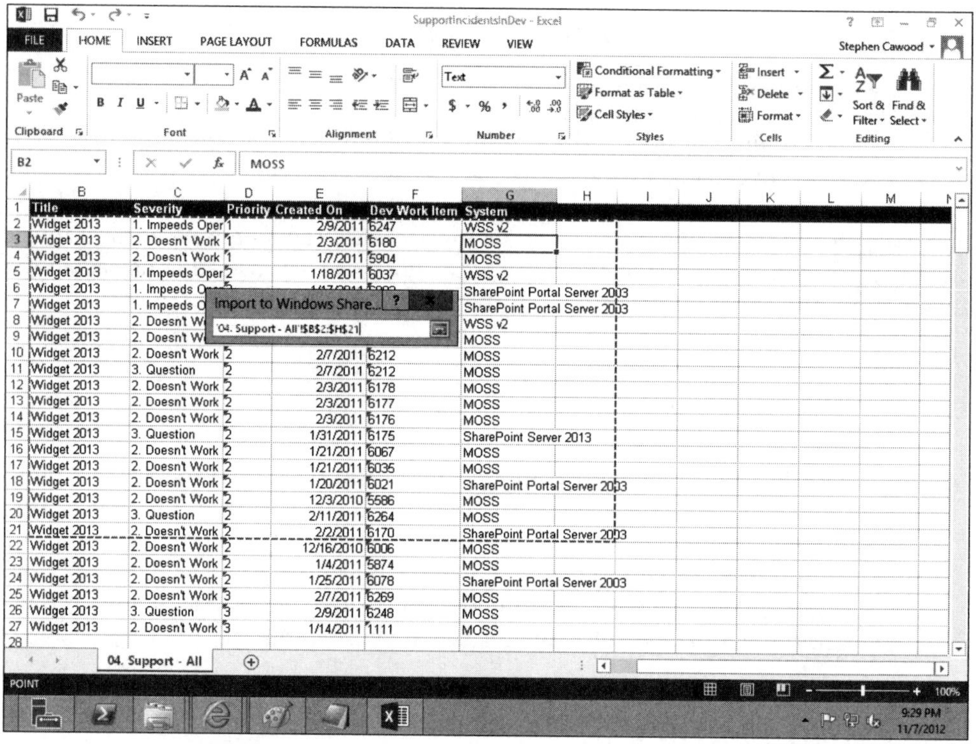

FIGURE 13-5 Choosing a range of cells to import

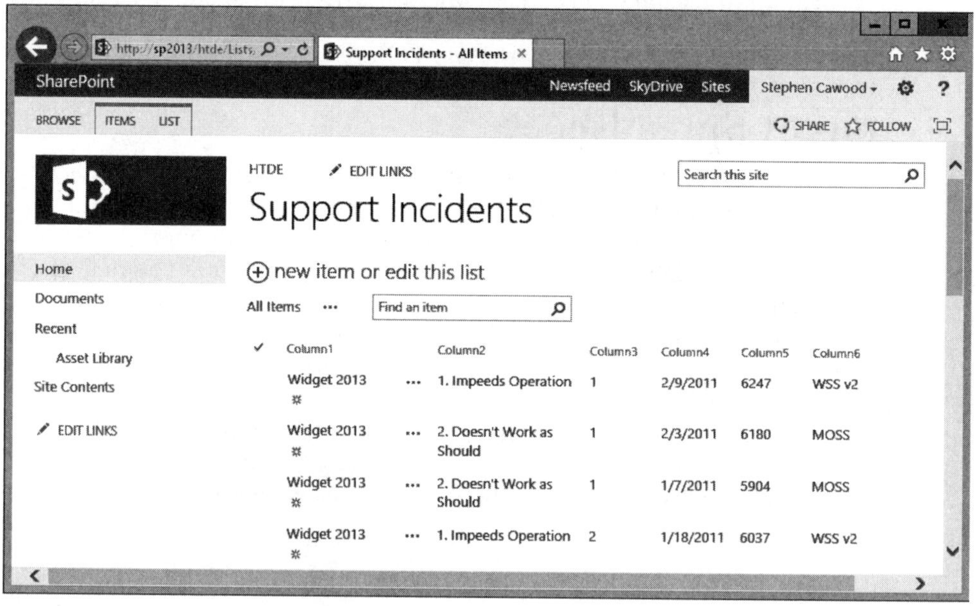

FIGURE 13-6 After importing an Excel spreadsheet

Issue Tracking

A list of issues or problems associated with a project or item. You can assign, prioritize, and track issue status.

An issue racking list is similar to a tasks list in that you can assign ownership of each item and then track its progress to completion. However, there are a few differences that make tracking issues easier using this type of list. One example is the fact that each issue item is assigned an issue ID, which is visible in the default view of the list. These unique IDs ensure that there is no confusion as to which issues are being discussed.

Links

A list of web pages or other resources.

A links list allows you to store URLs with a description and associated notes. The information that you add to each links list item offers benefits beyond storing the links in a browser's favorites.

Picture Library

A place to upload and share pictures.

The description from Microsoft for the Picture Library template doesn't really provide a full explanation of what these libraries can do. Picture libraries allow you to associate metadata with images, view images in a slide show, convert images to web format, add version control, and use metadata-based filtering. You can even add validation settings to allow you to specify parameters, such as height, that determine whether images can be added to the library. As with many types of lists, you can add optional folders for organization.

To start adding pictures to your picture library, simply drag your images to the area of the page that reads "drag files here" (see Figure 13-7). Of course, you could also browse for your images using the new picture option, but that's not as impressive.

After you upload the images, you can select the link to return to the library, where you'll see your images in the picture library (see Figure 13-8). Once the images have been loaded, you can start using features such as the slide show view.

As you learned in Chapter 3, you may not get the same upload options in all browsers. For example, mobile browsers generally don't have as many features as PC browsers. One of the useful features of the picture library is the ability to view the files in a slide show view. Simply choose the Slides option (see Figure 13-9).

Promoted Links

Using the Promoted Links app, you can create a list of links and specify how they will behave.

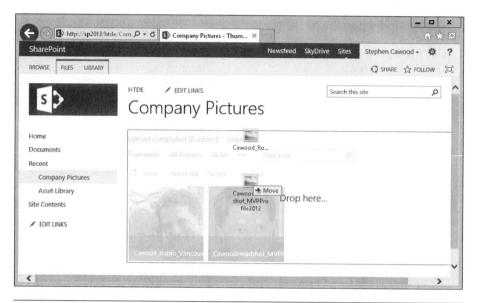

FIGURE 13-7 Choosing to upload multiple images

FIGURE 13-8 The picture library after uploading images

FIGURE 13-9   Selecting the slide show view

Report Library

A place where you can easily create and manage web pages and documents to track metrics, goals and business intelligence information.

Report libraries provide columns for useful report data, such as the owner, status, and report category. All of this data is meant to save you the trouble of adding these columns to a standard document library.

Survey

A list of questions which you would like to have people answer. Surveys allow you to quickly create questions and view graphical summaries of the responses.

Surveys allow you to poll other SharePoint users for their answers to questions you create. Survey lists are discussed in Chapter 4.

Tasks

A place for team or personal tasks.

Tasks lists are the workhorse of many types of sites in SharePoint. Whether you're creating a meeting workspace or a team site, you'll find that you'll automatically get a tasks list.

You don't need to be a proponent of Peter Drucker's management by objectives to understand the importance of tracking granular tasks. SharePoint tasks lists give you the ability to track who owns each task, view what the current priority and status are for each one, and even specify that one or more tasks are predecessors of other tasks (see Figure 13-10).

Note Tasks lists, unlike issues lists, can be connected to Microsoft Outlook, so that they can be managed from within the Outlook client.

Wiki Page Library

An interconnected set of easily editable web pages, which can contain text, images, and web parts.

Wikis have become mainstream over the past few years. They provide a frictionless, community-authoring environment. Wiki libraries are discussed in Chapter 4.

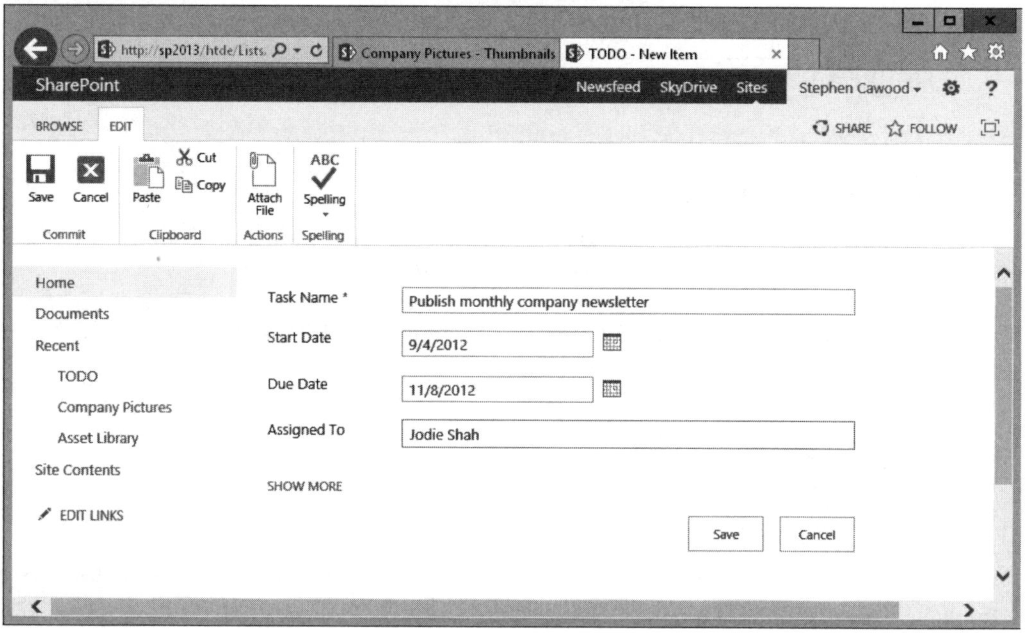

FIGURE 13-10   Creating a new task

Pages

There will be times when you don't need a whole site and a list isn't the right choice. You might want what some people refer to as a "landing page." Pages allow you to post content in a free-form manner. Pages are also the "items" you'll find under some apps. For example, wiki page libraries and publishing sites contain pages.

Page

A page which can be easily edited in the web browser using Web Edit. Pages can contain text, images, and wiki links, as well as lists and other web parts. Pages are useful for collaborating on small projects.

Obviously, formatted text is available when you create your page content, but you'll also be able to import media such as images, tables, audio, and video. You can even import web parts or SharePoint lists. Pages are created in the site pages library, which also supports the use of the wiki page format (see Figure 13-11).

Tip   Remember that the wiki functionality of adding page links also works on pages.

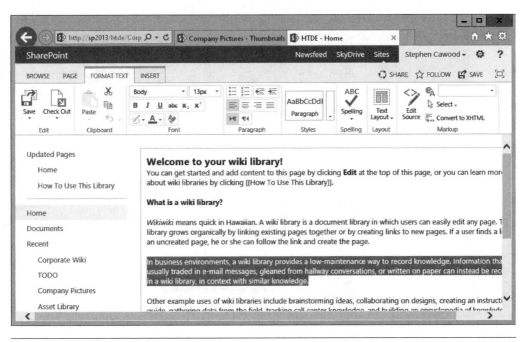

FIGURE 13-11   A page in edit mode

Web Part Page

A page which can display an aggregation of information from other sources. Web part pages can display many types of data, including lists, other web pages, search results, or data retrieved from other servers.

The first versions of SharePoint were called SharePoint Portal Server. The term *portal* is no longer in vogue, but the utility remains. Web part pages embody the idea that SharePoint can be used as a portal into diverse sources of information.

Web part pages contain zones, which can contain web parts. When you choose to create a web part page, you'll be asked to choose from a number of different layouts. Each layout contains a different organization option for your page (see Figure 13-12), or as the Create page dialog explains:

> "Select a layout template to arrange Web Parts in zones on the page. Multiple Web Parts can be added to each zone. Specific zones allow Web Parts to be stacked in a horizontal or vertical direction, which is illustrated by differently colored Web Parts. If you do not add a Web Part to a zone, the zone collapses (unless it has a fixed width) and the other zones expand to fill unused space when you browse the Web Part Page."

Numerous web parts come with SharePoint 2013. They are discussed in Chapters 8 and 12.

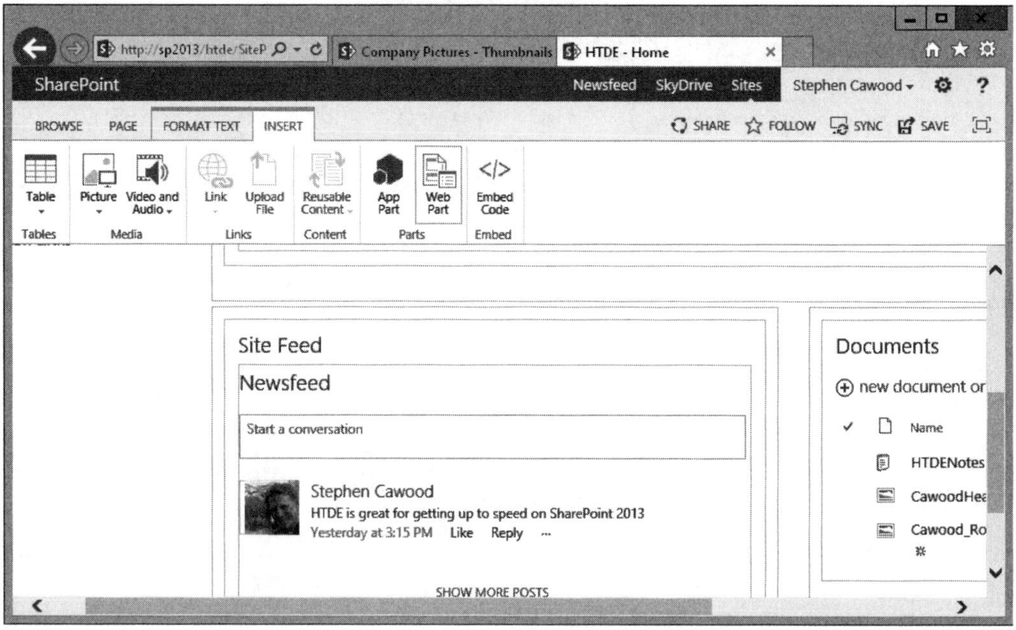

FIGURE 13-12 Choosing a web part page layout

Sites

When it comes to information architecture, sites are arguably the most important container in SharePoint planning. Site templates determine the features, apps, and pages that can be created in each area of your SharePoint server. In fact, when people talk about the problem of "SharePoint sprawl," they are generally referring to the creation of too many sites. If your sites are well planned, your users may not feel the need to keep creating more and more.

Remember that the site template is just a starting point. The idea is to choose the one that is closest to the final result you need for your project. However, you'll almost always need to add—or even remove—functionality to tweak the site to match your needs.

Collaboration

The Collaboration category contains site templates that are designed to enable teamwork.

Team Site

A site for teams to quickly organize, author, and share information. It provides a document library, and lists for managing announcements, calendar items, tasks, and discussions.

Team sites might be the most popular type of site in SharePoint. In fact, when people describe SharePoint, they are often describing the functionality found within a team site. When you create a team site, you'll find elements such as a document library, named shared documents, and a tasks list added for you.

Blog

A site for a person or team to post ideas, observations, and expertise that site visitors can comment on.

Blogs have become very popular over the past few years. They are discussed in Chapter 4.

Project Site

A site for managing and collaborating on a project.

This site template brings all status, communication, and artifacts relevant to the project into one place.

Community Site

A place where community members discuss topics of common interest.

Members can browse and discover relevant content by exploring categories, sorting discussions by popularity, and viewing only posts that have a best reply. Members gain reputation points by participating in the community, such as starting discussions and replying to them, liking posts, and specifying best replies.

Enterprise

The Enterprise category is not going to be used often by the average user. Generally, these sites are used for specific purposes and are added as part of a SharePoint governance plan that spans the entire organization.

Document Center

A site to centrally manage documents in your enterprise.

The best features of SharePoint document management can be found in the Document Center site template. As the home page explains, "Use this site to create, work on, and store documents. This site can become a collaborative repository for authoring documents within a team, or a knowledge base for documents across multiple teams."

Records Center

This template creates a site designed for records management. Records managers can configure the routing table to direct incoming files to specific locations. The site also lets you manage whether records can be deleted or modified after they are added to the repository.

The default content on the home page of a new Records Center site, listed next, encourages you to use the page to educate your colleagues about the records-compliance policies of your organization:

Add links to other organizational compliance sites, such as the following:

- *The definition of a record in your organization*
- *What happens to a record after it is submitted to the Records Center*
- *Steps users can take to comply with organizational policy*

Add information about records management topics, such as the following:

- *Your organization's compliance training site*
- *A site about organizational retention policies*
- *A list of records management contacts for each department*

Business Intelligence Center

A site for presenting business intelligence content in SharePoint.

If you're interested in the business intelligence site, refer to the article "SharePoint 2013 - The New Business Intelligence Center" on NothingButSharePoint .com (www.nothingbutsharepoint.com/sites/itpro/Pages/SharePoint-2013-The-New-Business-Intelligence-Center.aspx), or you can refer to the Microsoft TechNet page "What's new in business intelligence in SharePoint Server 2013" (http://technet .microsoft.com/en-us/library/jj542395.aspx).

Enterprise Search Center

A site for delivering the search experience. The welcome page includes a search box with two tabs: one for general searches, and another for searches for information about people. You can add and customize tabs to focus on other search scopes or result types.

As the description mentions, when you create a new Enterprise Search Center site, you'll get a general search box and another for a people search. However, you can add your own custom tabs and use the advanced options to filter your result sets (see Figure 13-13).

Basic Search Center

A site for delivering the search experience. The site includes pages for search results and advanced searches.

If you don't need the customization options in the Enterprise Search Center site, you might find that the Basic Search Center site template suits your needs.

Visio Process Repository

A site for teams to quickly view, share, and store Visio process diagrams. It provides a versioned document library for storing process diagrams, and lists for managing announcements, tasks, and review discussions.

This site template is reminiscent of the Document Center, but it is tailored to groups that work with Visio Process diagrams.

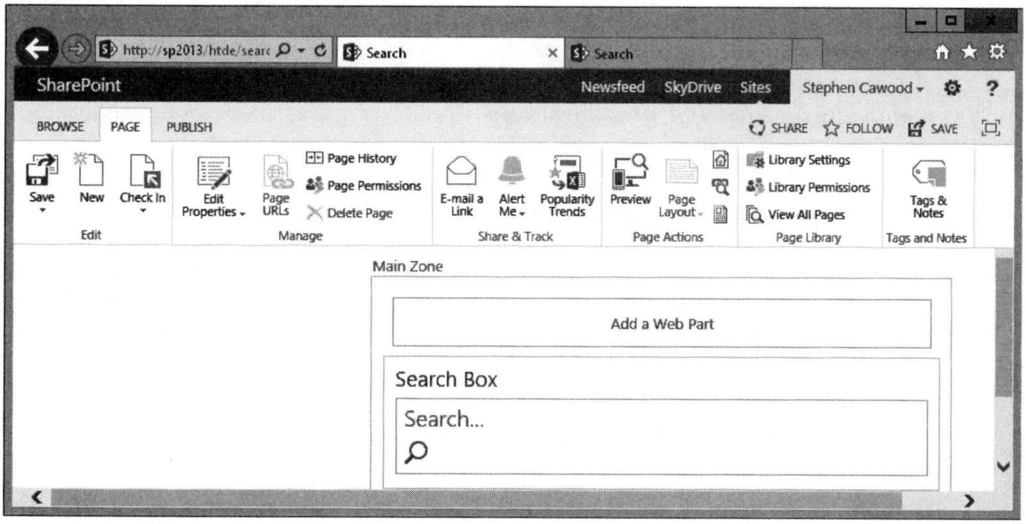

FIGURE 13-13 The search center page in edit mode

Publishing

The publishing category will be available only on sites where the publishing infrastructure feature has been enabled both at the site-collection level and at the site level. To activate the feature at the site-collection level, you will need to have site collection administrator rights. Activating the publishing feature is covered in chapter 11.

Publishing Site

A blank site for expanding your website and quickly publishing web pages. Contributors can work on draft versions of pages and publish them to make them visible to readers. The site includes document and image libraries for storing Web publishing assets.

Publishing site templates are discussed in Chapter 6.

Publishing Site with Workflow

A site for publishing web pages on a schedule by using approval workflows. It includes document and image libraries for storing Web publishing assets. By default, only sites with this template can be created under this site.

If you would like to add some more structure to your publishing experience, you might want to create a publishing site with workflow instead of a regular publishing site. As the name implies, edits under this type of site will need to be approved by a user who has sufficient rights.

If you created your initial site collection using the Publishing Site with Workflow template or the Collaboration Portal template, you will get these options. This template is often used for public-facing websites. It's discussed in Chapter 6.

Enterprise Wiki

A site for publishing knowledge that you capture and want to share across the enterprise. It provides an easy content editing experience in a single location for co-authoring content, discussions, and project management.

When you create an Enterprise Wiki site, the default home page content tells you everything you need to know about the site template:

"Use the Enterprise Wiki to create a single, go-to place for knowledge sharing and project management across the enterprise. Enterprise Wikis are simple to use, flexible, and lightweight in features. They are quick and easy to create, and you can easily add links to other information systems, corporate directories, or applications....

Working with content—text, graphics, or video—is as easy as working in any word processing application, such as Microsoft Word...."

The following are some other things you can do when working with Enterprise Wiki sites:

- Collaborate on wiki pages with other users
- Comment on a wiki page to enable discussion about the contents of the page
- Rate a wiki page to share your opinion about its content
- Categorize wiki pages to enable users to quickly find information and share it with others

Summary

This chapter provided an overview of pages, apps, and sites. It's unlikely that you'll need to use all of them, but it's best to know what your choices are when you plan and build out your SharePoint sites.

That's the end of the list of lists. (Yes, I know, they're now called "apps" but there's no pun in a list of apps). It's also the end of this book. I hope you found it useful. If you'd like to continue learning about SharePoint, the Appendix includes my list of favorite SharePoint learning sites and blogs.

A

SharePoint Resources

To help you continue your journey into the vast landscape of SharePoint subject matter, I've put together a reference list of some of my favorite SharePoint websites and blogs. Together they represent a treasure chest of knowledge. If you'd like to stay up to date on developments in the SharePoint community, the blog list below also serves as a great starting point for a list of SharePoint people to follow on Twitter.

Learning SharePoint

The following are some resources for getting started with SharePoint:

- **Microsoft SharePoint Website** http://sharepoint.microsoft.com/en-us/Pages/Resources.aspx
- **Microsoft Developer Network (MSDN), SharePoint Content** http://msdn.microsoft.com/en-us/library/fp161347.aspx
- **Microsoft TechNet SharePoint Content** http://technet.microsoft.com/en-US/sharepoint
- **SharePoint Pro Magazine** www.sharepointpromag.com

SharePoint Videos

The following are places for accessing training videos about SharePoint:

- **Microsoft SharePoint Website** http://sharepoint.microsoft.com/en-us/Pages/Videos.aspx?VideoID=25
- **Microsoft TechNet** http://technet.microsoft.com/en-us/library/cc262880.aspx
- **SharePoint-Videos** www.sharepoint-videos.com

Getting Help from the SharePoint Community

I am a strong believer in forums. Once they reach a certain critical mass—and SharePoint certainly meets that bar—they become 24/7 resources for any sort of question. One of my favorite techniques is to ask a question late at night and then go to bed knowing that people from around the world will post helpful answers while I'm sleeping—it's a great experience to wake up and have a solution waiting for me. To get help from the SharePoint community, try the following sites:

- **MSDN Forums** http://social.msdn.microsoft.com/Forums/en-US/category/sharepoint
- **StackExchange Forum** http://sharepoint.stackexchange.com
- **Nothing But SharePoint** www.nothingbutsharepoint.com
- **Yammer** www.yammer.com/spyam

Notable SharePoint Blogs

Here are some interesting SharePoint-related blogs:

- **itgroove staff blogs** www.itgroove.net/cms/company/learnmore/blogs
- **Microsoft SharePoint Team Blog** http://sharepoint.microsoft.com/blog
- **Mark D. Anderson** http://sympmarc.com
- **Becky Bertram** http://blog.beckybertram.com
- **Andrew Connell** www.andrewconnell.com/blog/
- **Spencer Harbar** www.harbar.net
- **Todd Klindt** www.toddklindt.com/blog
- **Mark Miller** www.nothingbutsharepoint.com/sites/eusp
- **Chris O'Brien** www.sharepointnutsandbolts.com
- **Joel Oleson** www.sharepointjoel.com
- **Yaroslav Pentsarskyy** www.sharemuch.com
- **Laura Rogers** www.wonderlaura.com
- **Paul J. Swider** http://paulswider.com
- **Raymond Dux Sy** http://blogs.innovative-e.com/sites/meetdux/meet-dux.aspx
- **Stephen Cawood's blog** www.geeklit.com

Professional SharePoint Training

The following are some resources for getting professional SharePoint training:

- **Mindsharp Training** www.mindsharp.com
- **Critical Path Training** www.criticalpathtraining.com
- **SharePoint Shepherd** www.sharepointshepherd.com

Sharing the Point charity http://sharingthepoint.org (a special shout-out to this group!)

Index